Hatnub: Quarrying Travertine in Ancient Egypt

EIGHTY-EIGHTH EXCAVATION MEMOIR

HATNUB: QUARRYING TRAVERTINE IN ANCIENT EGYPT

BY

IAN SHAW

WITH CONTRIBUTIONS BY PAUL T. NICHOLSON, PAMELA J. ROSE AND ROBERT JAMESON

ILLUSTRATIONS BY JULIAN HEATH

EGYPT EXPLORATION SOCIETY

2010

SOLD AT THE OFFICES OF
THE EGYPT EXPLORATION SOCIETY

3 Doughty Mews, London WC1N 2PG

www.ees-shop.com

© The Egypt Exploration Society 2010

A catalogue entry for this book is available from the British Library

ISBN 978-0-85698-187-6

Set in Adobe InDesign by Rutherford Press

Printed in Great Britain by Commercial Colour Press,
Angard House, 185 Forest Road, Hainault, Essex IG6 3HX

This book is dedicated to Albert Atkinson (1901-1980) and Michael Shaw (1928-2008), both very much missed

Contents

Illustrations		x
Acknowledgements		xiv
A Note on Geological Terminology		xv
Preface		xvi

1. The History of Previous Epigraphic and Archaeological Work at Hatnub

1.1	Introduction	1
1.2	The discovery and history of the study of Hatnub	3
1.3	Ancient toponyms associated with the Hatnub quarry region	6
1.4	The current condition of the site	8

2. Egyptian Exploitation of Travertine: its Definitions, Sources, Uses and Significance

2.1	Geological and chemical definitions of Egyptian travertine	11
2.2	The lexicography of Egyptian travertine	13
2.3	The ancient uses and symbolism of travertine	14
2.4	Egyptian sources of travertine other than Hatnub	19
2.5	Provenancing Egyptian travertine	24
2.6	Travertine workshops: excavation, ethno-archaeology and experimental work	25
2.7	To what extent was stone worked into artefacts at Hatnub?	27

3. The Quarry P Region at Hatnub ~ Ian Shaw, Robert Jameson and Paul T. Nicholson

3.1	Quarry P	31
3.2	The Old Kingdom quarry-workers' encampment immediately adjacent to Quarry P (structures P1–29)	35
3.3	The scattered groups of stone huts surrounding Quarry P	41
3.4	Structure S26 (excavated 7–9 October 1991)	64
3.5	Structure NW23 (excavated 12–13 February 1990)	67
3.6	Discussion	73

4. Quarries R and T at Hatnub

4.1	Quarry R	75
4.2	Quarry T	79

5. The Pottery ~ Paul T. Nicholson and Pamela J. Rose

5.1	The Old Kingdom pottery	81
5.2	The New Kingdom pottery	84
5.3	Pottery from structure S26	85
5.4	Pottery from structure NW23	91
5.5	Discussion	94

6. Religion and Ritual at Hatnub: Petroglyphs, Priests and Standing Stones

6.1	Petroglyphs	97
6.2	Stone alignments and orthostats	99
6.3	Shrines	101
6.4	Textual references to religion and ritual at Hatnub	105
6.5	Discussion	106

7. The Hatnub Quarry Roads and the Transportation of Travertine

7.1	The main Hatnub road	109
7.2	Evidence on stone transportation derived from the tombs of Weni and Thuthotep, and the Ma'sara quarries	115
7.3	Other quarrying and mining roads of the pharaonic period	117
7.4	Discussion	123

8. The Organization of Pharaonic Quarry-Workers at Hatnub: a Synthesis of the Archaeological and Textual Data

8.1	Sources of evidence for the organisation of quarrying expeditions	125
8.2	A typology of settlements and encampments associated with mining and quarrying	128
8.3	Planned and fortified quarrying settlements: organizational and defensive factors	129
8.4	Hatnub in the context of other quarrying and mining settlements	133

Appendices

1.	Chronology of the Site	135
2.	The Inscriptions	137
3.	The Graffiti	143
4.	Unprovenanced Texts	163
5.	Chronological List of all known Texts from Hatnub	167
6.	Texts formerly and currently in the collection of the Ägyptisches Museum, Berlin	169

Bibliography 171

Index 187

Illustrations

Photographs by the author unless otherwise stated.

0.1	Map showing the locations of major quarry-sites exploited in Egypt.	xx
1.1	Map of Amarna and the Hatnub quarries.	2
1.2	The Horus name and throne name of Khufu (Inscription II at Quarry P, Hatnub).	4
1.3	The Horus name and throne name of Pepi I (Inscription III at Quarry P).	5
1.4	Quarry P viewed from the northwest.	6
2.1	Map showing the principal travertine quarrying regions in Egypt.	10
2.2	Dry-stone hut A122 in the Quarry P settlement at Hatnub.	28
2.3	Some of the fragments of worked travertine from Hut A122.	29
3.1	Plan of Quarry P and the adjoining area of dense settlement.	32
3.2	View of the interior of Quarry P.	33
3.3	The small set of steps in Quarry P.	33
3.4	Sketch-plan of a rectangular structure near the entrance to Quarry P.	34
3.5	Elevation drawing of one of the walls of structure N1 in the Quarry P settlement.	34
3.6	The dense area of settlement beside Quarry P.	35
3.7	The deep, charcoal-filled midden situated between Huts P20 and P3.	37
3.8	Key-Plan of the entire Quarry P settlement region.	39
3.9	Cairn C1.	40
3.10	Cairn C3.	40
3.11	The stretch of high ground to the southwest of Quarry P.	40
3.12	Plan showing the groups of dry-stone structures S1–12 and N1–7.	42
3.13	Structure S1.	43
3.14	Plan of structures N1–21 (part of the Quarry P settlement).	44
3.15	Plan of structure N1, in the Quarry P settlement.	44
3.16	Plan of structures W1–51 and NW1–5 (part of the Quarry P settlement).	46
3.17	Structure NW3, a New Kingdom hut with *zir* emplacement to the left.	47
3.18	One of the large worked blocks of limestone in the New Kingdom encampment.	47

3.19	Plan of structures NW6–24 and NN1–52 (part of the Quarry P settlement).	50
3.20	The large, almost complete, hand-made basin from hut NN38.	52
3.21	Plan of the northwestern sector of the A1–179 group of structures.	54
3.22	Plan showing the southwestern sector of the A1–179 group of structures.	54
3.23	One of the discarded Old Kingdom beer jars.	55
3.24	Base of a Roman amphora, found in Hut A35.	57
3.25	Semi-worked travertine vessel from structure A97.	58
3.26	Structure A99, which has an unusually straight wall at its northeastern side.	58
3.27	The large roughed-out lump of travertine found in structure A99.	59
3.28	Plan showing the B1–46 group of structures.	59
3.29	Structure B1 containing four worked fragments of travertine.	60
3.30	The cylindrical and discoid worked fragments of travertine from Hut B2.	60
3.31	Meidum-type Old Kingdom bowl from structure B6.	61
3.32	Upright rim from a marl beer jar found in structure B14.	62
3.33	Old Kingdom spouted vessel from structure B18 (photograph).	62
3.34	Old Kingdom spouted vessel from structure B18 (drawing).	62
3.35	A simple-rim bowl from windbreak B27.	63
3.36	A Nile-silt jar from windbreak B27.	63
3.37	The multi-room structure S26; Room 2.	65
3.38	Room 2 of Hut S26, after excavation of unit 3.	65
3.39	Section along the western edge of squares A–B in Hut S26.	67
3.40	Excavated pit F1 (in Hut S26) and small-find H91/16.	67
3.41	Structure NW23.	68
3.42	Plan of structure NW23.	69
3.43	Structure NW23 before the removal of unit 1.	70
3.44	Squares A–C in NW23, after the removal of unit 1.	71
3.45	Squares A–C in NW23, after the removal of unit 2.	71
3.46	Section drawing in the excavated area of structure NW23.	71
3.47	Charcoal-dominated feature in square B of Hut NW23.	72
4.1	Plan showing Quarries P, Ra, Rb and T.	76
4.2	Plan of Quarry Ra, showing locations of Inscription XIII and Graffiti 50-2.	76
4.3	View of the entrance to Quarry Ra at Hatnub.	77
4.4	Part of the damaged graffiti in Quarry Ra.	77
4.5	One of the group of semi-subterranean huts northeast of Quarries Ra and Rb.	78
4.6	The relief and inscription incised on the wall of Quarry T.	79

5.1	Part of Kaiser's *Userkaf* pottery corpus: bowl types 107–114.	82
5.2	A complete Old Kingdom beer jar found on the surface within structure NW23.	83
5.3	An Old Kingdom bread-mould from structure B5 in the Quarry P settlement.	83
5.4	An Old Kingdom Meidum-type bowl from hut B6 in the Quarry P settlement.	83
5.5	New Kingdom vessels found in the Quarry P settlement.	85
5.6	Open-form vessel from the surface in Room 1 of structure S26.	87
5.7	Closed-form vessel from the surface in Room 1 of structure S26.	87
5.8	Old Kingdom silt ware jar found to the east of Room 5 of structure S26.	91
5.9	Beer jar.	91
5.10	Old Kingdom beer jar from structure NW23.	92
5.11	An Old Kingdom bottle from structure NW23.	92
5.12	Meidum-type bowl from structure NW23.	93
5.13	Old Kingdom closed-form vesse from structure NW23.	93
5.14	Old Kingdom pottery from the Wadi Gerrawi travertine quarries.	95
6.1	Cairn C7 and the 'foot' petroglyphs.	98
6.2	The petroglyphs below cairn C7.	98
6.3	A view of part of the W50 group of aligned standing stones.	99
6.4	A carefully carved standing stone found among the W50 group of alignments.	100
6.5	One of the largest standing stones at Hatnub (S42)	100
6.6	Shrine S2 from the south, with its stone lined 'avenue'.	101
6.7	Shrine S2 from the east.	102
6.8	Shrine N3 from the north.	102
6.9	Shrine N7.	103
6.10	Shrine S11a.	104
6.11	Shrine NW24.	104
7.1	View of a typical section of the main Hatnub road, crossing level terrain.	110
7.2	The major stone-built causeway between Hatnub and the Amarna cliffs.	110
7.3	One of the dry-stone way-side huts, to the north of the main Hatnub road.	111
7.4	The unfinished(?) causeway leading southwards from the main plateau.	112
7.5	A diagrammatic cross-section of the causeway shown in fig. 7.4.	112
7.6	The main stone-built causeway near the Hatnub travertine quarries.	114
7.7	A view of the side of the dry-stone causeway close to Quarry P.	114
7.8	Diagrammatic profile of the causeway close to Quarry P.	115
7.9	Rock drawing in the limestone quarries at Ma'asara.	116

7.10	The basalt-quarriers' road at Gebel Qatrani/Widan el-Faras.	117
7.11	One of the dry-stone ramps at the Gebel el-Asr gneiss quarries.	120
7.12	One of the encampments beside the road leading from Gebel el-Asr to Tushka.	121
7.13	One of the Gebel Gulab/Tingar roads used by quartzite quarriers.	122
8.1.	View of part of the fortified Old Kingdom settlement at Wadi Maghara.	130
8.2	Plan of the Middle Kingdom miners' fortress (site 9) at Wadi el-Hudi.	131
8.3	Part of the dry-stone wall surrounding the fortress (site 9) at Wadi el-Hudi.	131
App. 2	Inscription I.	137
App. 2	Inscription II.	138
App. 2	Inscription III.	138
App. 2	Inscription IV.	138
App. 2	Inscription V.	138
App. 2	Inscription VI.	139
App. 2	Inscription VII.	139
App. 2	Inscription VIII.	139
App. 2	Inscription IX.	140
App. 2	Inscription X.	141
App. 2	Inscription XI.	141
App. 2	Inscription XII.	141
App. 2	Inscription XIII.	142
App. 2	Inscription XIV.	142
App. 3	Graffito 33.	156
App. 3	Graffito 37.	157
App. 3	Graffito 40	157
App. 3	Graffito 46.	157
App. 3	Graffito 39.	158
App. 3	Graffito 43.	159
App. 3	Graffito 52.	162
App. 4	Unprovenanced Hatnub Inscription UT1.	163
App. 4	Unprovenanced Hatnub Inscription UT2.	164
App. 4	Unprovenanced Hatnub Inscription UT3.	165

Acknowledgements

I am extremely grateful to Barry Kemp for first suggesting that I undertake this work at Hatnub, and for providing a great deal of help, encouragement and advice during the various seasons of the survey, as well as during the period that I was working on my PhD dissertation on Tell el-Amarna. I am also grateful to the staff of the Egyptian Supreme Council for Antiquities at Cairo, Mallawi and Minya for their assistance in five seasons of fieldwork at Hatnub. Financial assistance was generously provided by the Mulvey Fund (Cambridge University), the Wainwright Fund (Oxford University), the Egypt Exploration Society (EES Centenary Studentship 1986), the Seven Pillars of Wisdom Trust, the Leverhulme Trust, the British Academy, and the Bioanthropological Foundation of California. Sponsorship in the form of an EDM total station was also generously provided by Balfour Beatty Ltd. I am indebted to Robert Jameson, who undertook much of the fieldwork jointly with me (with a level of enthusiasm beyond the call of duty, considering his specialisation in European prehistory), and also to Paul Nicholson and Pamela Rose, for their reports on the pottery (Chapter 5, and information on ceramics throughout the text), and to Julian Heath for the inking of most of the plans and drawings. Harco Willems provided very useful information on the travertine workings at Sheikh Said and Wadi Bershawi. Finally, I am as usual grateful to Ann, Nia and Elin for frequent reminders that 4500-year-old quarries are not necessarily the most important things in life.

A Note on Geological Terminology

There have been some attempts in recent years to rationalise and clarify the geological terminology used in Egyptology. There is nevertheless still considerable – and indeed somewhat unresolved – debate concerning the correct terms to be used for two types of rock that Egyptologists have usually described as 'Egyptian alabaster' and 'gypsum' respectively. The rock type commonly described as 'Egyptian alabaster' consists primarily of calcium carbonate ($CaCO_3$) and is therefore chemically quite distinct from 'gypsum', which is made up of calcium sulphate ($CaSO_4$). Since, however, 'Egyptian alabaster' is often opaque white in appearance, like 'gypsum', the two rocks – and objects made from them – can be relatively easily confused when examined visually (but see Chapter 2 below for a more detailed discussion of the differences between these two rock types and the simple tests that can be used to distinguish between them). The terminology for the two rock types is particularly problematic not only because they superficially resemble one another, and are occasionally mislabelled in museum displays and catalogues, but also because the geological term 'alabaster' can only be used to refer to 'gypsum' and not to 'Egyptian alabaster'. Consequently, a number of different terms have been suggested as less ambiguous ways of referring to 'Egyptian alabaster'. Dietrich and Rosalind Klemm (1991, 2008: 147) have suggested calling it 'calcite-alabaster', Christine Lilyquist (1995: 13) used the terms 'calcareous' and 'calcium-based rock' in a catalogue of stone vessels, while James Harrell (1990: 37) and Barbara Aston (1994: 43) have argued that it should be described as 'travertine'. As the title of this book indicates, I have chosen to use the term 'travertine', on the grounds that the definition provided by Aston and Harrell is the one that is most geologically precise (see Aston *et al.* 2000: 59), despite the fact that the term is less familiar to Egyptologists (and in spite of the fact that some Egyptologists still prefer to use the term 'calcite' in order to avoid confusion with Italian travertine from the Tivoli region).

Preface

In the last twenty years two regrettable gaps in Egyptological coverage have finally begun to be filled. One of these is the survey and excavation of sites in the Eastern and Western deserts and the Sinai Peninsula. The second is the *archaeological* (as opposed to textually based) study of quarrying and mining regions. This monograph on the quarrying site of Hatnub is intended to make a modest contribution to both of these worthy tasks.

I stress the word 'archaeological' above, because in Egypt, the lack of archaeological fieldwork relating to quarrying and mining contrasts sharply with the quantity of study devoted to the abundant surviving ancient texts commemorating these two activities (see, for instance, Couyat and Montet 1912–13, Anthes 1928, Gardiner et al. 1955, Sadek 1980–5, Seyfried 1981, Eichler 1993, and Hikade 2001). Many pharaonic mines and quarries have been investigated only by epigraphers recording the inscriptions and graffiti carved into the quarried walls. The archaeological remains of quarrying have received scant attention from Egyptologists over the last hundred years, although Petrie and Currelly (1906), Clarke and Engelbach (1930) and Caton-Thompson and Gardner (1934) are notable early exceptions. This is despite the fact that, unlike many more permanent settlements in the Nile Valley itself, the surface remains of quarrying and mining sites are often well-preserved *in situ*. There are therefore invaluable (and still relatively unexploited) opportunities to examine the geological and archaeological evidence concerning the procurement and processing of a great diversity of stone and metal. It should be noted, perhaps, that the disregard of quarrying sites is by no means peculiar to Egyptological work, since Ericson and Purdy (1984: 8) complained twenty-five years ago, with regard to world archaeology as a whole: 'our information on the activities at quarries and workshops ranks among the most abysmal'.

Pharaonic quarrying and mining sites are scattered across the Western Desert, the Eastern Desert, the Sinai Peninsula and southern Palestine (see fig. 0.1), typically incorporating settlements of varying size and permanence, as well as debris relating to the exploitation of the materials concerned. This body of data deserves to be examined methodically, for the procurement and uses of stone and metal lay close to the heart of the economy of pharaonic Egypt. Since the 1980s, a number of projects have begun to explore the full archaeological potential of Egyptian quarries and mines (see Rothenberg 1988; Castel and Soukiassian 1989; Harrell 1989; Arnold 1991; Harrell and Bown 1995; Shaw and Jameson 1993; Shaw and Bloxam 1999; Bloxam and Storemyr 2002; and Storemyr et al. in press). Others have concentrated on scientific provenancing of the minerals used in monumental structures, statuary and funerary equipment (Klemm and Klemm 1979; 1981; 1984; 2008; Bowman et al. 1984, Greene 1989; Middleton and Bradley 1989), or the study of pharaonic stone-working and masonry techniques, often using experimental methods (Moores 1991; Isler 1992; Stocks 1986; 1989; 1993; 2003).

Influences of quarrying and mining on our perception of ancient Egyptian history

Although opinions differ considerably as to the precise cultural and environmental factors in Egyptian prehistory that were responsible for the emergence of the state in the late 4th millennium BC (see, for instance, Helck 1987; Trigger 1987; Köhler 1995; Wengrow 2006), there seems little doubt that the control and exploitation of mineral resources was, at the very least, a crucial element in this process. Early Upper Egyptian 'proto-states' such as Naqada and Hierakonpolis apparently gained prosperity at least partly through their grip over the gold from the wadis of the Eastern Desert (Hoffman 1979: 339; Trigger 1983: 39–40; Rice 1990: 34–6) and the southward expansion of Egyptian territory, from at least the Early Dynastic period onwards, was motivated to some extent by the need to control the Nubian gold-mining regions.

The quarrying and use of certain materials have also often been regarded as important reflections of political and economic stability at various times during the pharaonic period. It has been argued that the fluctuating scale of limestone and granite quarrying in the Old Kingdom (c.2649–2134 BC) might have acted as a barometer of royal power and perhaps also of social cohesion (Kemp 1983: 86–9; Lehner 1985: 109–10), although of course it might respond to a number of other socio-economic features, such as the degree of centralisation of power or the extent to which the power of the elite was being expressed overtly in the form of impressive funerary superstructures. For some rulers, it is their act of sending out quarrying and mining expedition that has ensured the survival of any memory of their reign, as in the case of Nebtawyra Mentuhotep IV (c.1998–1991 BC), who would barely be known had he not sent an expedition to the Wadi Hammamat to quarry *bḫn*-stone (see Shaw 2002 for discussion of possible Middle Kingdom links between politics and quarrying expeditions).

Such textual sources as the annals of Thutmose III suggest that the prosperity and success of the Egyptian 'empire' in the late 2nd millennium may have been partially founded on the success of their Egyptian and Nubian gold mines. Janssen (1975: 153) suggests that 'the economic aspects of gold production are still largely obscure', but O'Connor argues that the mines of southern Egypt and Nubia were consolidated and expanded during the reign of Amenhotep III (c.1400–1350 BC), and that this underlines the importance of gold in Egypt's economic and diplomatic relations with western Asiatic neighbours (O'Connor 1983: 259–60, fig. 3.19).

The social and economic results of travertine quarrying were clearly not as explicitly connected with wealth-generation as gold and copper mining. However, the consistent popularity of travertine, particularly for funerary vessels (its whiteness and translucence connecting it symbolically with purity), must have ensured the reasonably regular organisation and dispatch of state-sponsored travertine quarrying expeditions. From the Early Dynastic period to the end of the New Kingdom, travertine was by far the most common type of stone used to make vessels for royal and private tombs (see section 2.3 below for statistics on this).

Quarrying and the ancient Egyptian economy

The control of mineral deposits was itself a valuable economic entity, sometimes forming part of the assets of temples or funerary estates. According to an inscription on the walls of a rock-temple of the early 13th century BC in the Wadi Abbad, about 35 km east of Edfu in Upper Egypt, the gold mines in the vicinity were owned by the temple of Seti I at Abydos (Schott

1961: 143–59). The temple endowment included not only the rights to the gold concession itself at Wadi Abbad, but also a large team of miners, their settlement and a well said to have been dug at the king's orders. Clearly the skilled workmen, their equipment and the yet-to-be-mined gold ore formed a single 'economic package' consisting of valuable mineral rights along with the means to exploit them.

The expensive procurement of stone and metal was therefore evidently part of the socio-economic bargain between the Egyptian ruler and his nobles (see Chapter 8); loyal members of the elite could rely on the king to provide raw materials for their funerary equipment. One way in which the well-known Old Kingdom official Weni served several 6th Dynasty rulers was by organising quarrying expeditions (including one to procure travertine from Hatnub) which resulted, appropriately, in the royal gift of a fine sarcophagus for Weni, carved from limestone deriving from the quarries at Tura (Sethe 1933a: 98–110; Lichtheim 1973: 18–23; section 7.2 below).

Like agriculture and bureaucracy, the procurement of mineral wealth was an essential part of the infrastructure of the pharaonic economy. However, it is an unusually quantifiable aspect of ancient Egyptian material culture, equally visible both in the form of texts and physical debris.

The Turin Mining Papyrus: a blue-print for the Egyptian quarrying expedition

The archaeological components of a pharaonic quarrying or mining site can be broadly categorized under seven headings: (1) traces of quarrying/mining activity, (2) remains of settlements/encampments, (3) facilities for provision of water, (4) arteries of transport/communication, (5) evidence of processing/manufacturing activities, (6) textual/pictorial memorials of the expeditions and (7) ritualistic/religious remains. All seven of these categories of evidence have been found at Hatnub.

The earliest surviving Egyptian map is an annotated pictorial record of an expedition to the quarries of Wadi Hammamat in the Eastern Desert to obtain $bḫn$-stone (this Egyptian term evidently being used to refer to a group of rock-types including siltstone and breccia - Aston *et al.* 2000: 58). The Turin Mining Papyrus, now in the Museo Egizio, Turin, dates to the mid-12th century BC; it identifies the essential elements of a group of gold mines – at a site now known as Bir Umm Fawakhir – as well as the principal $bḫn$-stone quarries, located further east in the Wadi Hammamat. It is therefore effectively an ancient record of a particular geographical context, which can be fairly confidently identified with a surviving archaeological site. Acquired by Bernadino Drovetti at the beginning of the 19th century, the fragments of the papyrus were first identified by Samuel Birch (1852) as a depiction of a gold mine in the Eastern Desert. In the 1980s, the textual and pictorial details of the document were re-analysed, and its meaning and archaeological context re-assessed (Klemm and Klemm 1988; Bradbury 1988; Harrell and Brown 1992). In an illuminating exposition of the text of the papyrus, Harrell and Brown not only clarified the date and purpose of the map but also settled once and for all the vexed question of its identification with a particular locality in the Wadi Hammamat.

However, the particularity of the document – as a record of an actual quarrying expedition at a specified time and place – is perhaps not as important as the insights that it provides into the ancient Egyptians' conception of a mining or quarrying landscape. Archaeologists are only rarely presented with the opportunity to observe a particular type of archaeological site through ancient eyes. From this point of view, perhaps the most satisfying aspect of the Turin Papyrus is that its hieratic annotations include all of the essential components of a quarrying or mining site listed above in relation to Hatnub.

The map incorporates colour-coded geological zones, the locations of the gold mines and *bḫn*-stone quarries, a miners' settlement, a cistern (or water-reservoir), three ancient roads, two locations associated with the processing and transportation of minerals, a shrine dedicated to 'Amun of the pure mountain' and a commemorative stele from the time of Seti I (c.1306–1290 BC) reminiscent of the inscribed rock-shrine at Wadi Abbad mentioned above.

There are few other pictorial or textual sources with which to compare the Turin Mining Papyrus. A number of surviving reliefs and paintings show the transportation of statues or stone blocks (see section 7.2 below) but the aim of these depictions is invariably commemorative and descriptive rather than explanatory – the artists would have seen no reason to illustrate the construction of quarry-roads, the digging of desert wells or the encampments occupied by the workers; their primary concern was with the finished product not the steps that led up to it.

The principal aim of most of the texts carved in the vicinity of mines and quarries was to draw attention to the individuals who had played a role in the successful completion of a task, just as the role of funerary reliefs and stelae was to perpetuate the existence of named individuals. However, the Turin Papyrus was evidently a document either created to assist in a *bḫn*-stone quarrying expedition in the reign of Ramesses IV, or at the very least composed in order to record the details of such an event (Harrell and Brown 1992: 88–93). It is this aspect of the Turin Papyrus that makes it more informative to archaeologists, since this means that it combines textual and pictorial elements in a diagrammatic rather than iconographic fashion; in other words its primary concern appears to be with the *process* of quarrying rather than the end-products.

The Turin Papyrus may constitute an ancient blueprint for the process of procurement, but inevitably numerous practical and logistical questions concerning quarrying and mining remain unanswered. Why, for instance, do methods of transportation vary from one site to another? Why are there so many different types of workers' settlements and encampments? Do these specialised sites differ for functional, chronological or geological reasons, or perhaps a combination of all three? It is the task of projects such as the Hatnub Survey to provide the kinds of archaeological evidence to help us to answer questions of this type.

In 1981, Hester and Heizer (1981: 24–6) pointed out that their ethno-archaeological work on the making of travertine vessels was severely constrained by the military restrictions that prevailed in Egypt in the early 1970s, preventing them from supplementing their ethnographic work with survey and excavation of ancient quarrying materials:

> *We focused in our 1972 research on the manufacturing process. We need much more first-hand information on quarrying activities. We also need more information on the social organization and economic structure within which the quarrying-manufacturing system operates…it is also to be hoped that any future research could involve visits to the alabaster quarries, excavation in the contemporary middens associated with the workshops and other aspects of this fascinating technology which were not available in the political climate of 1972.*

The Hatnub Survey is one of several projects, from the 1980s onwards, precisely geared towards achieving the kinds of aims set out by Hester and Heizer.

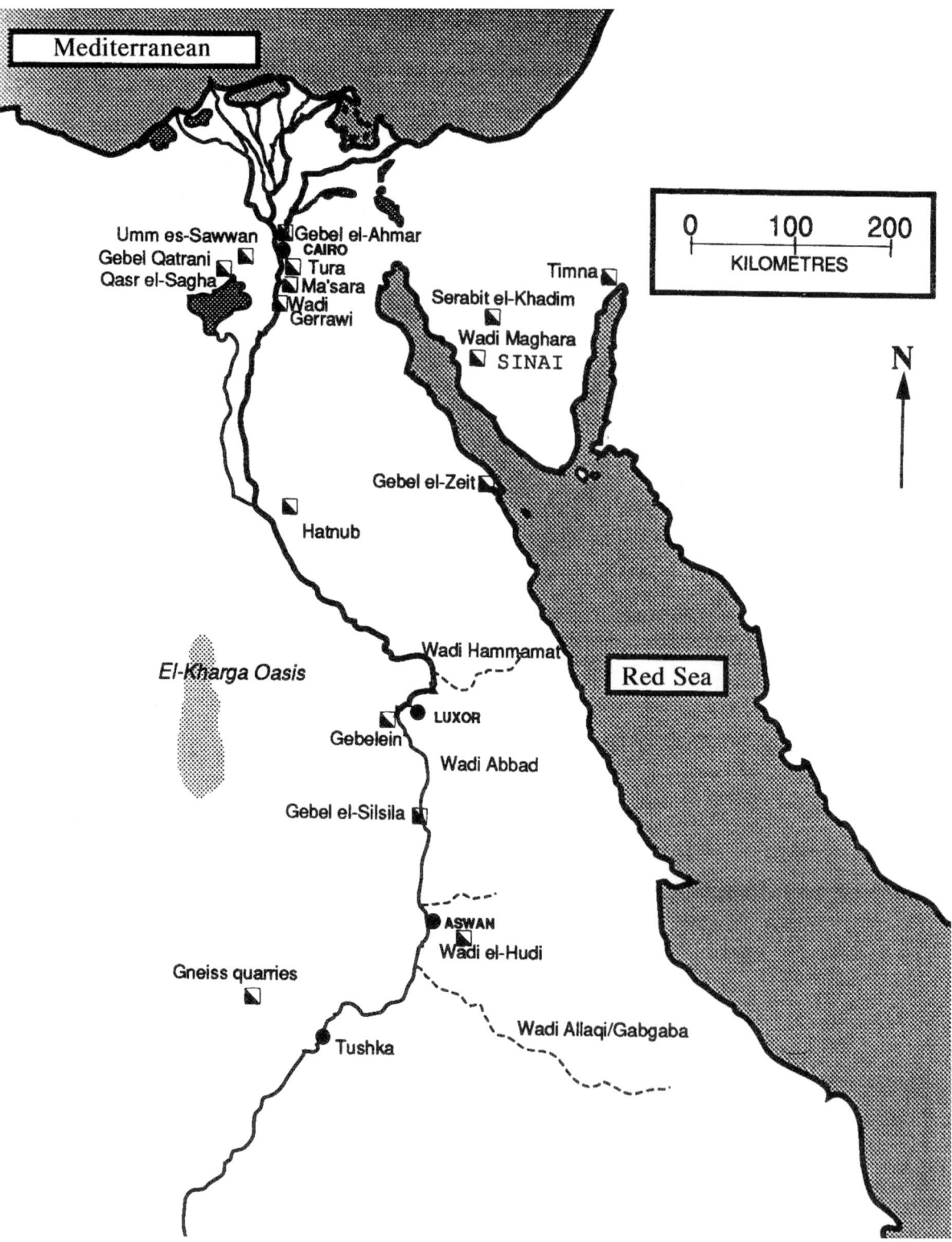

Figure 0.1. Map showing the locations of major quarry-sites in Egypt exploited during the pharaonic period, including Hatnub.

Chapter 1

The History of Previous Epigraphic and Archaeological Work at Hatnub

The Hatnub travertine quarries are situated around 16 km southeast of the city-site of Amarna, on the eastern side of the Nile in Middle Egypt (27° 33' N, 31° 00' E). The inscriptions, graffiti and archaeological remains at Hatnub indicate that this region of the Eastern Desert was intermittently exploited by the Egyptians for a period of about three thousand years, from at least the 1st Dynasty until the Roman period.

1.1 Introduction

There are three separate ancient quarrying zones at Hatnub, which were labelled P, R and T by Flinders Petrie when he included the site in his general map of the Amarna region in 1892 (see fig. 1.1). He provided a brief description of the site, including transcriptions of eight of the inscriptions and one of the graffiti in Quarry P (Petrie 1894: 3-4, pl. 42). Petrie also discussed a group of limestone and travertine quarries at the northern end of the Amarna plain, which have recently been examined in greater detail by James Harrell (2001a).

The inscriptions and graffiti at Quarries P and R were first recorded by Marcus Blackden and G. Willoughby Fraser (Blackden and Fraser 1892; Fraser 1894), who published facsimiles of 11 'inscriptions' (one hieratic and 10 hieroglyphic) and 21 'graffiti' (17 hieratic and two hieroglyphic). In 1907 the texts were more exhaustively investigated by Georg Möller, who recorded 15 inscriptions and 56 graffiti, producing facsimiles of each, as well as providing copies and translations (Möller 1908), which were eventually published by Rudolf Anthes (1928). Virtually all of the texts were inscribed or incised on the walls of Quarry P, where the large-scale incised cartouches of Khufu (fig. 1.2) provide the earliest *in situ* date for the exploitation of the quarries. With regard to dating, however, it should be noted that many Early Dynastic inscribed travertine vessels from the subterranean chambers of the Step Pyramid of Djoser at Saqqara specifically cite Hatnub as their place of origin (see Aufrère 2003: 7), thus probably indicating that the Hatnub quarries were in use from at least as early as the 1st Dynasty. Nine of the graffiti in Quarry P (Gr. 37, 39-41 and 44-8) and fragments of five others (collectively designated Graffito 48a) were removed from the quarry walls and became part of the Ägyptisches Museum und Papyrus Sammlung, Berlin (museum nos 18555-7 and 22609-19), although many of these were subsequently lost in the Second World War (see Appendix 6 for descriptions and bibliography of the Hatnub texts formerly and currently in the Berlin collection).

Fraser mentions traces of two inscriptions and 28 painted graffiti on the walls of the smaller Quarry R but he states that only one inscription and three of the graffiti were still legible, the rest

Figure 1.1. Map of Amarna and the Hatnub quarries (after Petrie 1894: pl. 42).

being visible only as depictions of men and offering tables. Three unprovenanced Middle Kingdom stelae probably deriving from Hatnub have also been published (see Appendix 4 below, figs A1–3; see Grdseloff 1951; Simpson 1958; Goedicke 1959; Simpson 1961; Posener 1968).

The texts at Hatnub provide many useful items of information concerning the size of the work-teams and the professions of the expedition members. These texts, and similar inscriptions at other quarrying and mining sites, such as the Sinai turquoise mines, suggest that there was a complex hierarchy of quarry-workers in the pharaonic period, involving as many as 25 different types of government officials, 11 varieties of local quarrying supervisors and numerous categories of skilled and unskilled workers (see Chapter 8 below).

The epigraphic evidence from Hatnub has been supplemented by a number of inscriptions in private tombs describing expeditions to the Hatnub quarries. The 'autobiography' of Weni from his tomb-chapel at Abydos, which was mentioned in the Preface, describes the quarrying of a very large travertine offering stone on behalf of the 6th Dynasty ruler Merenra (Sethe 1933a: 98–110; Lichtheim 1973: 18–23), and this is perhaps corroborated by Inscription VI at Hatnub, dating to the same reign (Anthes 1928: tf. 5, and see Appendix 2 below). The 12th Dynasty tomb of Thuthotep at Deir el-Bersha includes an annotated depiction of the transportation of a colossal travertine statue of the deceased from Hatnub, dragged along on a wooden sledge by lines of men pulling on ropes (see Newberry 1893: 17–26, pl. 15; Breasted 1906: 306–12; Badawy 1963; Jones forthcoming). Once again, the inscriptions at Hatnub itself seem to corroborate this funerary evidence, since a number of them commemorate quarrying expeditions sent by Thuthotep's family, the provincial governors of the Hare nome. The textual and pictorial data from the tombs of Weni and Thuthotep are discussed further in section 7.2 below.

Because only one inscription dating to the New Kingdom has been found at Hatnub, it used to be thought that the quarry had fallen into disuse after the Middle Kingdom, but our 1985–94 survey revealed substantial archaeological remains of New Kingdom quarrying expeditions (both at Quarries P and R). In addition, the date of some pottery shows that there was still some very limited activity at the site as late as the Roman period (see Fraser 1894: 76).

At the foot of a cairn marking the highest point in the area near Quarry P are votive sets of model steps and carved outlines of feet, and scattered throughout the Quarry P settlement are a number of small edifices approached by stone-lined paths, probably to be identified as shrines. The most impressive of these is a small hemispherical roofed building with a long approach path and a square entrance, too small to shelter a man but large enough for offerings to have been inserted. It is perhaps significant in this regard that several of the quarry inscriptions mention priests as members of the expeditions. Chapter 6 therefore discusses the surviving traces of the religious/ritualistic life of the quarry-workers.

Hatnub is linked with the Nile Valley by several dry-stone roads, one of which – the main route between the Old Kingdom quarries and the river – is marked at intervals with cairns and still clearly visible for much of its route (see section 7.1 below). At its northwestern end, in the el-Amarna plain, the first traces still visible in modern times (Kemp pers. comm.) are in the vicinity of Kom el-Nana, but it must originally have extended further to the west, presumably terminating in some form of harbour, the remains of which would now be buried beneath the modern cultivation. Petrie (1894: 3) claimed that the road was still 'traceable on the plain of Tell el Amarna' and that it 'must have started from a landing place a little to the south of el Amarieh', although it seems as if he bases this supposition not so much on any surviving remains beside the modern village of Amaria, but more likely simply by extending the trajectory of the perceived traces of the road in the desert to the east of the 18th Dynasty city at Amarna. To the east of Kom el-Nana, the road ascends the scarp face of the Eastern Desert and then heads southeastwards across undulating terrain. At two points along its route it had to be transformed into a causeway in order to bridge the larger wadis that interrupted its progress.

1.2 The discovery and history of the study of Hatnub

Hatnub (*ḥwt-nbw*: 'mansion of gold') is regularly mentioned in ancient Egyptian texts as the principal source of a stone called *bỉt* or *šs* (travertine), but for a long time its precise location was unknown. It was not until December 1891 that the site itself was rediscovered by Percy Newberry and Howard Carter, who were at that time undertaking epigraphic work at the Deir el-Bersha rock-tombs, at the same time as the first part of Petrie's 1891–2 season at Amarna. In

Figure 1.2. The Horus name and throne name of Khufu (Inscription II at Quarry P, Hatnub). As with other rock-cut texts and images in the quarry, significant damage has taken place since this inscription was recorded by Georg Möller in 1907.

late December 1891, G. Willoughby Fraser and Marcus Blackden, who had been working with Newberry and Carter at Beni Hasan and Deir el-Bersha, spent several days at the site copying the hieroglyphic and hieratic inscriptions in Quarries P and R; it was at this point that the site was identified as Hatnub, since the site-name was found to occur at least five times in the hieratic graffiti. Until this discovery, as Fraser (1894: 74) points out, the site's location had been 'generally and apparently wrongly supposed to be the alabaster quarries which lie in the eastern hills near Asyut' (see section 2.4 below for brief discussion of the Asyut travertine quarry).

T. G. H. James' biography of Howard Carter includes controversial discussion of Newberry's evident outrage that the find had been 'poached' by Blackden and Fraser (James 1991: 26–8), whose copies of the inscriptions (supplemented by two further visits in 1892) were published in 1894, in the same year that Petrie's publication of Amarna appeared. Francis Griffith also published translations of eight of the Hatnub graffiti in the second volume on Deir el-Bersha (Griffith 1894: 47–55, pls 22–3), adding some discussion concerning the various officials from the Hare nome (*wnw*) to whom the texts refer.

Since the published reports and unpublished letters and diaries of Newberry, Carter, Blackden, Fraser, Griffith and Möller/Anthes all focus almost entirely on the inscriptions and graffiti, the first archaeological work at the site was undertaken by Flinders Petrie in 1892, when he

Figure 1.3. The Horus name and throne name of Pepi I are barely visible in this photograph of the extremely vandalised remains of Inscription III at Quarry P.

included it in his general map of the Amarna region and provided brief discussion of it in the publication (Petrie 1894: 3–4). He provides some description of the main road linking the quarrying region at site P with the Amarna plain (as discussed above), which climbs up through the southern cliffs, passing to the south of boundary stelae R and S. He points out that there are also traces of a second quarry-workers' route, stretching between site R and the point on the main road several kilometres before it reaches site P. A more detailed archaeological survey of Hatnub was conducted by the German archaeologist Paul Timme, as part of a survey of the area in 1911, prior to Ludwig Borchardt's excavations at Amarna (Timme 1917).

Petrie describes Quarry P as 'an open circular pit with vertical sides, about 200 feet across and 50 feet deep', confirming that the corridor leading into it was decorated with many rock-cut inscriptions comprising Old Kingdom rulers' names and titles from Khufu onwards. He observes that the latest name at Quarry P seems to be that of a 12th Dynasty official, Sobekhotep, and therefore suggests that the quarry was perhaps abandoned at this date in favour of the pair of quarries at site R, about 1.5 km to the southwest. This may well have been the case, but it is now known not only that there is at least one New Kingdom inscription at Quarry P but also that there are significant surviving archaeological remains from the New Kingdom in its vicinity (see Chapter 3 below), suggesting that this region received a new lease of life at a much later date. Petrie briefly describes both the R quarrying site, where Middle Kingdom inscriptions and graffiti were found, and the undated quarry at site T (where a probable Roman rock-cut relief was discovered and recorded by Timme 1917: 45–7, abb. 50).

The most recent work at the site, the Hatnub Survey, which forms the main section of this monograph, took place over the course of five seasons between 1985 and 1994. The survey was initially conducted under the auspices of the University of Cambridge and the Egypt Exploration Society, and from 1992 onwards it was a project of the Institute of Archaeology, University College London (see Shaw 1986; 1987; 1990). The area around Quarry P was mapped in considerable detail, including the recording of surface remains and the excavation of two of the drystone structures (see Chapters 3–5 below).

Figure 1.4. Quarry P viewed from the northwest.

1.3 Ancient toponyms associated with the Hatnub quarry region

A number of different toponyms are associated either with the Hatnub quarrying region itself or with the general district around Amarna, where the Hatnub quarry road reaches the Nile valley. These are *ḥwt-nbw, pr-šs, ṯrtỉ* and *mrt-snfrw*.

ḥwt-nbw (mansion/temple/estate of gold; Hatnub)

The toponym Hatnub (*ḥwt-nbw*) is the one most frequently and straightforwardly associated with the travertine quarries 18 km to the southeast of Amarna. It is a matter of some debate, however, as to why this toponym was first applied to the quarries. Simpson (1977: 1043) and Harrell (2001b: 223) suggest that the phrase might refer to the golden-brown colour of the rock in this region, but Simpson also suggests that the application of this phrase to the travertine quarries might be alluding to the traditional association between Hathor and mining expeditions, as well as foreign countries and desert regions. The phrase *ḥwt-nbw* is also used to refer to:

- sarcophagus chambers
- temple workshops (probably with reference to gold-working taking place there, see Great Harris Papyrus 47, 2)
- a sculptor's studio mentioned in the tomb of Amenemhat at Thebes (TT82; Davies and Gardiner 1915: 58)
- chambers in temples where statues were placed (and where the 'opening of the mouth' ceremony was performed; see PT 1329 and Palermo Stone 5, 1)

- serapeum buildings at Memphis, Koptos and Dendera
- a celestial region mentioned in the Pyramid Texts
- a temple at Abydos (Sethe 1924: 68: 6)

Of these alternative meanings, the New Kingdom application of the term to a sculptor's studio, along with the references to temple workshops and statue-chambers, suggests that there was a link with craftwork and the fashioning of materials, both allusions that might be connected with the processing of travertine into funerary equipment and sculptures, and therefore might, by extension, refer to a source of this rock-type.

pr-šs (Ἀλαβαστρινη/Ἀλαβαστρων πολις, Alabastronpolis)

The 20th Dynasty *Onomasticon of Amenemope* mentions a settlement called *pr-šs*, which, given the presence of Hatnub, is assumed to have been located in the region of Amarna (see Gardiner 1947: II, 376). Kessler (1981: 106–7) suggests that the term may in fact not refer to Hatnub itself, but might actually designate a settlement associated with the travertine quarries to the northeast of Amarna (see section 2.4 below), which were exploited from the New Kingdom onwards. Kessler points out that these quarries can be reached via the Wadi Isbeida, therefore the Darb Isbeida region might have been the site of the ancient town or village *pr-šs*. It appears that *pr-šs* is probably to be identified with the Greek place-name of Ἀλαβαστρινη or Ἀλαβαστρων πολις, which is also usually assumed to be located somewhere in the region of Amarna, although Zawiyat el-Amwat is another possibility for Ἀλαβαστρινη (see Edmé Jomard's description of fragments of travertine found at Zawiyat el-Amwat in *Description* IV, 354, and see also Kessler 1981: 107).

Since neither Darb Isbeida nor Zawiyat el-Amwat are definitely associated with *pr-šs*, it is possible that the term might actually be referring either to Hatnub itself or to a settlement in the Amarna plain that served as the Nile-end of the travertine quarrying operations in the New Kingdom.

ṯrtỉ

The toponym *ṯrtỉ* seems to refer to a settlement associated in some way with the travertine quarries in the Middle Kingdom and perhaps earlier. Dieter Kessler (1981: 98) speculates that the word may derive from the botanical term *ṯrt*, meaning willow (*Salix safsaf*), while the determinative would usually be expected to refer to a place in the hilly region to the east of the Nile (as opposed to the flatter desert to the west).

Hatnub Graffito 49 refers to an expedition leader called Amenemhat, who worked at the quarries in the 31st regnal year of Senusret I, and held the title 'lord of *ṯrtỉ*' (Anthes 1928: 77; see also Appendix 3 below for a full translation), while another 'lord of *ṯrtỉ*' is mentioned on an unprovenanced 12th Dynasty stele assumed to be from Hatnub (see UT2 in Appendix 4 below), which was published by Simpson (1958, 1961). It is faintly possible that this toponym has survived in the name of Dairut (Coptic ⲧⲉⲣⲱⲧ, Greek Ταρ(ρ)ουθις), a small modern town located some 10 km south of Amarna, on the west bank. However, the most likely location of the original *ṯrtỉ* appears to have been near the modern village of Hawata, on the east bank of the Nile, at the southern end of the Amarna plain, given that it seems to be a harbour area at the northwestern end of the main Hatnub road (roughly where the so-called River Temple was constructed at the end of the Amarna period). The excavations at Amarna have yielded no traces of such an early settlement, which, if it existed, would probably lie beneath the modern agricultural fields by Hawata. Kessler (1981: 98) suggests that the 'columns of men from east and west' whom the inscriptions in Thuthotep's tomb at Deir el-Bersha claim to have conveyed a colossal travertine statue from Hatnub to Bersha, might have come from the region of *ṯrtỉ*.

mrt-snfrw

The toponym *mrt-snfrw*, which Anthes (1928: 20) assumes to be an alternative name for the Hatnub travertine quarries, occurs in Graffito 4 at Quarry P, although the literal meaning of the name may well be 'harbour of Sneferu', in which case it may be the specific name of the harbour at *ṯrtỉ* in the southern Amarna plain (see above). Goedicke (1965: 32–3) refers to a 'well of *mrt-snfrw*' in his translation of Graffito 4, which he interprets as a draft or copy of a letter written by a quarrying expedition leader to his superior (see Anthes 1928: 20). Goedicke assumes that in this instance the toponym *mrt-snfrw* is some kind of Nile valley terminus of the Hatnub road: 'As the alabaster quarries of Hatnub are at a distance of c.12 miles to the east of the Nile valley, those workmen could not make their entire approach by boat, but eventually had to leave the Nile and to "ascend" to the quarries. There was apparently an established road which is said to branch off the Nile at a point called "well of *mrt-snfrw*".' Günther Roeder (1959: 21) cites a 'quarry of King Sneferu's harbour'.

1.4 The current condition of the site

The Hatnub region has been protected for thousands of years primarily by its remoteness from the Nile valley, but unfortunately the late 20th century and early 21st century have seen a severe decline in the quality of preservation of its archaeological remains, rock inscriptions and graffiti. Even in the late 19th and early 20th century there were already signs of deterioration at the site. Anthes (1928: 2) notes that in the 15 years between the Blackden and Fraser survey of 1892 and the Möller work of 1907, the cartouche of Pepi I in Inscription III was stolen, Graffito 7 was evidently damaged by a Bedouin camp-fire, and several other graffiti were affected by soluble salt damage.

Unlike many other ancient sites in the Eastern Desert, which are severely affected by the rise of a modern trend for off-road tourism in convoys of four-wheel-drive vehicles, the most recent damage at Hatnub seems to derive from the significant resumption of quarrying in the 1980s (see Bloxam and Heldal 2007 for a similar problem at the Widan el-Faras basalt quarries in the northern Faiyum region). The modern quarrying companies are not interested in large blocks of travertine, but have tended to focus on obtaining large quantities of small chips for use in the production of small household tiles. In addition, the legally required move away from mud brick to limestone for new houses, has increased the level of quarrying activity in pursuit of good quality limestone. As a result, the main ancient quarry road between the Amarna plain and the quarrying regions P, R and T has suffered considerable damage due to the repeated movement of materials by heavy modern vehicles. At the quarries themselves, the remains of stone huts and the main causeway near site P had not yet been affected, by the time of our final season (1994), but there were many signs of vandalism in the main quarry at site R, with numerous inscriptions and graffiti on the quarry walls having been damaged, and, in some cases, totally destroyed. The site of quarry T had also been severely affected by modern quarrying activities.

Like other ancient quarrying sites in the Eastern and Western Deserts (e.g. the Khafra anorthosite gneiss and chalcedony quarries at Gebel el-Asr and the turquoise mines at Wadi Maghara), Hatnub is in desperate need of a great deal more official protection than it currently receives, and all such sites should ideally be inspected at regular intervals to keep a check on the overall site preservation.

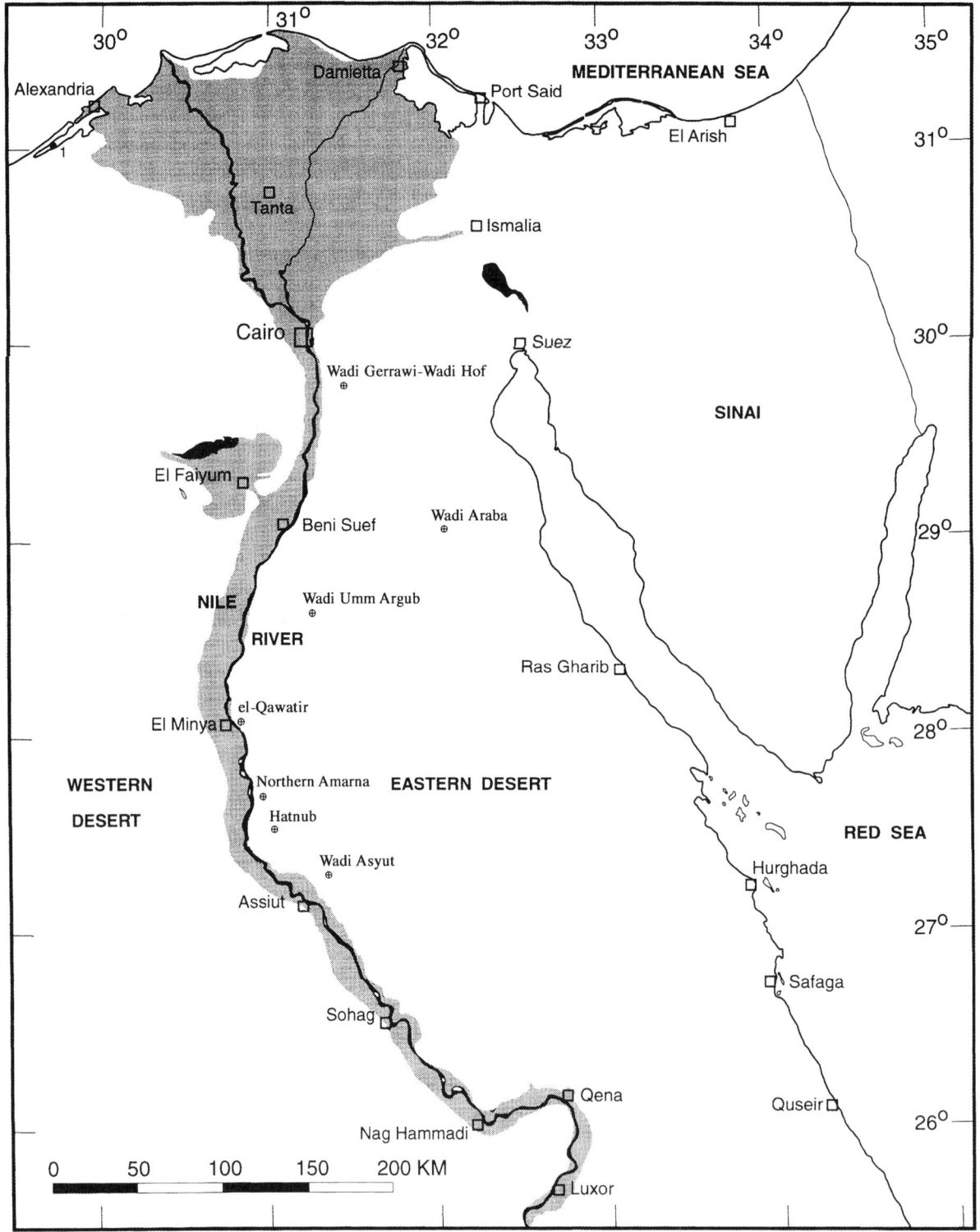

Figure 2.1. Map showing the principal travertine quarrying regions in Egypt (after Aston *et al.* 2000: fig. 2.1)

Chapter 2

Egyptian Exploitation of Travertine and the Geoarchaeology of Hatnub and Other Ancient Quarries

This chapter discusses a variety of issues relating to Egyptian travertine in general: its lexicographical and geological definitions, its uses and symbolism, its sources, and the methods by which it appears to have been worked.

2.1 Geological and chemical definitions of Egyptian travertine

Travertine is a sedimentary rock and a variety of limestone consisting largely of calcite (calcium carbonate, $CaCO_3$) or aragonite (another form of calcium carbonate). The travertine used in ancient Egypt is frequently described in archaeological monographs and papers as 'Egyptian alabaster' or simply 'alabaster'. This terminology, however, is incorrect, since true alabaster, as recognised by geologists, consists of gypsum (the principal ancient Egyptian quarries for which are located at Umm el-Sawwan in the Faiyum region - see Caton-Thompson and Gardner 1934). True alabaster (i.e. gypsum or calcium sulphate, $CaSO_4$, not travertine) is opaque white with occasional yellow patches or reddish brown veins caused by impurities; it can readily be distinguished from travertine both by its extreme softness (it can be scratched by a fingernail) and by the fact that it fails to effervesce in hydrochloric acid. Another major difference between true alabaster and travertine, is that the latter was used in Egypt for funerary vessels throughout the pharaonic and Greco-Roman periods, whereas alabaster-gypsum had only three phases of use: first, from the Predynastic to the 3rd Dynasty, secondly in the New Kingdom and thirdly in the Late Period. Many of the hundreds of inscribed travertine vessels from among the tens of thousands found in the subterranean chambers of the Step Pyramid of Djoser at Saqqara are inscribed with references to Hatnub (Lacau and Lauer 1961; Aufrère 2003: 7).

The fact that alabaster-gypsum was rarely used for funerary vessels in the later Old Kingdom, the First Intermediate Period, the Middle Kingdom, the Second Intermediate Period, and the Third Intermediate Period is another useful factor in distinguishing the true material of a funerary vessel, since the date of the item may sometimes be sufficient in itself to indicate whether it is made from alabaster-gypsum or travertine. On this point, it is worth noting that Barbara Aston's re-examination of the alabaster-gypsum quarries at Umm el-Sawwan led her to suggest that Gertrude Caton-Thompson (Caton-Thompson and Gardner 1934) was probably incorrect in dating the majority of alabaster-gypsum quarrying and vessel manufacture to the 3rd and 4th Dynasties, when in fact the pottery at the site dates largely to the 1st and 2nd Dynasties and Aston's study of vessels in museum collections suggests that virtually all date to the 1st–3rd Dynasties.

Some Egyptologists (e.g. Ruffle 1977: 164; Bourriau 1988: 144–5; De Putter and Karlshausen 1992: 44) prefer to use the compromise terms 'calcite' and 'calcite-alabaster' to refer to travertine, but these suggestions are somewhat problematic, since calcite is the name of a mineral (not a rock type) and calcite-alabaster is a hybrid name considered unsuitable by geologists. Barbara Aston (1994: 43), on the other hand, puts forward a convincing defence for the use of the word travertine, arguing that this terminology 'not only indicates the correct chemical composition, but has the additional advantage of implying a particular texture and mode of formation' (see also Aston *et al.* 2000: 59–60).

Percy Newberry wrote some brief comments on the re-discovery of the Hatnub quarries in an article in the *Morning Post* in 1923, in which he argued that the rock quarried at Hatnub should actually be described as 'aragonite'. However, one aspect of terminology that all Egyptologists and geologists seem to be agreed on is that the term aragonite is incorrect for either the Egyptian rock type traditionally described as 'Egyptian alabaster' or the mineral of which it is composed. Aragonite not only has a higher specific gravity than calcite but also has a different crystal structure, therefore both Lucas (1962: 59) and Petrie (1940: 98) agreed that it was incorrect in the Egyptian context, and Aston devotes extensive discussion to the arguments against using this term (Aston 1994: 44).

Egyptian travertine is a dense (non-porous) rock consisting entirely of calcite and is a variety known as 'calcareous sinter' (alternative names being 'calc-sinter' and 'onyx marble'). A porous, spongy-looking variety called 'calcareous tufa' occurs outside Egypt (e.g. at Tivoli in Italy), and is the rock type most frequently associated with the name travertine. The Egyptian deposits – made up of the same material as cave stalagmites, stalactites and other flowstone speleothems (i.e. secondary mineral deposits formed in caves) – originally formed in subsurface caverns and fissures in the Eocene limestone bedrock (Scoffin 1987: 151–2). There is some evidence suggesting that hot springs may also have played some role in the formation of the Egyptian travertine deposits. Harrell (1990: 39) points out that both Egyptian travertine, and the cavities in which it formed, probably date back to the Pleistocene epoch, when a considerably wetter climate prevailed in northeast Africa.

Travertine is an extremely versatile and attractive stone, which seems to have been consistently highly valued by the Egyptians since Predynastic times. Three variants of travertine are found in Egypt:

1) An opaque, milky white calc-sinter that is fine-grained (crystals < 1 mm) with little or no layering, which seems to have only rarely been used by the ancient Egyptians.

2) A frequently-used translucent coarse-grained, fibrous calc-sinter (coloured in shades of pale brown or yellowish- to orangey-brown with faint to marked layering).

3) A strikingly banded calc-sinter comprising an interlayering of the other two forms (see Akkad and Naggar 1964a; 1964b; 1965a; 1965b), which was also frequently used.

The brownish colouring of types 2 and 3 – derived from minute traces of iron oxide deposited by groundwater – fades to white after exposure to the sun. Harrell *et al.* (2007) undertook ultraviolet and gamma irradiation experiments to investigate the source of the brownish colour and the process by which it fades. Their work shows that natural radioactivity within the rock activates the colour centres, but that these are eventually deactivated by the ultraviolet component of sunlight. This seems to have happened in the case of the exterior walls of the Muhammad Ali Mosque (in the Citadel, Cairo), which was built between 1830 and 1848, using exterior and interior veneers of the interlayered type of travertine.

2.2 The lexicography of Egyptian travertine

As if the above discussion of geological debate concerning such terms as travertine and alabaster were not sufficiently confusing in itself, it is also necessary to cope with the complexity and ambiguity of ancient definitions and terms, in order to be able to reconcile the archaeological survival of travertine artefacts with textual references to this type of stone, and objects carved from it. Nicholas Postgate (1997) has demonstrated the many pitfalls of studying ancient Mesopotamian petrology, and the same situation clearly applies in an ancient Egyptian context. As Postgate (1997: 206–7) puts it, 'there are endless hurdles to negotiate…No single procedure is sufficient', and he goes on to argue that such criteria as function, form, substance and source can, in various situations, be the key to understanding the precise meanings and nuances of ancient terms that have been broadly categorized as 'geological' words. The Akkadian terms *parūtu* and *gišnugallu*, for instance, each appear to be used to refer to *both* alabaster gypsum and travertine in Neo-Assyrian building inscriptions. This suggests that Akkadian writers were not making any clear or consistent distinction between these two rock types, but simply treating the two words as synonymous general terms for precious white stone; as Roger Moorey (1994: 343) points out, 'the ambivalence of ancient scribal usage in this case is hardly surprising and reflects a dilemma still current'. Chapter 7 below, deals with quarry roads and transportation, in which several Assyrian palace reliefs depicting the transportation of travertine bull-sphinxes from quarries to city (by both land and river), in the early 8th century BC, are employed as non-Egyptian evidence placing the data from the Nile valley in a broader cultural context.

The earliest surviving Egyptian text to refer to travertine uses the word *šs* (Wb IV.540.10), and dates to the early 4th Dynasty (Petrie 1892: 13). The words *bȝt* and *šs* are both used to refer to travertine during the Old Kingdom, but by the Middle Kingdom *šs* is the word that is most commonly used. It was Brugsch (1862: 12) who first stated that *šs* should be translated as 'alabaster' (by which he seems to have meant travertine, rather than alabaster-gypsum), demonstrating this usage on the basis of a dedicatory inscription on a travertine shrine in the temple of Ramesses II at Abydos. The word *bȝt* is employed to refer to travertine in Graffiti 3, 6, 7 and 9 at Hatnub, all but one of which date to the reign of Pepi II (the odd one out being Gr. 9, which dates to the First Intermediate Period).

According to Harris (1961: 78), 'apart from its regular occurrence in the *ḥtp dȝ nsw* formula, *šs* is stated to be the material of buildings, stelae, statues, vessels, headrests and other objects, and occurs in at least two contexts which seem to suggest that the Egyptians regarded it as one of the semi-precious stones'. Rudolf Anthes (1928: 7) suggested that a third term for travertine was the phrase '*rwdt* stone of Hatnub', which would literally have meant 'hard stone from Hatnub'. However, Montet (1930) argues convincingly not only that this does not make sense in geological terms (since travertine is a soft stone) but also that the reading of the sign as *rwdt* is erroneous, and that the sign is actually *šs* followed, rather unusually by the feminine suffix *-t*. The addition of this suffix to produce the alternative spelling *šst* (Wb IV.541.6–10) does occur in a number of other texts (see Harris 1961: 78, n.1 for six instances of *šst*).

Harris (1961: 77) also discusses the frequent use of the epithets *wꜥb* ('pure'), *bḳ* ('white') and *n ḥwt-nbw* ('of Hatnub') to qualify the terms *šs* and *bꜣt*, in the same way that *nfr* is often used to qualify the words for limestone and sandstone. Similarly, Sethe (1933b) points out that the use of the phrase *šs wꜥb n ḥwt-nbw* ('pure travertine from Hatnub') seems to deliberately parallel the expression *inr ḥḏ nfr n ꜥin.w* ('fine white (lime)stone from Ainu [i.e. Tura/Ma'asara]'). It is unclear whether this descriptive phrase *n ḥwt-nbw* always meant that the travertine derived from Hatnub specifically or whether it simply became a convenient way of indicating the high quality of the stone in question. This suggestion is made by Harris (1961: 77), but primarily as a means of explaining the use of the phrase in the New Kingdom, when he believed that there was little or no quarrying at Hatnub itself. Since the 1985–94 survey at Hatnub indicates that the site was exploited in the New Kingdom, it now seems more likely that the phrase indicates the actual source of the stone (or alternatively, that it may sometimes indicate actual provenance and sometimes quality, depending on the specific context). As noted above, many of the inscribed Early Dynastic travertine vessels from the Step Pyramid at Saqqara specifically refer to Hatnub, presumably as an indication of their provenance (Lacau and Lauer 1961; Aufrère 2003: 7).

Barbara Aston (1994: 44) lists five travertine artefacts that actually bear hieroglyphic inscriptions identifying the material of which they are composed as *šs*: a chapel of Amenhotep I from Karnak (Pillet 1923: 113–17), an offering slab of Thutmose III from Karnak (Legrain 1903: 225–6), a shrine of Amenhotep II from Karnak (Van Siclen 1986), a shrine of Ramesses II from the temple at Abydos (Brugsch 1862: 12), and a 'lion-bed' of Ahmose II from the Apis House at Mitrahina (Jones and Jones 1982: 53). These objects and their inscriptions make it clear that the word *šs* was used to refer to travertine, whereas the term *ḳd* (or *ḳꜣḏꜣḏꜣ*) was applied to alabaster-gypsum in the New Kingdom at least (Harris 1961: 90–1). Note that Harris (1961: 91) also cites one example of the use of *ḳꜣḏꜣḏꜣ* in place of *ḳd* (Ostr. Cairo 25521 rt.) and argues that this confirms the likelihood that the Egyptian term *ḳd* derives from the Akkadian *gassu*, from which the Greek γυψος, and therefore ultimately also the word gypsum itself, stem.

In the Roman period, the term 'alabaster' (derived from the Greek ἀλαβαστρος) began to be used to refer to Egyptian travertine, but this original meaning of the word was evidently forgotten during the Middle Ages, when 'alabaster' acquired its modern definition and began to be applied to a variety of gypsum visually resembling travertine. It is unclear how the term ἀλαβαστρος first emerged. Several writers, including Alfred Lucas (1962: 60) and Rosemarie and Dietrich Klemm (1981: 11), have suggested that it might have come from the town or region of Alabastron mentioned by Pliny (*Natural History* Book 36 XXXVII: 54 and V: 11). However, it seems much more likely that the reverse is the case, i.e. that the town/region is named after the stone (as in the discussion of the toponym *pr-šs* in section 1.3 above). Kurt Sethe (1933b: 888–9) suggests that ἀλαβαστρος might derive from the Egyptian phrase *ꜥꜣ n bꜣstt* ('vessel of [the goddess] Bastet'), but this remains very much a hypothesis, unsupported by any real proof.

2.3 The ancient uses and symbolism of travertine

Egyptian travertine is a relatively soft stone, which had many uses, ranging from the lining and paving of buildings (e.g. the valley temple of Khafra at Giza, and the mortuary temple of Unas at Saqqara) to the creation of colossal statues, such as the one that was depicted in the tomb of

Thuthotep at Deir el-Bersha (Newberry 1893: 17–26 - see also section 1.1 above and 7.2 below), and the making of receptacles, particularly unguent vessels. In addition, travertine was commonly employed throughout the pharaonic period for other small objects such as canopic jars, statuettes, shabtis, offering tables, bowls and dishes. The earliest known example of canopic equipment, a chest from tomb G7000x, the 4th Dynasty burial of Hetepheres at Giza (Cairo, Egyptian Museum, JE52452; Reisner and Smith 1955: 21–2, pl. 44), was carved from travertine.

Uses of travertine within Egypt

In the late Predynastic and Protodynastic periods, travertine was primarily used for funerary vessels and mace-heads. About 16% of 300 protodynastic vessels listed by Alfred Lucas (1962: 47) were carved from travertine, making it the third most popular material from which to carve vessels at that date (after limestone, 36%, and basalt, 21.5%). By the Early Dynastic period travertine was by far the most common stone used for funerary vessels, both in royal and private tombs (but see Aston 1994: 47 for a discussion of the problems in assessing quantities of materials used for funerary equipment at Abydos and Saqqara).

In one 1st Dynasty tomb at Saqqara, dating to the reign of Aha, over 90% of the total of 653 stone funerary vessels were made from travertine, and in the slightly later 1st Dynasty tomb of Hemaka at Saqqara half of the 384 stone vessels were of travertine. The further increase in popularity of travertine vessels in the Old Kingdom is indicated by the fact that $c.$30,000 travertine vessels were found in one subterranean gallery of the Step Pyramid complex of Djoser at Saqqara (Firth and Quibell 1935: 76–7), and this material accounted for the entire group of 38 vessels in Queen Hetepheres' 4th Dynasty tomb at Giza (see Reisner 1931: 139–40 for further discussion of the growing preference for travertine funerary vessels in the Old Kingdom). The popularity of travertine vessels in the Old Kingdom is in curious contrast to the complete dearth of alabaster gypsum vessels during this period, despite the fact that many were made from alabaster gypsum during the Early Dynastic period. The use of travertine for funerary vessels clearly still prevailed in the New Kingdom, in that 76 of the 79 vessels in Tutankhamun's tomb were carved from this stone (el-Khouli *et al.* 1994).

Since the predominant colour of travertine is white, it seems to have been regarded as a symbol of cleanliness, purity and therefore also sanctity. Hence it is not surprising that travertine was frequently the material of choice for religious and funerary equipment. It also evidently acquired certain connections with pregnancy and milk, as in the case of several small vessels carved in the forms of misshapen pregnant women, often with one hand rubbing the abdomen. These vessel types, the so-called *Gravidenflasche*, presumably held ointment, and may perhaps be linked with two medical 'prescriptions' in Papyrus Ebers that are thought to have been intended to stimulate the production of breast milk (P.Ebers 808–9, see Brunner-Traut 1970; von Deines 1976).

There is evidence to suggest that in certain contexts travertine might have been imbued with more complex symbolism, as in the case of the two block statues found in the mastaba-tombs of Hetep and Ihi, near Teti's pyramid at Saqqara. One of these figures was carved from travertine and the other from diorite, therefore Eggebrecht (1966) argued that the two different stone types may have symbolised the rising sun (travertine) and the sun in the night-sky (diorite).

Spence (1999: 115) points out that, 'Textual sources ... associate only three terms with the colour of building stone: black, white and red'. She goes on to suggest that these colours are deliberately employed symbolically in Egyptian buildings, rather than being simply decorative. Whereas black and red building stones (such as basalt and silicified sandstone) are associated with darkness/underworld and danger/blood/sun respectively, a white stone such as travertine was associated with light and purity (Aufrère 1991: 695-8). Red stones (e.g. pink granite and silicified sandstone) appear to have had magical, liminal connotations and were therefore particularly used for temple doorways and false doors, whereas travertine was more frequently used for paving (e.g. the floors of Khafra's valley temple and Sahura's mortuary temple).

Gardiner (1930: 167) first made the point that, when the term *šs* is used in lists of offerings in funerary inscriptions (e.g. 'thousands of travertines'), it refers not to pieces of the stone itself but to the various different vessels characteristically carved from this material. He suggests that this was done partly because there were no doubt several different shapes of vessel represented, but partly also because the material was clearly regarded as an important factor, and this practice is echoed by the references to *alabastra* in the Roman period, such as those in Pliny's *Natural History* (see section 2.2 above).

Because large blocks were difficult to obtain from quarries, travertine was only occasionally used for sarcophagi, statues and naoi. The sarcophagus of the 3rd Dynasty ruler Sekhemkhet (still *in situ*, see Goneim 1956: 99-132) and that of the 4th Dynasty Queen Hetepheres (Cairo, Egyptian Museum, JE51899, see Reisner and Smith 1955: 16, pls 4, 43) were both carved from travertine, as was the much later sarcophagus of Seti I of the 19th Dynasty (now in the Soane Museum, London, see Budge 1908). Myriam Wissa (1997) discusses the sarcophagus of Sekhemkhet, arguing that its sheer size as a monolithic piece of carving suggests that it might have come from the large Quarry P at Hatnub, although there are no known inscriptions or graffiti at this site dating as early as the 3rd Dynasty (see Appendices 3-5 below).

From the 3rd Dynasty, there are two libation tables of the reign of Djoser (Cairo, Egyptian Museum, CG 1321), and the main court of the 5th Dynasty sun temple of Nyuserra at Abu Ghurob contains a massive travertine altar comprising a disc surrounded on each side by four carved examples of the hieroglyphic sign *ḥtp* ('offering'), thus giving the whole item an unusual cruciform shape. From the same period there is the travertine altar of Sahura (Wartke 1977), and in the 6th Dynasty mortuary temple of Teti at Saqqara there is a badly eroded travertine altar still *in situ*, originally decorated with the royal titulary and personifications of the nomes (Malek 1986: 77). From the Middle Kingdom, two important examples of travertine naoi have survived: one from the temple of Mentuhotep II at Deir el-Bahari, and the base of another from the Senusret I phase of the Karnak temple. Travertine was also used for the embalming tables of the Apis bulls at Memphis, mostly dating to the 26th Dynasty (Jones 1990).

Travertine royal and private statues are known from the Old Kingdom onwards, notable royal examples being fragments of several figures of the 4th Dynasty ruler Khafra (e.g. Boston MFA 21.351 and Hildesheim Roemer and Pelizaeus Museum 5415), the well-known statuette of Pepi II on his mother's lap (Brooklyn 39.119), the 18th Dynasty colossal sphinx at Memphis (Mitrahina Museum), the dyad of Amenhotep III and the god Sobek, from the temple of Sobek at Dahamsha (Luxor J155), a statue of Seti I from the Karnak cachette (Cairo, Egyptian Museum, CG 42139), and part of a colossal seated statue of Ramesses II (Louvre A22-N22). Statues of non-royal individuals include two 5th Dynasty figures in the Egyptian Museum, Cairo (CG 132 and 134), several statues of provincial governors of the First Intermediate Period and Middle Kingdom (e.g. Boston 1971.20, Brussels MRAH E5596), and the statue of the God's Wife of Amun, Amenirdis (Cairo, Egyptian Museum, CG 565). There are also several 6th Dynasty travertine sculptors' models from Kom el-Dara (Louvre E17276 and E25212). It appears, however, that only a relatively small number of private statues carved from travertine have survived from the New Kingdom, perhaps suggesting a decline in popularity of the sculptural use of travertine at that date.

Travertine had a number of significant architectural uses. It was sometimes employed from the Early Dynastic period onwards for pavements and wall-linings in temple passages and rooms, as noted above in the brief discussion of colour symbolism. A particularly well-preserved example of a travertine pavement has survived in the Valley Temple of the 4th Dynasty King Khafra at Giza, where it was no doubt chosen for maximum contrast with the black granite walls. It was also used extensively for small Middle and New Kingdom shrines (such as those of Senusret I, Amenhotep I/Thutmose I and Thutmose III in the open-air museum at Karnak - the three shrines mentioned above, in section 2.2, in Aston's list of items explicitly identified as being made from *šs*). In the late 4th century BC, a travertine funerary building was constructed at Alexandria; this structure, discovered in the Catholic Cemetery of Terra Santa in *c.*1914, was thought by Achille Adriani to be the antechamber of Alexander's tomb (Adriani 1940: 15–23), but his hypothesis remains unconfirmed. It measures around 5×5 m in area, and incorporates some very large blocks of travertine including one (forming the floor of the building) that measures 4.62×3×0.7 m.

Finally, possible indications of the medicinal use of travertine, presumably in powdered form, have survived in the form of the phrases *dkw n šs* and *ỉmt n šs*, which occur in Papyrus Ebers (e.g. P. Ebers 69: 19, 86: 3 and 87: 5) as well as other documents (e.g. verso of P. Smith 21: 6). There is also some evidence for the employment of travertine in the preparation of ointments applied to the skin (P. Ebers 714–15, P. Hearst 153–4; see Halioua and Ziskind 2005: 33).

Travertine vessels as elite exports

Elaborate travertine vessels seem to have played an important role in Egypt's elite contacts with the outside world, either through straightforward commerce or, more often, through the diplomatic exchange of gifts between ruling families. Travertine's economic influence can also be seen in the frequent use of this stone type for weights used in the evaluation and exchange of commodities both within Egypt and beyond its borders. Lemaire and Vernus (1978) have pointed out that the sign ϐ/Ϗ frequently appearing on inscribed weights in Iron Age Israel, might have derived from the Egyptian hieroglyphic determinative used to refer to travertine artefacts.

In the 5th and 6th centuries BC, when Egypt was a satrapy in the Achaemenid empire, there appears to have developed a vogue among the Persian elite for the acquisition of large inscribed Egyptian travertine vessels (Westenholz and Stolper 2002). In 1936 Georges Posener published descriptions of six vessels of this type bearing the name of Darius I, thirty-five with the name of Xerxes, and five with the name of Artaxerxes, but others have been found since the 1930s, including a quadrilingual vessel bearing the name of Artaxerxes which was found at Orsk in southern Russia in 1971, and a vessel bearing the name of Xerxes found at the foot of the western staircase in the Mausoleum at Halicarnassus (Posener 1936). It has been suggested that these vessels became popular because they were used to hold the regular supplies of Nile water for the Great King's table (which the Egyptians are said to have been obliged to send as tribute).

The appreciation by non-Egyptians of Egyptian excellence in the carving of travertine can clearly be traced much earlier, and instances of the diaspora of such vessels outside Egypt range from the jar of Pepi I found on Crete, several inscribed with the name of the Hyksos ruler Khian, which were found at Boghazköy and Knossos, and those excavated from the tombs of the rulers of Byblos in the late Bronze Age (the latter proving extremely useful in the process of synchronizing the chronologies of Egypt and the Levant). Many of these 'exported' vessels are decorated with inscriptions incorporating royal titularies and references to the ḥb-sd, or royal jubilee festival (Minault-Gout 1997), while some are inscribed with 'drinking songs' (Jansen-Winkeln 1989).

It is interesting also to note the likely cultural effect of the many Egyptian travertine vessels exported to Syria-Palestine. Rachael Sparks (2001, 108), for instance, draws attention to the possible impact on local choice of materials:

Although Palestinian workshops exploited regional gypsum resources, there was no attempt to widen their repertoire to include other local materials such as limestone. Like their preference for purer white varieties of gypsum, this single-mindedness probably reflects a continued desire to select materials with a strong visual similarity to imported Egyptian calcite vessels. These imports provided the chief inspiration for the development of this industry, and continued to influence the style and shapes of Palestinian versions throughout the course of the Bronze Age. The fact that this influence does not extend to manufacturing techniques implies that Egyptian influence came via trade goods, rather than through the arrival of Egyptian stone vessel craftsmen to the region.

Some of the travertine vessels imported by Minoans are mentioned above, and they appear to belong to two specific phases: EMII-III (roughly corresponding to the Egyptian Old Kingdom) and MMIII-LMIA (Second Intermediate Period–early 18th Dynasty). As Phillips (2001: 80) points out, 'The travertine alabastron was the ultimate Bronze Age container for oils, unguents and perfumes before the later invention of glass'. She also discusses two crucial questions relating to these imports: (1) whether they were imported primarily for themselves or for their contents, and (2) what influence the styles and shapes of Egyptian vessels might have had on locally made Minoan ones. She concludes that, since many are exotic, often 'antique', vessels they are highly likely to have been prized for themselves (Phillips 2001: 80-1). As far as the second question is concerned, she lists their primary uses as religious and funerary offerings, but notes that some vessels were converted and embellished by Minoan craftsmen, with one example (an Egyptian 'baggy' alabastron converted into a Minoan ewer) being imported, reworked then re-exported from Crete to Mycenae, where it was excavated from a Late Helladic IB shaft grave (Phillips 2001: 81-2). Warren (1967: 199; 1969: 125) even argues that raw blocks of Egyptian travertine were exported to vessel-making workshops in Crete, on the basis of waste fragments found in the Knossos excavations of 1957-61. In a later article Warren (1989: 8) specifically suggests that this imported travertine was being worked by Minoan craftsmen in part of the town-site at Knossos. However, Lilyquist (1996: 140) argues that such stone might equally well have been imported from some closer part of the east Mediterranean, such as Cyprus. Ultimately this conundrum may perhaps be solved by the application of chemical provenancing techniques (see section 2.5 below, as well as Barbieri *et al.* 2002)

2.4 Egyptian sources of travertine other than Hatnub

Small deposits of travertine occur sporadically in the Eocene limestones of the Nile Valley and adjacent desert (mainly Eastern) plateaus between Cairo and Esna. Both Klemm (1984: 1278) and Harrell (1989: 5–6) have listed the principal known occurrences of travertine in Egypt, comprising the Wadi Gerrawi and Wadi Hof (near Helwan), Wadi Araba, Wadi Umm Argub (near Wadi Sannur and Wadi Moathil, southeast of Beni Suef), el-Qawatir (near Minya), northern Amarna (Gebel Sheikh Said and Wadi Bershawi), Hatnub (near Mallawi), Wadi Asyut and Gebel Rokham (near Asyut) and in the cliffs on the west bank at Luxor. There are also sources of travertine in the Sinai Peninsula (see Beadnell 1927: 83; De Putter and Karlshausen 1992: 44), but these appear never to have been exploited by the ancient Egyptians.

A total of nine ancient Egyptian travertine quarries are known (see fig. 2.1). The Hatnub quarries lie roughly in the centre of a region known as 'Alabastron' in the Roman period, stretching from Minya in the north to Asyut in the south, that was identified in Pliny the Elder's *Natural History* (1st century AD) as the source of the so-called *alabastra*, unguent vessels made of travertine - *hunc aliqui lapidem alabastriten vocant, quem cavant et ad vasa unguentaria, quoniam optume servare incorrupta dicatur. Idem et ustus emplastris convenit. nascitur circa Thebas Aegyptias et Damascum Syriae* (Pliny: *Natural History*, XXXVI: 60-61); *Alabastritis nascitur in Alabastro Aegypti et in Syriae Damasco candore interstincto variis coloribus* (Pliny *Natural History*: XXXVII: 143). The ancient Alabastron region broadly corresponds to the 145 km-long stretch between Minya and Asyut, which Lucas (1962: 60) identifies as the main concentration of Egyptian travertine sources.

Wadi Gerrawi-Wadi Hof (N 29° 48.5´, E 31° 27.4´)

Wadi Gerrawi, near Helwan, is the site of the northernmost ancient Egyptian travertine quarry, which was probably exploited primarily in the Old Kingdom (see Mackay 1915; Murray 1945–6; Hellström 1951; Dreyer and Jaritz 1983; Garbrecht 1983, 1999). The Wadi Gerrawi-Wadi Hof quarries, although less remote than those at Hatnub, are said to have been linked with the Nile by a long road, some traces of which evidently still survived in the late 19th century, when they were described by Adolf Erman (1885: 623–4). The Wadi Gerrawi quarry itself centres on a thick vein of travertine, varying between 0.5 and 3 m in width, which passes vertically through the surrounding limestone bedrock.

The Wadi Gerrawi region is equally well-known for the Sadd el-Kafara, a massive stone dam built across the wadi, about 3 km west of the quarries, dating to the early 4th Dynasty. Both the dam and the quarries were rediscovered in 1885 by Georg Schweinfurth, who was the first to suggest a direct link between the two (see Erman 1885: 623; Schweinfurth 1885; 1922: 228–9). He argued that the dam (115 m wide and 14 m high) might have been constructed in order to create a reservoir for the quarry-workers' use, although a considerably more likely possibility is that the dam was intended to prevent flash-floods from affecting some area of settlement or important ritual structure much further to the west. When Rosemarie and Dietrich Klemm studied the site in the 1970s, they suggested that the latter hypothesis was more likely (Klemm and Klemm 2008: 148), although they also mentioned the possibility that this body of water could have been used to transport stone blocks to the Nile. Klemm and Klemm (2008: 148) argue that there are no definite archaeological indications that the travertine quarries were contemporaneous with the Old Kingdom dam, as many scholars have tended to assume, but this seems to fly in the face of the dating evidence from pottery published both by Ernest Mackay (Petrie and Mackay 1915: 38-9) and Gunther Dreyer and Horst Jaritz (1983).

Henning Fahlbusch (1986) re-examined both the Sadd el-Kafara dam and the Wadi Gerrawi quarries, taking into account the geography and geology of the region, and also the building phases discernible in the construction of the dam. In a variation on the Klemms' hypothesis concerning use of the dammed water for floating stone blocks, he suggests that the dam facilitated the creation of mud paths, allowing travertine blocks to be transported more easily from the quarry to the Nile valley.

There are two obvious ancient travertine workings in Wadi Gerrawi, one about 4 km to the east of the dam and the other 2 km further to the east, reflecting the fact that the vertical band cuts across the wadi at these two points. The travertine still remaining at the site seems to be browner in colour than the surviving material at Hatnub, although chemical provenancing would need to be undertaken to confirm or deny the possibility that this is a genuine basis for distinction between the rock types at these two quarries.

Mackay, who worked at Wadi Gerrawi in 1912, mentions the presence of 'scraps of Old Kingdom pottery' scattered on either side of an ancient path leading along the southern side of the wadi, and linking an Old Kingdom settlement near the dam with the quarrying area at the head of the valley (Petrie and Mackay 1915: 39). Mackay also mentions 'numerous stone shelters' in the immediate vicinity of 'the quarry' (it is unclear whether he is referring to the western or eastern quarry), as well as 'Roman pottery' lying on the ground surface near the shelters (although he points out that the Roman sherds might relate to exploitation of an outcrop of gypsum at the top of the nearby cliffs). He specifically mentions that no pottery dating later than the 4th Dynasty was found anywhere in the vicinity of the Wadi Gerrawi quarries. Another piece of dating evidence took the form of a small piece of travertine 'roughly hacked' into the form of a stone vessel identified by Mackay as an 'Old Kingdom offering jar' (Petrie and Mackay 1915: 40).

The archaeological survey undertaken by Dreyer and Jaritz (1983) focussed primarily on the workers' settlement near the dam. It is unclear whether this settlement was mainly used by dam-builders or quarry-workers (or both), but in this connection it is worth noting that Garbrecht estimated that the dam might have taken 10–12 years to build, so there would certainly have been some need for local accommodation for construction workers. The dam settlement consists of about fourteen dry-stone buildings, four of which were very large structures, perhaps serving as 'barracks-blocks' or communal cooking/eating areas. The four larger buildings ranged in area from $c.1000$ m^2 (Bau II) down to 450 m^2 (Bau IV), while the smaller buildings were between 10 m^2 and 30 m^2.

Wadi Araba (near Wadi Askhar el-Qibli; N 29° 4.75´, E 32° 3.1´)

The travertine quarries in Wadi Araba were evidently exploited during the Roman period, but there appear to be no surviving traces of their use during the pharaonic period.

Wadi Umm Argub (near Wadis Sannur and Moathil; N 28° 38.1´, E 31° 15.9´)

The modern and ancient travertine quarries of Wadi Umm Argub are situated about 60 km into the Eastern Desert to the southeast of the city of Beni Suef. Lucas (1962: 60) claimed that 'there are not any signs of ancient working', only quarrying from the time of Mohammed Ali in the early 19th century AD, but he may have based this claim on a reading of Sethe (1933b) rather than personal experience, since Klemm and Klemm's visit to the site in the 1980s confirmed Rateb's assertion that there were hieroglyphic inscriptions at Wadi Umm Argub, thus indicating that the quarries were in use during the pharaonic period (Klemm and Klemm 2008: 149). On the basis of several rock-cut and painted scenes with accompanying inscriptions, as well as distinctive chisel marks on the quarry walls, the Klemms date this phase of use of the site to the Late Period.

There are six main travertine quarrying areas spread across the Wadi Umm Argub, and although some of these are still in use, the remains of dry-stone huts of the pharaonic period have survived (for plan of site see Klemm and Klemm 2008: fig. 224, after El Naggar 1962). In the easternmost cluster of quarries, there was a Greek inscription (the name Ἄμμον) as well as a rock-cut human figure accompanied by largely illegible pharaonic hieroglyphic inscriptions (Klemm and Klemm 2008: figs 225–6). The Klemms also located a smaller ancient quarrying area, unaffected by modern quarry work (but known to modern workers as 'the quarry of the statues'), about 2 km to the northwest of the main quarrying region. There they found a crudely executed offering scene (Klemm and Klemm 2008: figs 227–8) incorporating three elements: a standing figure holding out *nw*-vessels, a possible depiction of a seated deity, and a kneeling figure holding out offerings, the whole scene measuring c.110×50 cm. Unfortunately the accompanying lines of hieroglyphic inscription have been rendered illegible by vandalism. This quarry is also decorated with a rock-cut stele bearing roughly carved reliefs of two standing deities, each with a different feathered headdress, accompanied by rock-cut hieroglyphs recording an offering to Osiris made by a man named Wahibra. The Klemms (2008: 150) suggest that thorough archaeological survey at this site would doubtless result in further evidence of pharaonic travertine quarrying activities.

The modern importance of the occurrences of travertine at Wadi Umm Argub is indicated by the use of the commercial term 'Beni Suef alabaster' to refer to the stone as a commercial product. As with the recent quarrying in the Hatnub region, the stone is primarily converted into domestic tiles and flagstones, as well as supplying the widespread tourist trade in antique-style vessels (see section 2.6 below). Since the Wadi Umm Argub travertine tends to be naturally white with dark bands (see Akaad and Naggar 1965a, 1965b for petrographic and geological analyses), the tourist-trade vessels are often varnished and painted with yellow or ochre to achieve a more convincingly 'ancient' appearance. The similarity with Hatnub evidently also extends to the condition of the ancient track leading to the quarries, which, as at Hatnub, is currently heavily rutted by constant movement of modern quarry-trucks back and forth.

El-Qawatir (near el-Minya; N 28° 6.2´, E 30° 49.2´)

The large el-Qawatir area of ancient travertine quarrying is situated in the Eastern Desert, about 5 km east of the modern city of Minya. The geological sources here, like those at Wadi Gerrawi, occur as long vertical strata rather than the more lens-like clusters of material at the other sites (including Hatnub itself). Some of the ancient workings are therefore more shaft-like than at other travertine quarries, occasionally incorporating rock-cut steps for the workers to descend into them, and rectangular apertures in the walls that presumably held the ends of wooden beams. Rings, hewn roughly into the rock, were presumably intended to support hanging lamps.

Although the surviving rock-cut texts at the site date only to later periods (consisting of demotic and Coptic graffiti), Klemm and Klemm (2008: 152) argue that the ancient activity at the site can be dated from the Old Kingdom through to the late New Kingdom, on the basis of chronological changes in the distinctive patterns of chisel marks on the walls of the quarries, with earliest activity evidently taking place at the southern end of the region. It is in the southern part of the workings, about 1 km from the edge of this travertine stratum, that a few pharaonic-style rock-cut stelae have been found, but their inscriptions (presumably either hieroglyphic or hieratic) have unfortunately been entirely weathered away.

The Klemms point out that the probable relatively continuous level of activity at the el-Qawatir quarries for much of the pharaonic period suggests that these workings might once have even rivalled the more famous ones at Hatnub as an ancient source of travertine.

Northern Amarna (Wadi Bershawi and Gebel Sheikh Said: N 27° 41.37´, E 30° 54.3´; Wadi el-Zebeida: N 27° 42.37´, E 30° 56.06´)

When Sir John Gardner Wilkinson made his second visit to the Amarna region in 1826, he and James Burton conducted a survey of the cliffs at the northern end of the site, which corresponds to the region of Wadi Bershawi and Gebel Sheikh Said (Thompson 1992: 68–9). They found an ancient travertine quarry roughly halfway between the Gebel Sheikh Said tombs and the Amarna North Tombs. This quarry is clearly visible in a sketch of the cliffs made by Wilkinson (Wilkinson 1843: II, 72; Ricci 1932: 475). It was presumably partly on the basis of this discovery that Wilkinson describes the entire city as Alabastron.

In 1891, Wilkinson's quarry was re-examined by Petrie, who designated it 'Alabaster Quarry G'. He describes it as 'an open pit of alabaster, of large width but not deep… approached by a sloping trench from the west', and notes some possible niches where stelae may once have been located in the walls of the quarry. It was on the basis of the style of one illegible surviving stele that Petrie tentatively dated Quarry G to the Middle Kingdom (Petrie 1894: 4).

In 2007–8, Quarry G, sometimes also described as the site of Maghara, Abu Aziz, was re-examined by a team under the direction of Harco Willems (the Katholieke Universiteit Leuven Mission to Deir el-Bersha - Willems pers. comm.). It is now said (*contra* Petrie 1894) to have two basic phases of exploitation, first the Old Kingdom, and secondly the New Kingdom-Third Intermediate Period. An ancient road leads from this quarry into the Nile valley, and there is an inlet from the river that may have served as a harbour. Evidence includes extensive archaeological remains from the time of Khufu (including a bakery area) and an area where travertine vessels were being made *in situ*, perhaps during the New Kingdom and Third Intermediate Period.

Petrie also mentions a 19th Dynasty travertine quarry, 'Alabaster Quarry L', which is said to be inscribed with the names of Ramesses II and Merenptah (Petrie 1894: 4). He points out that large amounts of travertine seem to have been used for the public buildings at Akhetaten, raising the question as to which quarry served as the Amarna Period source. Probably the answer to this is partly provided by the archaeological evidence from the 1986 Hatnub survey, which indicated an 18th Dynasty phase of quarrying (see sections 3.3.3 and 5.2 below).

In the course of a study of the entire quarrying region in the cliffs to the north of Amarna, in 2000, the American geologist James Harrell located twelve individual quarries (Harrell 2001a). Nine of these (numbered 1, 2 and 4–10) were evidently sources of limestone for the city at Amarna, while two others (11 and 12) produced only travertine, and the other (3) produced both limestone and travertine (Harrell 2001a: 36). Harrell's quarries 3 and 11 seem to correspond to Petrie's quarries G and L respectively. The third travertine quarry (12) is situated beyond the plateau, in the Wadi Bershawi (Klemm and Klemm 2008: 158-61). This is a very large set of New Kingdom travertine workings in the Wadi Barshawi, which was reportedly partially destroyed in January 2009 by workmen involved in the construction of a new tarmac road passing through the wadi. Harrell (2001a: 38) dates his Quarries 3 and 12 to the Middle Kingdom, but Willems (pers. comm.) identifies Quarry 3 as Old Kingdom and New Kingdom/Third Intermediate Period and Quarry 12 as predominantly New Kingdom.

Wadi Asyut (N 27° 18.75´, E 31° 20.7´)

The quarry in Wadi Asyut is the southernmost of the known ancient Egyptian sources of travertine (although the modern Wadiyein travertine quarries in the cliffs of western Thebes might perhaps also have been exploited in ancient times, see section 2.6 below). It appears to have been exploited both in the early 18th Dynasty (attested by an inscription of Queen Ahmose-Nefertari, the wife of the first 18th Dynasty ruler, Ahmose), and much later, from the time of Muhammad Ali (AD 1805–48) onwards. It was visited by Arthur Weigall (1911) and W. F. Hume (1912) in the early 20th century. Hume (1912: 72) describes it as being 'an easy baggage camel day's journey from the village of Arab Hatim, on the borders of the desert road eastward of Assiut', while Klemm and Klemm (1979: 126) describe its location as 25 km eastwards from the Nile, along the Wadi Asyut.

Hume notes that, like Hatnub, the Asyut quarries are linked with the Nile valley by a stone-built road, but assumes that in this instance the road was built in the 19th century AD. His description of the travertine itself sounds very similar to the occurrences at Hatnub, comprising 'a compact lenticular mass or vein, which has no definite relation to any particular bed in the strata' (Hume 1912: 72), unlike the vertical band of travertine at Wadi Gerrawi. He estimated that, if the main mass of travertine were solid throughout, there might have been some 19,000 cubic metres of the stone still *in situ* (in the early 20th century AD), and he also notes the presence of a 'large number' of finely worked blocks of travertine lying in the vicinity, each between one and two cubic metres in volume. Akaad and Naggar (1964a, 1964b) have provided analyses of the petrography and formation of the travertine at Wadi Asyut, on the basis of which they confirm that Egyptian travertine is essentially a type of cave deposit.

2.5 Provenancing Egyptian travertine

There have been relatively few attempts to provenance Egyptian travertine based on petrological and/or geochemical analyses. As much as anything else, this situation is indicative of the more general fact that relatively few ancient Egyptian rock-types of any kind have been the subjects of scientific provenance studies. Some work has been undertaken on different types of limestone. Meyers and van Zelst (1977), for instance, used INAA to identify trace element 'signatures' allowing them to distinguish between limestone artefacts coming from the Theban region and areas to the north of Thebes, while Middleton and Bradley (1989), used a combination of thin-section petrography, SEM-EDS and XRD to distinguish between limestone objects originating from the Thebes/Abydos, Deir el-Bersha and Cairo areas. The most contentious Egyptian stone provenancing investigation involved analyses of quartzite by Heizer *et al.* (1973), Bowman *et al.* (1984) and Stross *et al.* (1988) using thin-section petrography and INAA, and by Klemm *et al.* (1984) using thin-section petrography, XRF and AAS. In addition, in an ongoing provenancing study of Egyptian obsidian, Bavay *et al.* (2000) have used laser ablation inductively coupled plasma mass spectrometry to analyse obsidian artefacts and quarry samples from Egypt, Ethiopia and Syria; their results indicate that the northern part of the East African Rift Valley in Ethiopia was the most probable source for Egyptian artefacts, given that two trace element ratios (Th/Ta and Th/U) were found to be very similar in the Egyptian and Ethiopian samples, and quite different to those found in the Syrian artefacts.

In the early 1970s, el-Hinnawi and Loukina (1972) used XRF (X-ray fluorescence spectrometry) to try to source ancient Egyptian travertine artefacts to specific quarries or regions. They noted that Egyptian travertine exhibited a variety of structures the most common of which were: botryoidal structure, banding (alternating translucent and white bands of different sizes) and cockade structure. The mineralogical composition of the translucent bands has been determined as magnesian calcite and that of the milky-white bands as normal calcite. Differences in the Ca/Mg and Sr/Ca ratios between both types of bands have been noticed and are attributed to differences in the solubilities of Ca-, Mg-, and Sr-carbonates.

During the 1970s, Rosemarie and Dietrich Klemm undertook petrographic and geochemical analysis of the principal ancient sources of travertine (summarised in Klemm and Klemm 2008: 165–6), and more recently Barbieri *et al.* (2002) compared petrography and strontium isotope analysis as methods of provenancing Egyptian and Minoan travertine artefacts, concluding that strontium isotope analysis provided a fairly reliable way of distinguishing between Egyptian calcite (from Eocene host rock) and Cretan calcite (primarily deriving from much more complex geological contexts), whereas petrography had previously been a highly unreliable method for differentiating between the two.

In the 1980s, Barbara Aston (1994) used thin-section petrography to analyse many of the rock types used for stone vessels from the late Predynastic period to the end of the Old Kingdom. On the basis of samples of rocks from the ancient quarries, as well as the relevant geological information, she was able to determine the provenance of many of the materials. In the case of travertine, however, she was somewhat pessimistic: 'Despite the fact that much is known about ancient travertine quarries and potential travertine sources, at this point in time it is still impossible to say from which source a particular travertine vessel derives. Because the texture and mineral composition of travertine do not vary significantly, thin sections are not particularly helpful in differentiating travertine from various quarries' (Aston 1994: 46). Not only did she encounter problems with the process of distinguishing between the products of different quarries, but even when she was potentially able to do so, as in the case of the characteristic colours of stone at Hatnub and Wadi Gerrawi (white and red-banded at Hatnub and brownish at Gerrawi), she found that these colours did not correlate very well with the stone vessels that were actually manufactured in the Old and Middle Kingdoms, since these were most frequently made from yellow and white banded travertine. Although it is possible that such yellow-banded rock might simply have been quarried away entirely at both of these sources, she feels that this is unlikely given the dearth of yellow-banded waste chips at either Hatnub or Gerrawi. It is possible, however, that the yellow-banded stone might have been obtained from other sources, such as el-Qawatir or Asyut, from which Aston was unable to obtain samples (which raises the intriguing possibility that the greatest quantities of travertine for ancient vessel production may have come from neither of the best-known ancient quarries). James Harrell's website includes colour photographs of samples from many ancient travertine quarries in Egypt (see Harrell n.d.).

2.6 Travertine workshops: excavation, ethno-archaeology and experimental work

Stone vessels were the products of one of the earliest specialised forms of craftwork in ancient Egypt, and thus became firmly established as one of the most characteristic products of Egyptian craftsmen from the early Predynastic period onwards (there are already examples of stone vessels in Badarian burials, c.4500–3800 BC). Ironically, it seems to have been in these earlier periods that many of the most impressive hard-stone vessels were produced; by the late Old Kingdom fewer stone vessels were being made, and most of these were carved from the softer stones. The precocity of Egyptian craftworkers in this area of technology appears to be confirmed by the fact that the Egyptian term for 'craftsman' (*ḥmwty*) is written with a determinative sign in the form of a drill, and was initially used only to refer to producers of stone vessels.

Until the appearance of Barbara Aston's *Ancient Egyptian Stone Vessels* in 1994, the only general publications on this topic were the catalogue of stone vessels in the Egyptian Museum, Cairo compiled by Friedrich von Bissing (1907) and a typological study of stone and metal vessels by Flinders Petrie (1937). A few other publications have appeared in recent years, but all these have concentrated on specific periods (see, for example, el-Khouli 1978 on Early Dynastic vessels; Reisner 1931; 1932; and Bernard 1966–7 on Old Kingdom vessels; el-Khouli et al. 1994 on the vessels from the tomb of Tutankhamun; and Lilyquist 1995 on Second Intermediate Period and New Kingdom vessels). Aston's study of the materials and forms of ancient Egyptian stone vessels combines field survey and petrographic analysis to produce a thorough study of changing materials and forms. A number of insights into processes of hollowing out the interiors of travertine vessels have been provided by ethno-archaeological and experimental studies (see Hester and Heizer 1981; Stocks 1986a; 1986b; 1993; 2003a; and 2003b).

The initial stages of travertine vessel production clearly consisted of a process by which the fragment of stone was roughly shaped and smoothed with stone tools (probably flint chisels, punches and scrapers). As far as the next stage of the process is concerned, the British experimental archaeologist Denys Stocks has studied such pictorial evidence as hieroglyphic symbols representing boring tools (Stocks 1993: fig. 3) and depictions of the use of the so-called twist-reverse-twist drill (or TRTD) in various tombs, including that of Mereruka at Saqqara (6th Dynasty; Duell 1938), that of Pepyankh at Meir (6th Dynasty), and those of Rekhmira at Thebes and Iby at Thebes (18th Dynasty and 26th Dynasty; see Stocks 1986b: fig. 1). On the basis of such depictions, Stocks succeeded in creating modern replicas of the figure-of-eight stone borer and the TRTD, thus producing an experimental limestone vessel. With a height of 10.7 cm and a diameter of 10 cm, the vessel took 22 hours and 35 minutes to make (including the exterior shaping, interior tubular drilling and stone boring).

Stocks found that bow-driven tubes produced a tapering drill core, whereas the use of the TRTD resulted in a parallel-sided core, as in the case of an un-catalogued alabaster gypsum vase in the Petrie Museum. Although bow-driven tubes would have been five times faster than the TRTD, they would have provided insufficient leverage and control, and Stocks' experiments showed that the vessels could actually be broken by the additional mechanical stresses involved in using a bow.

Although there are many so-called 'traditional' travertine workshops, producing modern replicas of ancient vessels and sculptures, on the west bank at Luxor (Hester and Heizer 1981), there has so far been little archaeological evidence for the working of travertine (hence Stocks' experimental work described above). Some partially worked fragments and piles of debris have survived *in situ* at Hatnub, but travertine workshops usually seem to have been situated in urban areas rather than in the desert locations where the stone was extracted. This is in quite striking contrast to the situation at the Umm el-Sawwan alabaster gypsum quarries, in the northern Faiyum, surveyed and excavated in 1928 by Gertrude Caton-Thompson. She found numerous tools and partially drilled and fashioned vessels in working areas scattered across the region adjacent to the quarries (Caton-Thompson and Gardner 1934; see fig. 8.2). The tools at Umm el-Sawwan principally comprised crescent-shaped flint borers used to carve out the interiors of cylindrical alabaster gypsum vessels. This particular tool type was initially published by Jacques de Morgan in 1897 (de Morgan 1897: 114) and John Garstang (1903), but it was at Umm el-Sawwan that flint borers were first found in large numbers.

An Old Kingdom stone-vessel workshop was excavated on the island of Elephantine in 1999, providing evidence for the techniques used to produce large numbers of vessels from the local granite. This workshop also suggests that funerary vessel making may have been extensively undertaken at provincial towns, close to the actual quarries, rather than being focussed almost entirely on workshops near the Memphite necropolis (see Arnold and Pischikova 1999: 129, n.23).

In 1972, the discovery of a crescent-shaped tool by a French archaeological surveyor working in the southwest corner of the mortuary temple of Ramesses II (the Ramesseum) in western Thebes, led to Fernand Debono's excavation of a 19th Dynasty stone vessel-making workshop (Debono 1993-4). Throughout Debono's published report the term 'alabaster' is used to refer to the principal material being worked, although it seems clear from some of the bibliographical references (and the assertion that it was probably quarried in an area about 5 km east of the Valley of the Kings) that gypsum is meant. Debono also makes frequent references to Caton-Thompson's tools and workshops at Umm el-Sawwan.

Although travertine and alabaster gypsum were used to make similar items (i.e. mainly funerary vessels and unguent jars), different toolkits seem to have been required for the drilling of the two rock types, since they were 3 and 2 respectively on the Mohs scale of hardness (4.5 and 1.25 on the 'absolute' scale of hardness). Modern experimentation involving the attempted drilling of gypsum and travertine vessels with flint or chert crescent-shaped borers has demonstrated that such tools would not have been capable of drilling harder stones such as travertine, which are instead likely to have been hollowed out with a reed tubular drill in the earliest periods, and later with a copper tubular drill (Stocks 2003a: 139–40). With travertine vessels, the brittleness of the stone would have presented an additional difficulty to the use of flint borers.

In 1972, Thomas Hester and Robert Heizer undertook a thorough ethnographic and technological study of the modern 'alabaster' workshops at the Upper Egyptian village of Sheikh Abd el-Gurna on the west bank opposite Luxor, both in order to record a unique modern cottage industry and in an attempt to gain new insights into ancient techniques of vessel carving and drilling. Hester and Heizer (1981) note that the modern travertine quarrying took place all year round, involving a group of six men and a single donkey. Although Hester and Heizer were told that the source of the travertine was 'the mountains of Nag' Hammadi, on the way to Akaba', an alternative, more convenient source would have been a small quarry located about 5 km west of Wadiyein, a wadi branching off from the Valley of the Kings, as mentioned by Lucas (1962: 60). This is probably the same quarry that Barbara Aston (1994: 46) visited 'on the edge of the western cliffs opposite Luxor', describing it as 'now worked out'. Aston also makes two useful points about this Luxor quarrying area: first, that there was no evidence for this travertine being worked in ancient times, and, secondly, that the stone there was mainly white or brown in colour, without any bands (which ties in to some extent with Lucas's assertion that the Wadiyein travertine was a 'white translucent' type).

Finally, as previously noted (see section 2.3 above), there appears to be evidence for a workshop dedicated to the production of stone vessels at the Minoan site of Knossos, including some examples perhaps made from imported Egyptian travertine (Warren 1989: 8).

2.7 To what extent was stone worked into artefacts at Hatnub?

Opinions differ as to the quantity of stone-sculpting or vessel-making that took place at ancient Egyptian quarry sites (as opposed to such work taking place at royal and temple workshops/studios in cities such as Memphis or Thebes), and in practice it seems likely that *in situ* sculpting varied according to date, material and location, and perhaps through other factors too. The survival of debris from vessel-making, including occasional unfinished vessels, indicates that the quarry-workers transformed a certain amount of the travertine into vessels *in situ* at Hatnub (e.g. in structure A122 in the Quarry P settlement, see figs 2.2–3, and see also section 3.3.7 below), but there is no real evidence of the creation of any large-scale objects, such as statues, in the vicinity of the quarries. It might be noted that recent work (as yet unpublished) by the Katholieke Universiteit Leuven Mission to Deir el-Bersha has revealed a New Kingdom travertine vase-making workshop at the Maghara Abu Aziz travertine quarries, midway between Sheikh Said and northern Amarna (Harco Willems pers. comm.).

One type of evidence for the extent to which items were carved in advance of transportation takes the form of a number of surviving depictions of the movement of statues, the best-known being the scene in the tomb of Thuthotep at Deir el-Bersha, showing a colossal statue of the

Figure 2.2. Dry-stone Hut A122 in the Quarry P settlement at Hatnub, from the south, showing extensive traces of stone vessel production.

deceased being dragged along by lines of workers pulling on ropes (Newberry 1893: 17–26, pl. 15). The principal difficulty in interpreting such scenes, however, is the fact that pharaonic-period artists often portrayed objects in their finished form even when, in reality, they were still incomplete – this is particularly evident from the many scenes in which objects are being manufactured in temple workshops. It is therefore uncertain as to whether Thuthotep's travertine statue, for instance, was actually completely carved at the Hatnub quarries, or simply shown in its finished state as an artistic convention. Breasted (1906: I, 309) argues vehemently that the sculpting of the Thuthotep colossus was unlikely to have taken place at Hatnub:

> *That the statue would be sculptured in the desert quarry, nearly a day's journey from water and supplies, then to run the risk of the long and dangerous transportation to Eshmunen [i.e. el-Ashmunein], as is usually supposed, is a priori exceedingly improbable. The inscription is also clearly against this supposition. The scene depicts the arrival of the statue at its destination, and naturally the inscription begins with that event, which it describes in six lines. Then (l.6) it reverts to the work of getting the stone from the quarry, and says distinctly that on leaving the quarry the statue was "a squared block." After this the ships for the river transport are referred to, and then Thuthotep mentions his arrival "in the district of this city" (doubtless Eshmunen).*

A similar point is made by Badawy (1963), who also refers to the text accompanying the Thuthotep scene, and specifically the description of the statue as *ist twt pn ifd*, arguing that this implies that the statue was just a squared block until it reached Hermopolis Magna (or Deir el-Bersha).

Betsy Bryan, however, argues that 'statues were largely completed in or near quarries and… shipped to distant sites', pointing out, for instance, that there were 'chief sculptors among

Figure 2.3. Some of the fragments of worked travertine from Hut A122.

Ramesside quarry expedition personnel' (Bryan 1992: 138–9) and also that 'calcitic works are homogeneous as a stylistic group and were very likely sculpted in or near the quarries'. Furthermore, in the case of statues carved from 'soft sedimentary rock' such as travertine, she makes the point that there might have been particular geological reasons for such work practice: 'Both limestone and alabaster [i.e. travertine] lose moisture quickly after quarrying and consequently harden, so they must be sculpted soon after separation from their source for maximal exploitation of their subtleties' (Bryan 1992: 146; see also Arnold 1991: 42–7).

The archaeological evidence for some quarry-site carving of hard-stone items is fairly convincing, with the survival of near-complete colossal statues in the southern granite quarries on the east bank at Aswan, an inscribed obelisk of Seti I at the Gebel Gulab quartzite quarries (Habachi 1960), and a statue of an unknown 25th Dynasty king in the Tumbos granite gneiss quarry (Dunham 1947). At Hatnub, however, despite the Thuthotep visual evidence mentioned above, there are relatively few surviving archaeological traces of sculpting or stone-vessel-fashioning at the site (although see section 3.3 below, for discussion of a likely Old Kingdom stone-working area beside Hut S1), suggesting that the stone was largely carried back in the form of blocks and lumps, to be transformed into vessels and other items at the various points of use. Further confirmation for this possibility in the case of Hatnub is suggested both by the Ramesseum vessel-making workshops described in section 2.6 above, and also by Abdel-Aziz Saleh's excavation of a set of apparent workshops south-south-east of Menkaura's pyramid at Giza, consisting of a large open courtyard and several small house-like buildings (Saleh 1974). A large collection of fragments of travertine (including an unfinished column base) were found in the courtyard, and it seems likely that these were being carved and polished for use in the nearby pyramid complex of Khafra, particularly in the Valley Temple. Rainer Stadelmann (1981: 67) has suggested that the structures excavated by Saleh may perhaps correspond to the so-called *ḥmwt-smit*, 'desert workshop', which is mentioned in workmen's graffiti on the granite wall-blocks of Khafra's Valley Temple (Reisner 1931: 277).

Chapter 3

The Quarry P Region at Hatnub

Ian Shaw, Robert Jameson and Paul T. Nicholson

In the brief overall description of the site of Hatnub in Chapter 1 above, it was pointed out that there were three principal areas of quarrying, and that Petrie named these quarries P, R and T in 1892 (see fig. 4.1). This chapter describes Quarry P and the various archaeological remains extending for several square kilometres around it.

3.1 Quarry P

Quarry P, by far the largest of the ancient workings at Hatnub, is still surrounded by huge spoil heaps of travertine chippings. It was originally a subterranean quarry but the roof has largely fallen in, leaving a roughly oval pit, entered via a sloping passage from the north (see fig. 3.1 for a plan of the quarry and its immediate vicinity, and see fig. 3.2 for a view from the interior of the quarry, showing the considerable amount of debris inside it, and also showing part of the entrance). The initial (northernmost) section of the entrance corridor is 9.2 m wide, then it gradually narrows as it descends towards the main quarry pit, so that the width roughly halfway down (parallel with Inscription VI) is 7.2 m. Just before the pit itself the corridor width shrinks to around 6 m. The main quarry pit has a maximum length of $c.70$ m, a maximum width of $c.50$ m, and its depth is $c.15$ m on average. Fraser (1894: 75) described Quarry P as 'an immense circular pit, like an English chalk-pit ... over 100 feet deep and 40 or 50 yards in diameter'.

It seems likely that, as Fraser argued, the quarry roof probably fell in at some date between the 4th and 6th Dynasties, on the basis of inscribed fragments included among the debris: 'there is an XIth or XIIth dynasty inscription on one fallen mass, and a dated VIth dynasty inscription on another' (Fraser 1894: 75). This raises the possibility that some inscriptions or graffiti from before the 4th Dynasty might be buried beneath the debris, but the process of removing the fallen stone to determine this possibility would be a considerable task.

Quarry P lies in a slight depression, and the surrounding plateau, which extends over several square kilometres to the west, northwest and southwest, was peppered with the small drystone huts that housed the quarry-workers, with a particularly dense area of occupation on top of the spoil heaps immediately beside the quarry. In the section of the spoil heaps immediately to the southwest of the entrance corridor, at a point about two-thirds of the way between the beginning of the corridor and the main quarry itself, is a low cairn (C9). About 100 m to the north of cairn C9, a small set of steps are carved into the southwestern side of the entrance corridor (see fig. 3.3), presumably allowing the workers to move from the quarry to the area of dense settlement without having to walk to the northern end of the corridor and then double back.

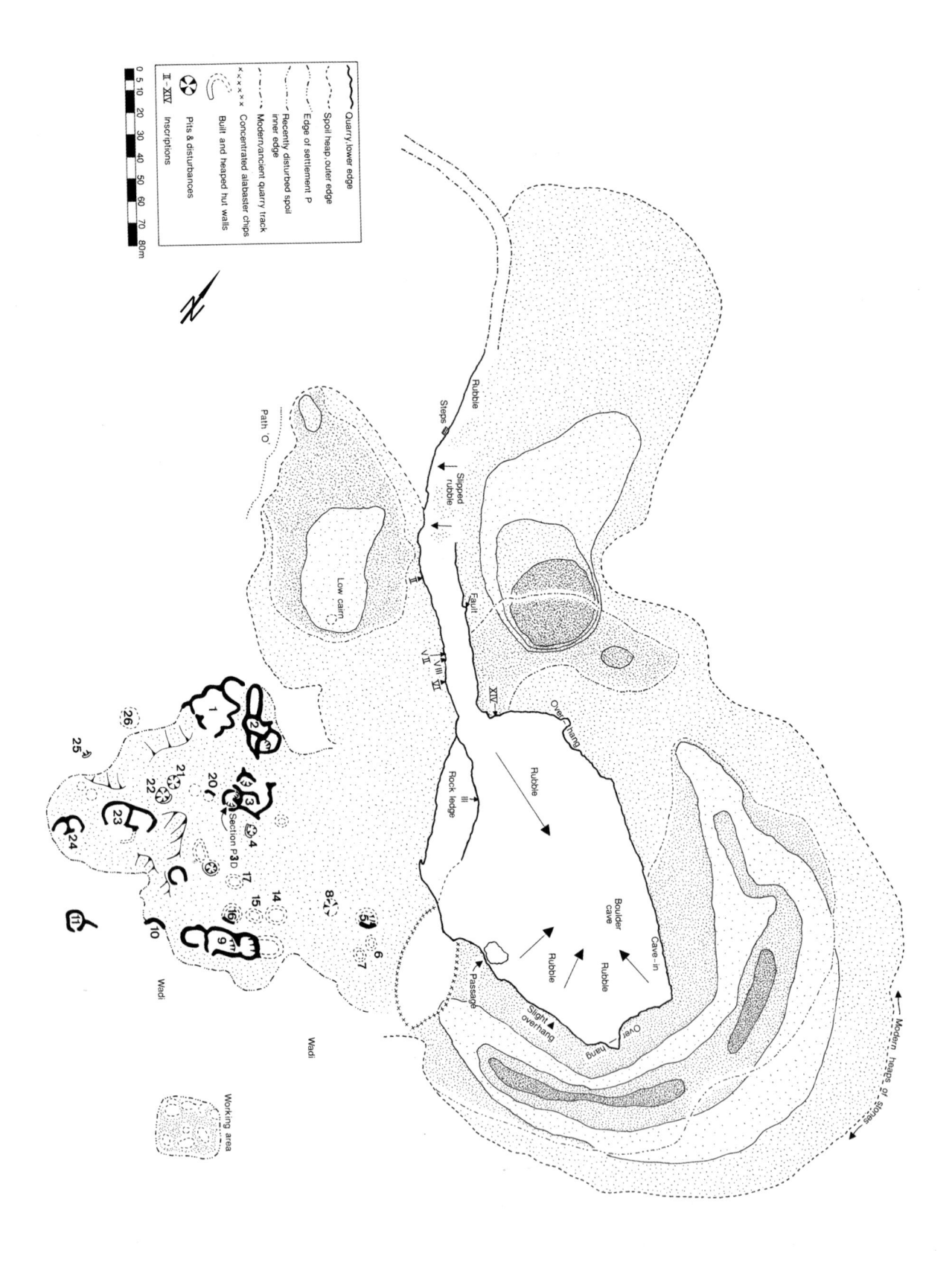

Figure 3.1. Plan of Quarry P and the adjoining area of dense settlement.

Figure 3.2. View of the interior of Quarry P, showing the large amounts of debris inside it, presumably deriving mainly from a collapsed roof. The entrance corridor is visible, stretching from the centre towards centre right.

Figure 3.3. The small set of steps carved into the southwestern side of the entrance corridor to Quarry P.

Anthes (1928: tf. 2, skizze 7) records the presence of a rectangular building measuring '16 paces by 10 paces' (i.e. presumably around 15 × 9 m), which was said to be near the entrance passage to Quarry P, but no traces of it were visible during our survey seasons, and Anthes gives no indication as to its precise location. This was presumably a dry-stone structure, although Anthes does not specify the material; his sketch plan (fig. 3.4) shows that it was subdivided internally into one large rectangular room with four smaller rooms leading off it. Anthes' plan is curiously rectilinear, in contrast to the other structures at Hatnub, but this may perhaps simply be the style of the sketch rather than a true indication of the nature of the building itself.

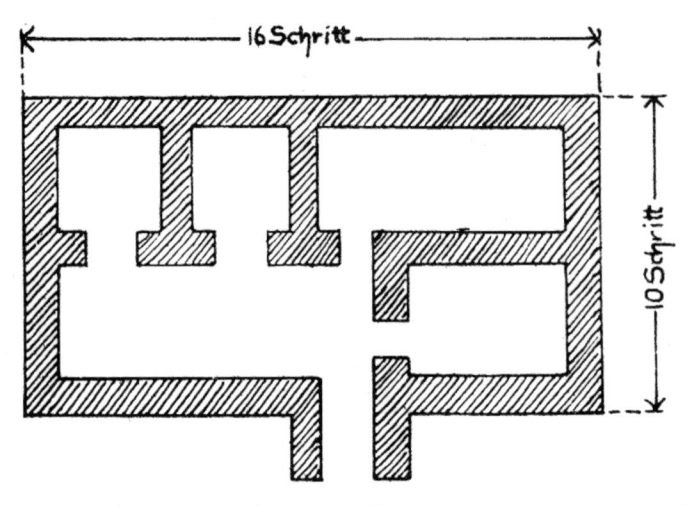

Figure 3.4. Sketch-plan of a rectangular structure that originally stood near the entrance to Quarry P (adapted from Anthes 1928: tf. 2, skizze 7).

Most of the area of dense settlement adjacent to the quarry dates to the Old Kingdom (judging from associated pottery), although several New Kingdom potsherds have also been found there. Elsewhere in the Quarry P region, there was also an encampment dating to the New Kingdom (see section 3.3.3 below) and there are a few traces of post-pharaonic activity in the region (see sections 3.3.4 and 3.3.8 for discussion of Roman and Coptic remains). The Hatnub Survey project from 1985 to 1994 included the study and mapping of these scattered groups of structures. Every hut was given an alphanumeric label referring to its geographical location and the order in which it was added to the survey, and each of the structures was recorded individually on a 'feature sheet', including a sketch-plan, dimensions and basic description of the building and any associated artefacts.

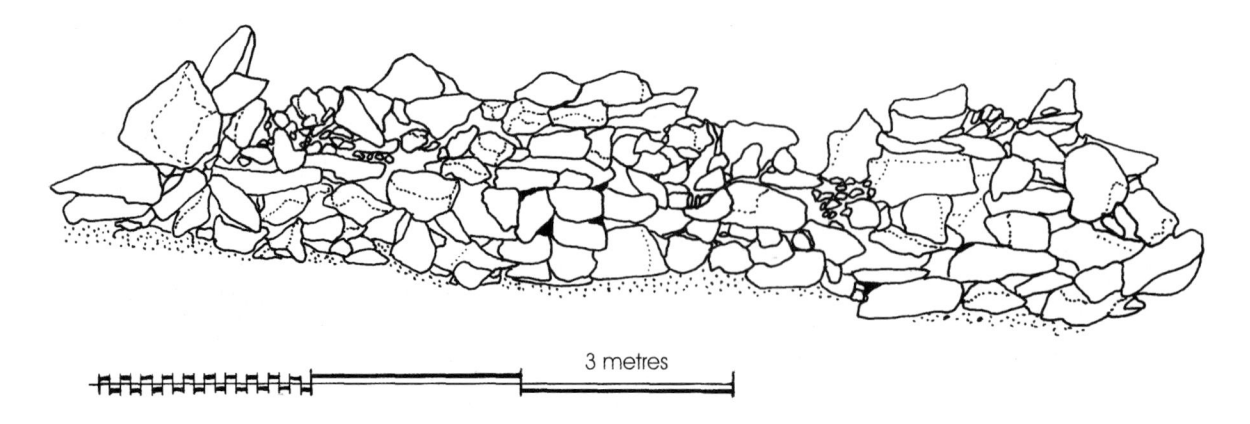

Figure 3.5. Elevation drawing of one of the walls of structure N1 in the Quarry P settlement.

The walls of the stone huts are made up of large un-worked limestone boulders, the spaces between being packed with smaller stones and grit (see fig. 3.5, showing an elevation drawing of one of the walls of structure N1). Many of the huts' walls are still preserved to heights of well over a metre, and numerous associated artefacts, particularly pottery vessels, are very well preserved, due to the site's isolation. The surface scatters of travertine chips, potsherds, hammerstones and lithics can be used to analyse different spatial zones of human activity across the site. There are several different types of structure at Hatnub, ranging from simple crescent-shaped windbreaks (with barely enough space for a single individual to crouch or lie) to multi-roomed buildings that might have accommodated eight or nine workers (e.g. structures S1 and N1 near Quarry P). The surface concentrations of stone chips and sherds suggest that some rooms may have been used for working rather than sleeping. There are also, in addition to the huts, many circular patches of cleared or flattened ground (often up to 2 m in diameter) that may represent either the remains of very low shelters, or, more plausibly, small working areas.

3.2 The Old Kingdom quarry-workers' encampment immediately adjacent to Quarry P (structures P1–29)

The most densely concentrated area of occupation is immediately adjacent to the west and southwest sides of Quarry P. Since most of the huts here (labelled P1–29, see figs 3.1 and 3.6) were built on top of the travertine and limestone spoil heaps created by the ancient quarrying, we can probably assume that they date to a period some considerable time after the initial creation of Quarry P, although the comparatively early date of most of the pottery suggests that there may not have been too long a delay. The density of this settlement, and its proximity to the quarry, sharply differentiate it from the surrounding settlement, suggesting that it may have served some specific function, perhaps as an administrative centre, or at least as accommodation for a core group of skilled workers. Almost all of the huts in the concentrated encampment by Quarry P are multi-roomed, with the numbers of chambers varying from two to nine. The encampment area as a whole showed clear signs of disturbance, and it was sometimes difficult to relate pottery clearly to the huts.

Figure 3.6. The dense area of settlement immediately to the south of Quarry P.

Comparisons with other quarrying sites

Other quarrying and mining settlements seem to have been characterised by a similar pattern of a concentrated encampment surrounded by scattered groups of huts. At the Wadi el-Hudi amethyst mines, the scattered huts of sites 14, 15 and 12 contrast with a dense fortified habitation zone at site 9 and a hilltop settlement at site 5 (Fakhry 1952, Shaw and Jameson 1993). At the turquoise mines of Wadi Maghara there is not only a group of about 125 stone huts comprising a hilltop settlement opposite the mines but also a smaller group of huts with thicker walls down in the wadi, which, according to Petrie and Currelly (1906: 38–40), might have been occupied by the expedition leaders. E. S. Thomas (1909: 110) mentions that 'some of the [mining] towns are composed of groups of huts, in others they lie scattered along the wadi edge, some have stone wall enclosures and watch towers… It has been surmised that scattered huts are relics of Arab occupation while the grouped ones belong to Ptolemaic and other slave-working ages'. Despite the over-simplification and inaccuracy of the final sentence, Thomas's comments present a recognisable image of the variability in patterning of quarrying and mining encampments (see section 8.3 below). The settlement patterning at Hatnub Quarry P therefore seems to be broadly comparable with the situation at several other Old and Middle Kingdom quarrying sites.

Pottery

During the 1985 and 1991 seasons Pamela Rose and Paul Nicholson undertook pottery surface surveys of the Quarry P region, focussing on those structures that contained larger quantities of potsherds. Diagnostic pottery was often difficult to locate but most of the ceramics seem to be consistent with a date in the Old Kingdom.

The 1991 survey included five of the huts in the dense quarry-workers' encampment adjacent to Quarry P (structures P3C, P11B, P20, P23 and P24). Structure P3C contained a very coarse, obviously hand-made Old Kingdom vessel in chaff-tempered silt ware. P11B contained sherds from at least one Old Kingdom beer jar, and body sherds from open forms of vessels, which had been red-burnished both inside and out. P20 contained Old Kingdom bread-moulds and a possible New Kingdom sherd. P23 contained a red-slipped Old Kingdom jar; a Meidum-type bowl with red burnished slip inside and out (and very sharp carination) and beer jar sherds. Finally, P24 contained the rim of a Meidum-type Old Kingdom bowl and body sherds from a large wheel-made vessel, probably a *zir* of New Kingdom date. These ceramics therefore suggest that the settlement immediately beside Quarry P was occupied intermittently throughout the whole sequence of expeditions at the site, from the early Old Kingdom to the New Kingdom.

Charcoal from a midden beside Hut P20

Beside Hut P20 there was a deep midden containing strata of debris and ash (fig. 3.7), from which a large sample of charcoal was taken. This charcoal was analysed by Dr Rainer Gerisch (see Gerisch 2004), who was able to detect traces of a number of different types of wood, including acacia (*A. nilotica* and *albida*), tamarisk and various desert shrubs (e.g. *Zilla spinosa* fruits). The combination of *Acacia nilotica* and tamarisk is also found in charcoal samples from the Kom el-Nana region at Amarna, and Gerisch (pers. comm.) notes that 'the presence of *A. nilotica* and

The Quarry P Region at Hatnub   37

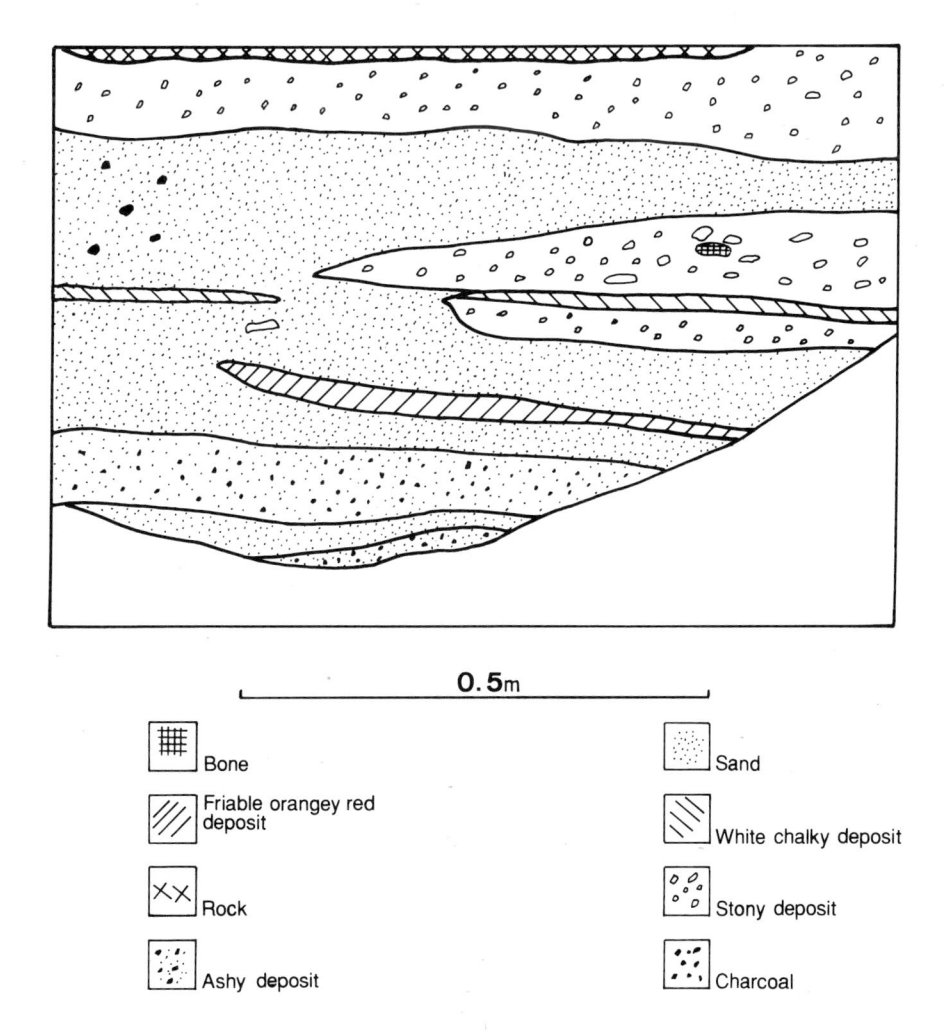

Figure 3.7. Photograph and section drawing of the deep, charcoal-filled midden situated between Huts P20 and P3, in the dense settlement immediately adjacent to Quarry P.

A. albida, which have higher demands on water supply, indicates that at least part of the fuel should have come from the Nile valley'. Table 3.1 shows the percentages of different species of wood represented in the sample of 953 pieces of charcoal larger than 6.3 mm long.

Wood species of charcoal	No. pieces (>6.3mm)	%
Acacia nilotica	665	69.78
Acacia sp.	52	5.46
Faidherbia albida (formerly *Acacia albida*)	20	2.10
Leptadenia pyrotechnica	1	0.11
Tamarix sp.	63	6.61
Zilla spinosa	2	0.22
Zygophyllum sp.	1	0.11
Indeterminate	100	10.49
Bark	49	5.14

Table 3.1. Quantity and percentages of species of wood represented in the sample of charcoal from the midden beside Hut P20 (figures provided by Rainer Gerisch).

Gerisch's analyses of the charcoal samples suggest that the wood used as fuel at Quarry P, presumably for baking and cooking to feed the workforce, seems to have been primarily brought from the floodplain of the Nile Valley to the quarry region of Hatnub. This assumption is based on two aspects of the evidence. First, there were twenty charcoal pieces of *Faidherbia albida*, a tree that is highly reliant on the availability of water and (apart from two isolated examples reported in recent times in the Eastern Desert) is almost exclusively limited to the floodplain of the Nile Valley. Secondly, nearly 70% of the charcoal pieces were identified as *Acacia nilotica*, which occurs in modern times as a tree (varying from 3 to 10 m in height) along the Nile and canal-banks, in the oases of the Western Desert, and in the Western Desert on moist ground.

In the section of the funerary text of Weni dealing with his expedition to Hatnub, it is pointed out that some of the expedition team-members were left in the Nile valley to build transport ships from acacia, using the timber available in the floodplain (Sethe 1933a: 98–110; Lichtheim 1973: 19; see also section 7.2 below).

Gerisch also suggests that some wood supplies could have been procured from directly alongside the quarry road on which the travertine blocks were transported. Stands of acacia trees (*Acacia sp.*) are sometimes found in the wadis of the Eastern Desert, and therefore might have been exploited by the quarrying expeditions, while *Zilla spinosa* and *Zygophyllum sp.* are typical desert shrubs, potentially available in the vicinity of Hatnub. It is interesting to note that, apart from the presence of *Faidherbia albida*, the general composition of the Hatnub charcoal sample closely resembles those taken from a temple area of the late 18th Dynasty at nearby Amarna. This reinforces the idea of the temporary quarrying communities at Hatnub as centrally controlled groups, whose resources were not obtained locally but brought in from the Nile valley.

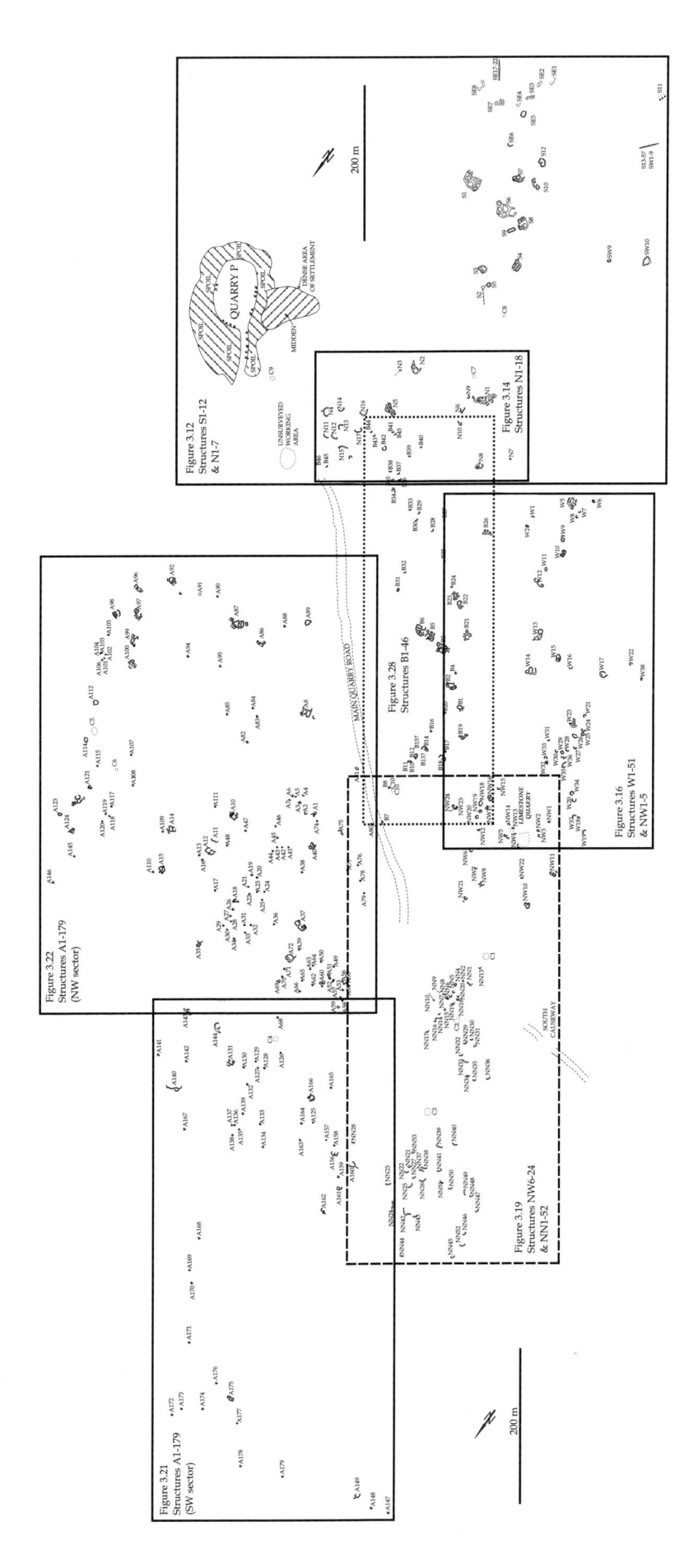

Figure 3.8. Key-Plan of the entire Quarry P settlement region.

Figure 3.9. Cairn C1, situated on a plateau just to the south of the main road leading to Quarry P (with Cairn C2 visible on the horizon to the left).

Figure 3.10. Cairn C3, situated in the centre of the NN group of huts, to the southwest of the main quarry road.

Figure 3.11. The stretch of high ground surmounted by two cairns (C7-8), to the southwest of Quarry P.

3.3 The scattered groups of stone huts surrounding Quarry P

Apart from the dense concentration of 29 dry-stone shelters built on top of the spoil heaps beside the quarry itself (Huts P1–29, described above), there were also about 470 dry-stone structures of various types scattered across an area of several square kilometres primarily to the west, northwest and southwest of Quarry P (see fig. 3.8). Generally speaking it is clear that the workers' encampments are situated in the terrain immediately to the north and south of the main quarry road leading from the direction of the Nile valley $c.16$ km to the northwest. There was obviously no reason for the settlement to expand very far to the south or east of Quarry P since this would have taken the quarry-workers further away from civilisation and unnecessarily deeper into the desert. There are also ten very large stone cairns located at various points across the area to the west of the quarry, presumably providing landmarks for those approaching the region from the Nile. One cluster of three cairns occupies a plateau just to the south of the main quarry road (labelled C1–3; see figs 3.9–10); a single cairn (C4) lies $c.160$ m to the north of the road; and a pair of cairns (C5–6) are situated on high ground $c.550$ m to the northwest of Quarry P and $c.320$ m to north of the road. A pair of smaller cairns (C7 and C8) were situated at either end of a stretch of high ground ('the peak' in fig. 3.11) about 300 m to the southwest of Quarry P. Cairn C9 is located immediately beside the southern edge of the entrance to Quarry P. Finally, cairn C10 is located among the group of nearly sixty windbreaks (B1–59) to the south of the main quarry road, between the New Kingdom encampment and the N1–21 group of huts.

The groupings of dry-stone structures identified and surveyed between 1985 and 1994 were S1–57, N1–21, W1–51, NW1–24, NN1–49, SE1–22, E1–4, SW1–10, A1–179 and B1–59. Each of these groups is discussed below in general terms, providing information on specific structures when they are of particular interest either in terms of architecture, function, location, or associated artefacts. The alphanumeric labels of specific stone structures (e.g. N1, SW20 etc.) are printed in bold when first mentioned, so as to make it easier to locate descriptions of specific structures within the text.

3.3.1 Structures S1–57

Dry-stone structures S1–57 are located to the south and southwest of Quarry P. They occupy an area between the quarry, the main quarry road, and the long area of high ground with cairns C7 and C8 at either end (see fig. 3.12). Most of the features labelled S1–57 are multi-room structures, ranging in size and complexity from the two-room S12 (7.0 × 6.2 m) to the nine-room **S1** and seven-room S6. The group also includes three 'ritual' structures (S2, S5 and S11) and one large rectangular area (S9), the latter probably serving more as a working area than as a sleeping shelter. Features S42–57 are all small orthostats, some in roughly aligned rows (see section 6.2 below), situated on the flattish ground between Huts S15 and S16.

The feature labelled **S1** (21.2 × 15.8 m, see fig. 3.13) is a very large multi-room hut located near the southern end of the plateau. Like some of the other multi-room huts, it appears to be a virtually self-contained area of habitation, consisting of areas for sleeping, working and refuse disposal. The main structure is a roughly circular cluster of nine rooms, with individual walls varying in height from a few centimetres to over a metre. About three metres north of the main building is an area of very low stone alignments forming the outlines of four oval spaces (total

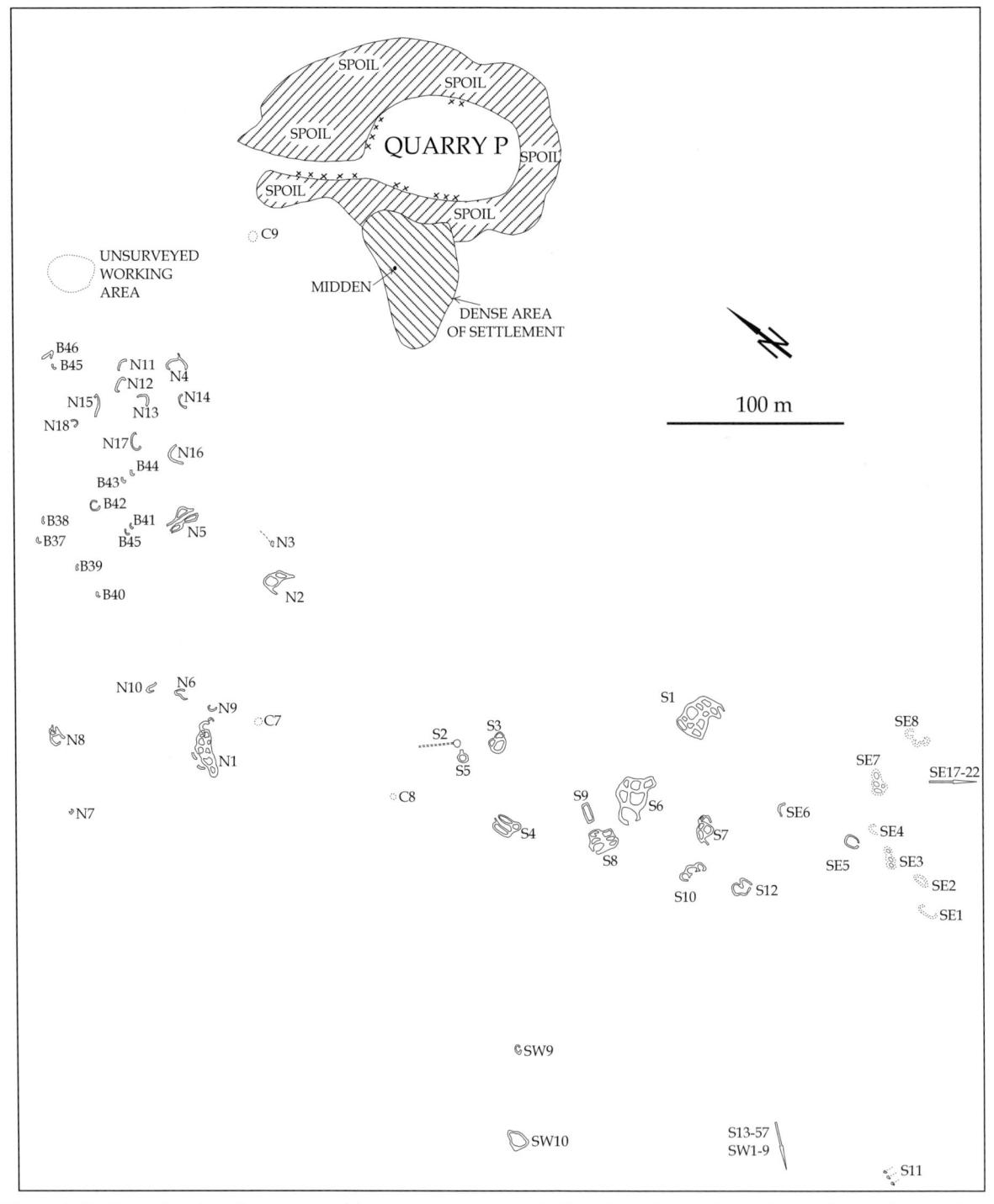

Figure 3.12. Plan showing the groups of dry-stone structures S1-12 and N1-7, and their relationship to Quarry P.

area roughly 11 × 10 m), which, judging from the thick layers of travertine débitage, constituted a stone-working area. Adjacent to this area, about a metre to the north, is a low midden heap consisting of sand, limestone pebbles, Old Kingdom sherds, alabaster chips and ash. The whole feature might perhaps be interpreted as the temporary quarters of a gang of eight or nine ẖrtyw-nṯr (stone-cutters), as mentioned in some of the inscriptions and graffiti on the walls of Quarry P. Sinai stele 85 (Gardiner *et al.* 1955: 17), states that the workmen are divided into groups of ten, each headed by an *ỉmy-r sꜣ* ('foreman'), a title that also occurs in six other Sinai stelae.

The seven-room Hut **S6** (25.4 × 17.8 m) is the second-largest dry-stone structure at Hatnub. It is located only about 30 m to the west of structure S1. It contained a number of concentrations

Figure 3.13. Structure S1, a large multi-room hut near the southern end of the plateau near Quarry P.

of travertine chips and Old Kingdom sherds. Two other large structures are situated nearby: **S7** (15.6 × 9.5 m), a six-room hut about 25 m to the southeast of S6, and **S8** (15.9 × 11.9 m), also six-roomed and about 10 metres to the west of S6, both containing a number of concentrations of travertine chips and Old Kingdom sherds. **S9**, midway between S6 and S8, and slightly to the north, is a smaller, though more unusual, feature consisting of a very low rectangular wall (8.6 × 5.8 m); its function is unclear, and a shallow hole excavated in the northeastern corner is probably modern.

Most of the other stone shelters in this part of the site are fairly small and lacking in pottery, but three other multi-room structures (S26–8, part of a large group comprising Huts S23–8) are worthy of mention, both architecturally and in terms of their finds. First, **S26** (11.0 × 7.2 m) is a very regularly and carefully constructed seven-room structure; this impressive complex, well-sheltered from the prevailing wind by the natural topography, is built over three 'terraces' on a slope descending from southwest to northeast, with a drop of around 0.4 m between each 'terrace'. Large quantities of travertine chips were found throughout, as well as numerous Old Kingdom sherds, including at least one beer jar and a shouldered vessel. The excavation of one of the rooms within Hut S26 is described below in section 3.4.

The two-room Hut, **S27** (total area 13.5 × 2.6 m), consists of an unusual, 10 m long, roughly rectangular, barrack-like structure, with an attached squarish room at the southeastern end (*c*.2.6 × 2.6 m). There are three entrances to the hut, one in each of the long sides of the 'barrack' room and one in the southern side of the smaller squarish room). The structure contains only a small quantity of travertine chips but a reasonable number of Old Kingdom sherds, including the base of a beer jar. Structure **S28**, a three-room building constructed on a slope descending from north to south, contained only a very small quantity of travertine fragments and sherds. In

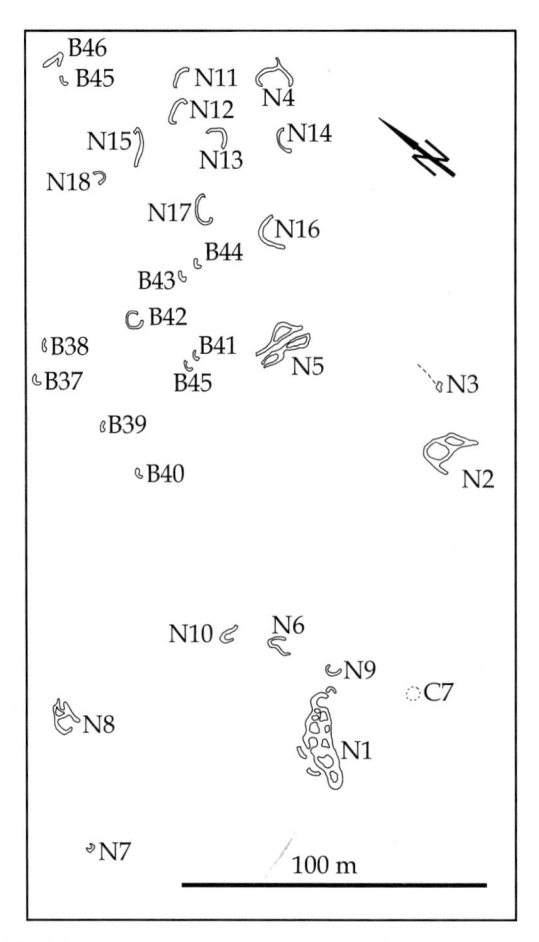

Figure 3.14. Plan of structures N1-21 (part of the Quarry P settlement).

Figure 3.15. Plan of structure N1, in the Quarry P settlement.

the northernmost room there was a very small concentration of travertine chips, as well as the rim and part of the body of a *c.*20 cm-high globular jar dating to the Old Kingdom.

3.3.2 Structures N1–21

This group of 21 features, comprising a mixture of structural types, from multi-room huts down to rough stone alignments, is located in the area to the west of quarry P and to the south of the main quarry road. There are 13 crescent-shaped windbreaks (N4, N6 and N9–18 and N22) and four multi-room huts (N1–2, N5 and N8). The other four features, comprising three shrine-like structures (N3, N7 and N20), and a roughly aligned row of four standing stones (N21), are discussed in Chapter 6 below.

The largest of the multi-roomed huts in this group is **N1** (25.8 × 15.2 m; see figs 3.5 and 3.15). Its overall floor area of over 390 m^2 makes it the most extensive at Hatnub as a whole. It is situated almost at the foot of the peak and cairn (point C7) and comprises ten rooms, the southern one containing a thick accumulation of travertine chips as well as sherds from Old Kingdom vessels. The nearby structure **N2** consists of three rooms, and also contained a reasonable quantity of sherds and travertine chips.

Hut **N4** (6.0 × 4.2 m) is a semi-circular windbreak built onto a kind of terrace of large stones, and lies at the end of an ancient path leading to/from the shrine-like structure N3. The neck of an Old Kingdom vessel, a large fragment of travertine, and many small chips were found inside N4. Structure **N5** (14.0 × 9.2 m) is a cluster of three basic rooms with a 'passage' running between two of the rooms and the third. The passage is littered with very small travertine chips, suggesting its intensive use as a working area. The structure itself is unusual in that it incorporates about a dozen large slabs of limestone. Just to the north of N1 and about 60 m to the west of N2 is **N6** (6.5 × 4.2 m), a relatively large crescent-shaped windbreak located on a slight rise in the ground at the foot of the main peak (D on the map). **N8** (7.1 × 4.1 m) is a three-roomed structure with very few traces of travertine fragments or potsherds.

3.3.3 Structures W1–51 and NW1–5 (including the New Kingdom quarry-workers' encampment)

The second season of survey at Hatnub (in March 1986) focussed on the mapping of an area of previously unrecorded New Kingdom occupation, which had been initially identified by Pamela Rose during the 1985 survey. This area (fig. 3.16), stretching westwards from the main area of Old Kingdom occupation (N1–21 and S1–57), and circumscribed to the north by the main quarry road, comprised a group of about twenty-five stone shelters with ceramic assemblages dating almost entirely to the New Kingdom (W18–38 and NW1–5), as well as another seventeen shelters containing a mixture of Old, Middle and New Kingdom pottery (W1–17).

Walking west from the main peak and cairn (point C7 in fig. 3.12), passing Hut N7, the ground gradually rises towards a pair of small dry-stone structures W1–2, situated on a small plateau, with a small northwest-southeast oriented wadi to the south. Windbreak **W1** (3.5 × 2.7 m) is just a short distance to the west of the shrine-like structure N7 (aligned between it and the main peak). **W2** (5.6 × 4.2 m) is a low roughly rectangular structure with an entrance at its eastern end.

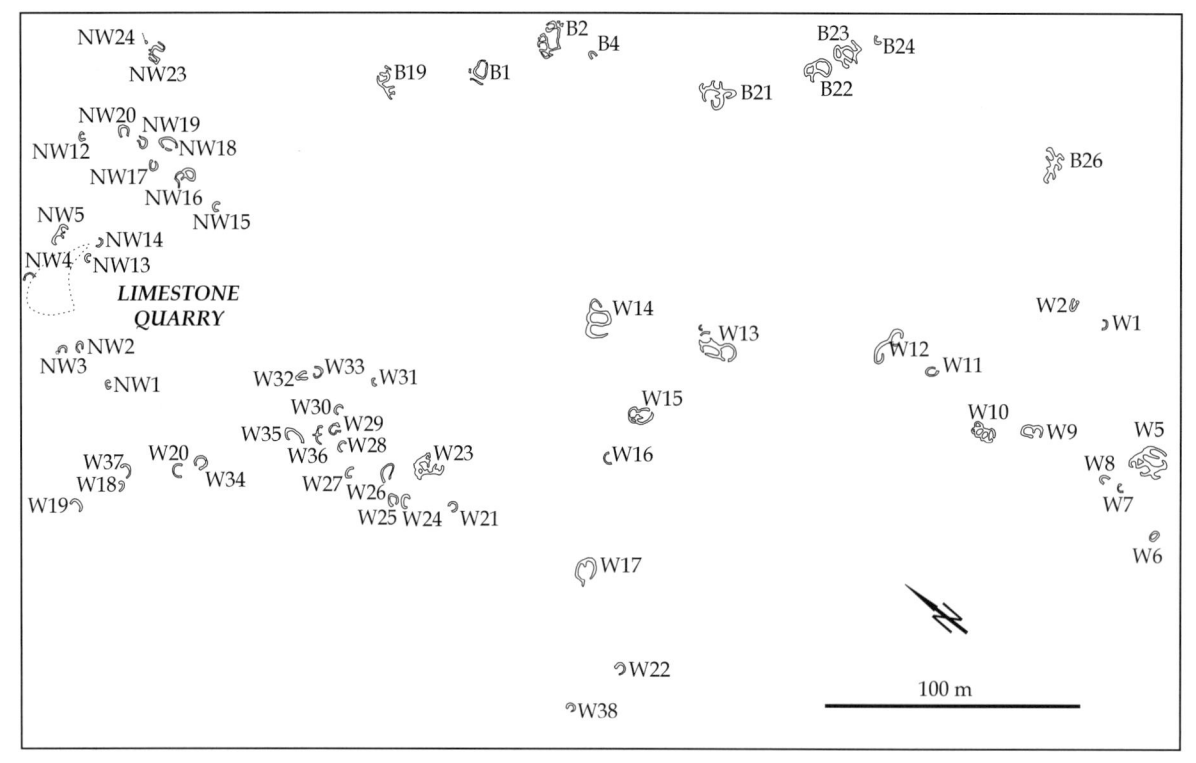

Figure 3.16. Plan of structures W1–51 and NW1–5 (part of the Quarry P settlement).

The next structures, slightly to the northwest, are **W3–4**, two poorly preserved crescent-shaped windbreaks (4.3 × 2.6 m and 3 × 2.5 m respectively), and to the south is a small basin at the southern end of the wadi, within which are three large windbreaks (**W6–8**: 4.9 × 4.6 m, 3.3 × 2.1 m and 4.4 × 3.8 m) and a large six-room structure (**W5**: 11.9 × 9.5 m). If one moves back northwards along the eastern side of the wadi, there is first an oval two-roomed hut (**W9**: 7.9 × 4.5 m) on a kind of natural terrace, and then, parallel with windbreaks W3–4, a high-walled five-room structure (**W10**: 7.9 × 6.2 m) which is the largest and best preserved of the multi-roomed clusters in this group. The walls of Hut W10 reach an average height of 1.1 m, and immediately to the north an extensive surface layer of travertine chips indicates an area in which stone artefacts were being roughed out (a theory reinforced by the surface find of a rough hammer-stone). The pottery found in Hut W10 includes a bread-mould (three sherds of which join, while two others do not, suggesting that more than one mould may have been present), a Meidum-type bowl rim, sherds from a red-slipped closed form, a 'gaming counter' or lid, and the very badly eroded base of an open-form vessel, red-burnished both inside and out.

A few metres to the north of Hut W10 is a large roughly circular hut (**W11**: 5.5 × 4.5 m), situated on the floor of the wadi, which gradually becomes shallower at its northern end. Roughly 15 m further on from W11 is a large two-roomed hut (**W12**: 7.9 × 5.2 m) containing large numbers of travertine chips. About 50 m to the west of W12 is a three-room hut (**W13**: 10.4 × 7.2 m) with an adjacent small windbreak. W13 contained five New Kingdom sherds from wheel-made silt-ware jars, as well as sherds of Old Kingdom vessels. Hut **W14** (12 × 5.3 m), about 30 m to the northwest of W13, is a low-walled three-room hut, and just outside its entrance is a dense concentration of travertine chips and Old Kingdom sherds, some of them in Meidum ware. Hut **W15** (7.3 × 4.3 m), c.30 m to the south of W14, consists of three rooms and contains both Old Kingdom and New Kingdom pottery, including the shoulder, handle and neck of a cream-slipped marl-clay New Kingdom amphora. Hut **W16** (4.6 × 2.8 m), a crescent-shaped

Figure 3.17. Structure NW3, a New Kingdom hut with *zir* emplacement to the left.

Figure 3.18. One of the large worked blocks of limestone in the New Kingdom encampment near Quarry P.

windbreak some 15 m to the northwest of W15, contained, Old Kingdom sherds as well as three siltware sherds from New Kingdom jars with knife-scraped bases, and several cream-slipped New Kingdom body sherds. A badly preserved two-room hut, **W17** (7.8 × 5.1 m), just a short distance to the south, contained sherds of Old Kingdom vessels.

To summarise the above description: the seventeen shelters W1–17, containing potsherds of both Old Kingdom and New Kingdom date, are located in a narrow wadi running from southeast to northwest and situated about 200 m to the west of cairns C7–8. These shelters comprised nine simple circular or crescent-shaped shelters and eight of the multi-room clusters typical of Old Kingdom occupation at Hatnub. While most of the shelters in this part of the site contain Old Kingdom sherds, there are three (W13, W15 and W16) that contain both Old and New Kingdom pottery. These three structures are the only part of the settlement containing traces of both major phases of use. It appears that the New Kingdom quarry-workers in this instance expanded beyond their own encampment (i.e. structures W18–38 and NW1–5) to occupy at least a few of their predecessors' shelters. It is clear, however, that, apart from this slight overspill to the south of their core area, the New Kingdom workers were clustering together some distance away from Quarry P, and well away from the core of the Old Kingdom settlement. The reasons for this very definite separation are at present unclear, although one possibility is that Quarry P itself had been essentially worked out by that date, therefore the New Kingdom expeditions were exploiting other stone sources.

All but four of the main group of New Kingdom shelters are single-roomed circular or crescent-shaped types (the exceptions being W19, W23, W36 and NW5), and the materials used are generally loosely assembled slabs and boulders, as opposed to the more carefully and densely constructed combinations of smaller stones and pebbles from which the majority of the Old Kingdom shelters are made. Figure 3.17 shows **NW3**, a standard crescent-shaped New Kingdom structure with a small emplacement for a water storage vessel (or *zir*) in the left foreground. The New Kingdom structures vary in size from 2.7 × 0.8 m (**W31**) to 14.1 × 10.7 m (**W23**, a sprawling nine-room hut), the average area being around 6 square metres. The impression given by the New Kingdom encampment is therefore of a set of very short-term shelters rapidly thrown together by individuals, whereas the typical Old Kingdom structures seem to be more sprawling and labour-intensive buildings intended perhaps to house gangs of workmen (e.g. N1, S8 and W10).

Another distinctive feature of this cluster of New Kingdom shelters is the presence of an area evidently devoted, rather unexpectedly, to the quarrying and carving of limestone. Three large worked blocks of limestone were still *in situ* among the huts themselves (see fig. 3.18). It is possible that this evidence for limestone quarrying provides at least one reason why the New Kingdom encampment is situated so far away from the travertine quarry itself, although, on the other hand, it seems highly unlikely that any limestone quarrying expedition would have chosen to exploit this stone in the vicinity of comparatively remote travertine quarries rather than quarrying it from the cliffs much closer to the Nile valley. Several flint tools were found on the modern ground surface near the New Kingdom encampment (see table 3.2 below). These tools are difficult to date precisely, and may possibly even pre-date the pharaonic activity (although this seems unlikely). The best current hypothesis as to their purpose is that at least some of them were used by the New Kingdom quarry-workers to dress the nearby slabs of limestone.

Find Number	Description	Provenance
H86/1	Pair of large flint tools	Surface, between the knoll and the main New Kingdom encampment (W18–38 and NW1–5)
H86/2	Pair of small flint tools	Surface, on the knoll between the W and NW groups of huts
H86/3	Large flint tool	Surface, immediately to the southeast of the knoll between the W and NW groups of huts
H86/4	Small flint blade, with serrated edges	Surface, beside Hut W31
H91/4	Flint tool, dark brown	Surface, Hut W51
H91/5	Flint tool, pale brown (re-used as core for bladelets)	Surface, Hut W51
H91/6	Basalt, small lump	Surface, Hut W51
H91/7	Flint flake, dark brown (with limited retouch on edge)	Surface, Hut W51
H91/8	Flint flake (with distinct platform and possible retouch along edge)	Surface, Hut W51 (just outside entrance)

Table 3.2. The flint and basalt surface finds from the W and NW groups of huts.

Some general comments can be made concerning the nature of the New Kingdom pottery in this part of Hatnub. It should be noted that the New Kingdom ceramics are accompanied by sufficient examples of Old Kingdom sherds to suggest that at least some of the New Kingdom occupation is secondary. The Old Kingdom pottery from this part of the site mainly consisted of Meidum-type bowl rims, red burnished body sherds from open forms, and occasional fragments of beer jars. The most obvious types of New Kingdom pottery at the site were:

1) Long necked 'vase' type vessels in a cream slipped and burnished marl III:2 with a single handle and Amarna J-type rim. These are entirely consistent with an 18th Dynasty date and are well-known, though not common, at Amarna.

2) Beer jars with angular/faceted, knife-scraped bases.

3) Clearly wheel-made body sherds, mostly in Nile silt fabric I:1, but clearly distinct from the material viewed elsewhere at Hatnub and assigned to the Old Kingdom.

4) Cream-slipped and burnished marl body sherds possibly from amphorae, meat jars or vases.

5) Simple-rim bowls usually with red slip, their bases more carefully finished than those dating to the Old Kingdom.

Structure **W51** (2.7 × 3.0 m) is an unusually shaped structure, comprising essentially two rooms, one L-shaped and the other, almost back-to-back with it, a typical crescent-shaped windbreak. It lies just to the southeast of feature **W52**, a group of orthostats (see section 6.2 below), and in fact some of the stones from which Hut W51 is built are unusually tall and triangular, suggest-

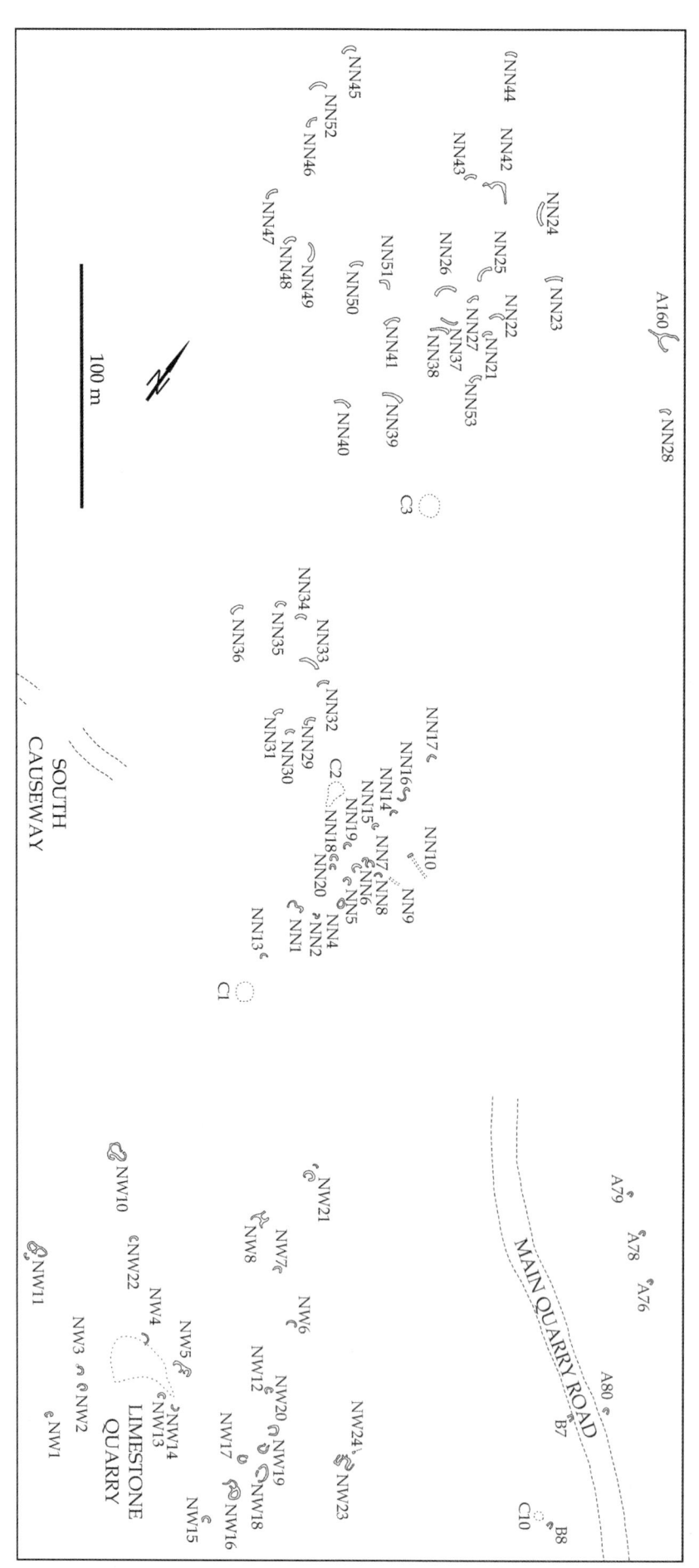

Figure 3.19. Plan of structures NW6–24 and NN1–52 (part of the Quarry P settlement).

ing that some orthostats may have been re-used for it (and it is even possible that the latter are in their original positions and that the hut was constructed around them without actually disturbing the original alignment). Hut W51 is also unusual because of the presence of a number of lithics on the surrounding ground surface (see table 3.2). Two of these flint tools (H91/7-8) were found just on the edge of the L-shaped room, and the rest (H91/4-6) were scattered to the southwest of the hut, in association with what appears to be a roughed out, quarried block of limestone, as well as the remains of an Old Kingdom beer jar.

3.3.4 Structures NW6-24 and NN1-52

To the north and west of the New Kingdom encampment (W1-38 and NW1-5), the Old Kingdom settlement resumes, generally following the course of the main quarry road as it heads northwestwards, away from Quarry P. Most of these huts are single-roomed circular structures, but a large three-roomed complex (**NW23**, see figs 3.39-40) occupies a small knoll near the centre of the plateau, containing a larger than usual quantity of sherds, and with several different ancient pathways leading up to it from several directions. The northern wall of the rectangular central room (flanked by two smaller ones) was over a metre in height. To the northwest, on the western face of the knoll, is a semi-circular area probably used for working travertine, judging by the large quantity of stone chips scattered across the surface.

The excavation of structure NW23 is discussed in section 3.5 below, while Chapter 5 includes further discussion of the New Kingdom pottery from the W and NW groups of structures in the Quarry P region. The possible importance of structure NW23 is indicated by the proximity of a small shrine-like feature (**NW24**), consisting of a pointed stone (28 cm high) with an approach path (120 cm long and 50 cm wide) consisting of two parallel lines of stones. In addition, one extra component distinguishes NW24 from the other features of this type: a stone-built emplacement behind the pointed stone, which may have been used to deposit ritual offerings, thus perhaps serving a similar purpose to the dome-shaped shrine S2 described in section 6.3 below.

The NN group of 52 built features is scattered across the area of the plateau dominated by a group of three very large cairns. Most of these NN huts are windbreaks, and they are situated in the area between the main quarry road and cairns 1-3 (see fig. 3.8, the main site map). Each of these cairns is about 5 m in diameter and about 2.5 m high at their centres. In at least twelve instances there are rough paths worn out in the ground between particular NN huts and the main quarry-road, and in five cases windbreaks (**NN1-2** and **NN11-13**) are incorporated into the side of the western section of road. Two of the NN features (**NN9-10**) take the form of the characteristic parallel lines of stones leading up to small upright stones, usually described as 'shrines' (see sections 6.2 and 6.3 below for further discussion of ritual alignments/orthostats and shrines). NN9-10 are located roughly midway between cairn C1 and the main road.

NN22, a large windbreak with a smaller windbreak attached to it, contained sherds making up most of an Old Kingdom Meidum-type bowl, as well as fragments of travertine both inside and outside the hut. Many potsherds were scattered across the surface between NN21, NN22 and another large windbreak **NN23** (6.7 × 5.1 m), the latter containing fragments from an Old Kingdom beer jar as well as travertine chips. **NN29-36** are a group of huts to the west of cairn C2, all but NN30 and NN33 being simple windbreaks.

The large windbreak **NN37** had a large limestone boulder immediately to the south of it, and a concentration of travertine chips just to the north. It contained a red-burnished closed form of vessel, the base of a beer jar, a fragment of a Meidum-type bowl, broken just above the carination, and the rim of another Meidum-type bowl. Hut **NN38**, a carefully constructed two-room building, contained a spherical hammer-stone, just inside the entrance of the northeastern room, and there is a large area to the east of both rooms' entrances which seems to have been deliberately cleared of pebbles. The hut also contained wheel-made body sherds of silt-ware, a red-burnished body sherd from an open-form vessel, fragments of beer jars, some highly eroded bowl fragments, a Coptic wheel-made sherd in chocolate-brown silt-ware, with white crosses and dots painted on it (the only clearly Coptic sherd so far found at Hatnub), and a large, almost complete, hand-made basin made in a very coarse silt ware, showing a clear join between the rim and body (a cross is incised on the outer surface of the basin, just below the join between these two parts, see fig. 3.20). No similar fragments or fabrics similar to this basin were encountered either in this hut or elsewhere at Hatnub – it is believed to be Old Kingdom, on the basis of similar vessels excavated in recent years at Dahshur and Giza. Hut **NN42**, a three- to four-room building with a dense concentration of travertine chips immediately to the west, contained a spherical hammer-stone (*c.*100 mm in diameter), the rim of a Meidum-type bowl, and several beer-jar sherds.

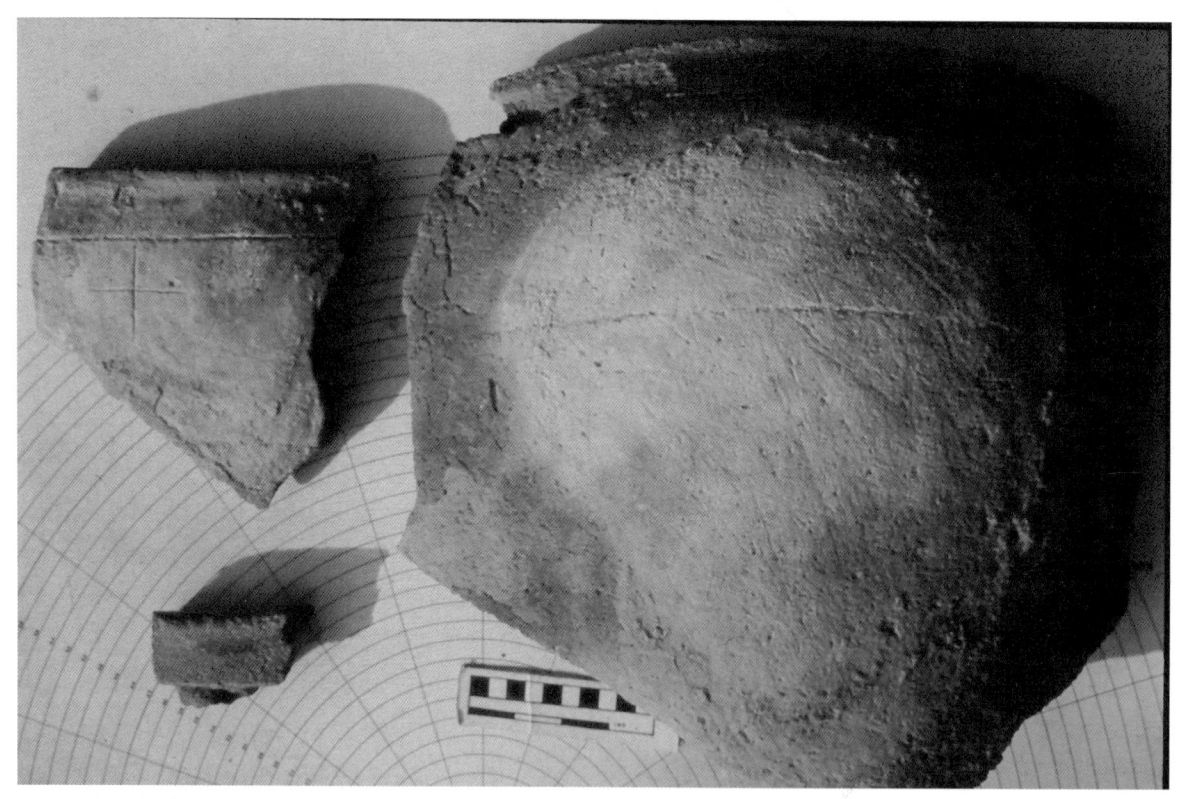

Figure 3.20. The large, almost complete, hand-made basin from hut NN38, which is thought to be Old Kingdom, on the basis of similar vessels found at Dahshur and Giza. A pre-firing pot-mark, in the form of a cross, was incised on the shoulder.

3.3.5 Structures SE1–22 and E1–4

At the furthest southeastern extent of the Quarry P settlement are six crescent-shaped wind-breaks (**SE17–22**) a short distance to the southeast of the small cairn marked C8 on the main map. Only a small quantity of travertine chips and a tiny number of potsherds (probably all from a single Old Kingdom vessel) were found in this cluster of windbreaks. A short distance to the west of this cluster of habitation is a pair of round huts (**SE12–13**) containing Old Kingdom pottery. Close by are two small windbreaks (**SE14–15**), and, a short distance to the southwest, a large windbreak (**SE16**) with travertine chips and Old Kingdom potsherds. To the northwest of SE16 is a large group of structures: **SE1**, a large, low-walled windbreak; **SE2**, an oval hut with fairly high walls; **SE3**, a three-room hut; **SE4**, a small windbreak; **SE5** (5.3 × 5.1 m), a large round hut with high walls and a dense concentration of travertine chips; **SE6** (2.5 × 1.8 m), a small windbreak containing very few sherds or travertine chips; **SE7**, a four-room hut; **SE8**, a tight cluster of three low windbreaks; **SE9**, a three-room hut; **SE10**, a vague feature comprising travertine chips and potsherds, which was presumably a working area; and **SE11**, another low windbreak. A small group of four structures were situated further to the east (**E1–4**).

3.3.6 Structures SW1–10

This group of ten dry-stone windbreaks is situated to the west of huts S13–14 in a small wadi running initially in a roughly north-south orientation, then turning west, and finally curving round to resume its north-south. The wadi peters out as it climbs the slope towards the gap between Huts S4 and S8. Huts SW1–10 are scattered across this small wadi and the plain that lies beyond it, to the west.

In the small wadi are Huts **SW1–2**, a pair of crescent-shaped windbreaks placed close together. About 10 m to the north of SW1–2, still in the small wadi, is **SW3**, a tight cluster of three round huts, in the southwest corner of which is a roughly constructed emplacement with a diameter of about 18 cm, presumably intended to support a pottery storage vessel, although no sherds have survived. On the plain to the west of the small wadi, about 14 m to the west of SW3, is a two-roomed hut (**SW4**), comprising one high-walled inner structure to the north, and a more poorly built, low-walled outer room; associated with SW4 are Old Kingdom potsherds in Meidum ware, and a large quantity of travertine chips. To the west of SW4 is a semi-circular windbreak, **SW5**, with a possible emplacement at the northern end of the eastern wall (i.e. facing Hut SW4). This emplacement contains a few rim-sherds of an Old Kingdom vessel, probably a beer jar, and there are also five large fragments of travertine in the vicinity. To the south of windbreak SW5 is a roughly oval structure (**SW6**), built on a south-facing slope; it contains a thick concentration of potsherds and travertine chips, and has a clear entrance on its southern side.

About 15–20 m to the west of Hut SW6, beyond a very shallow north-south oriented wadi, is another roughly oval structure, **SW7**, with a wall jutting out from it, evidently protecting a small stone emplacement. Hut SW7 contains some large lumps of travertine and Old Kingdom sherds. At the southern end of the shallow wadi just mentioned, at the point where it joins the deeper wadi in which Huts SW1–3 are located, is structure **SW8**, a roughly rectangular hut built up against the western slope of the shallower wadi. It contains only a very small quantity of tiny travertine chips and a few undiagnostic Old Kingdom sherds.

About 18 m to the northwest of Hut SW7 is a small oval hut, **SW9** (4.6 × 3.3 m), containing a reasonably large quantity of travertine chips of varying sizes, as well as some large sherds from an Old Kingdom round-based jar. To the north of SW9, the ground rises up to a knoll, then

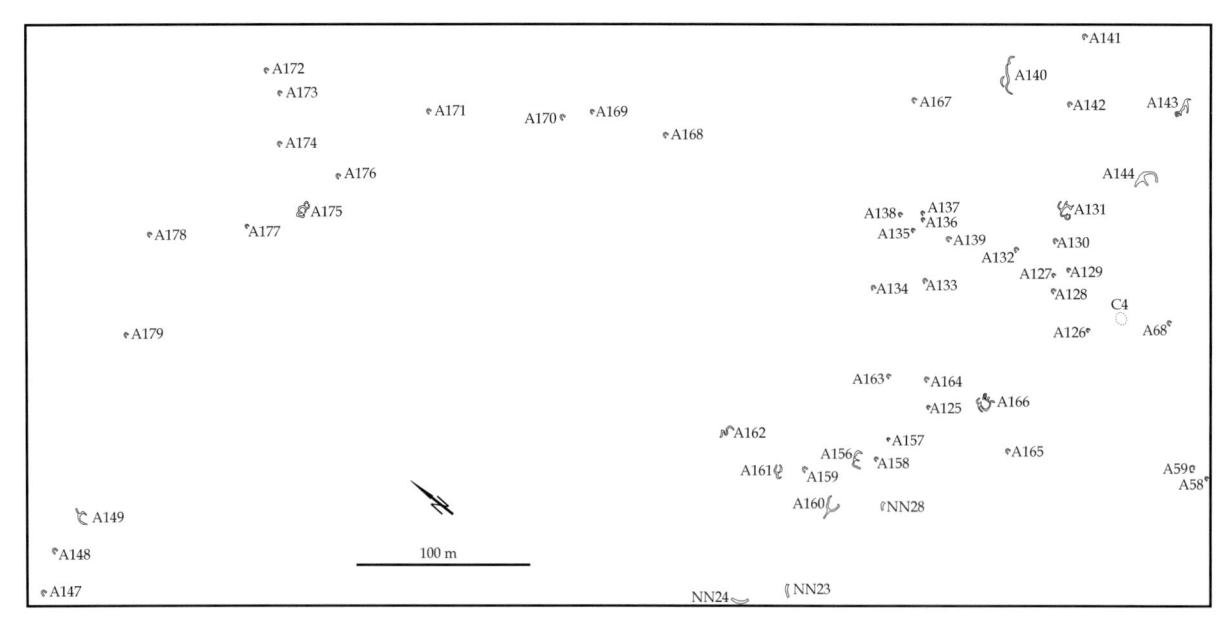

Figure 3.21. Plan of the northwestern sector of the A1–179 group of structures (part of the Quarry P settlement).

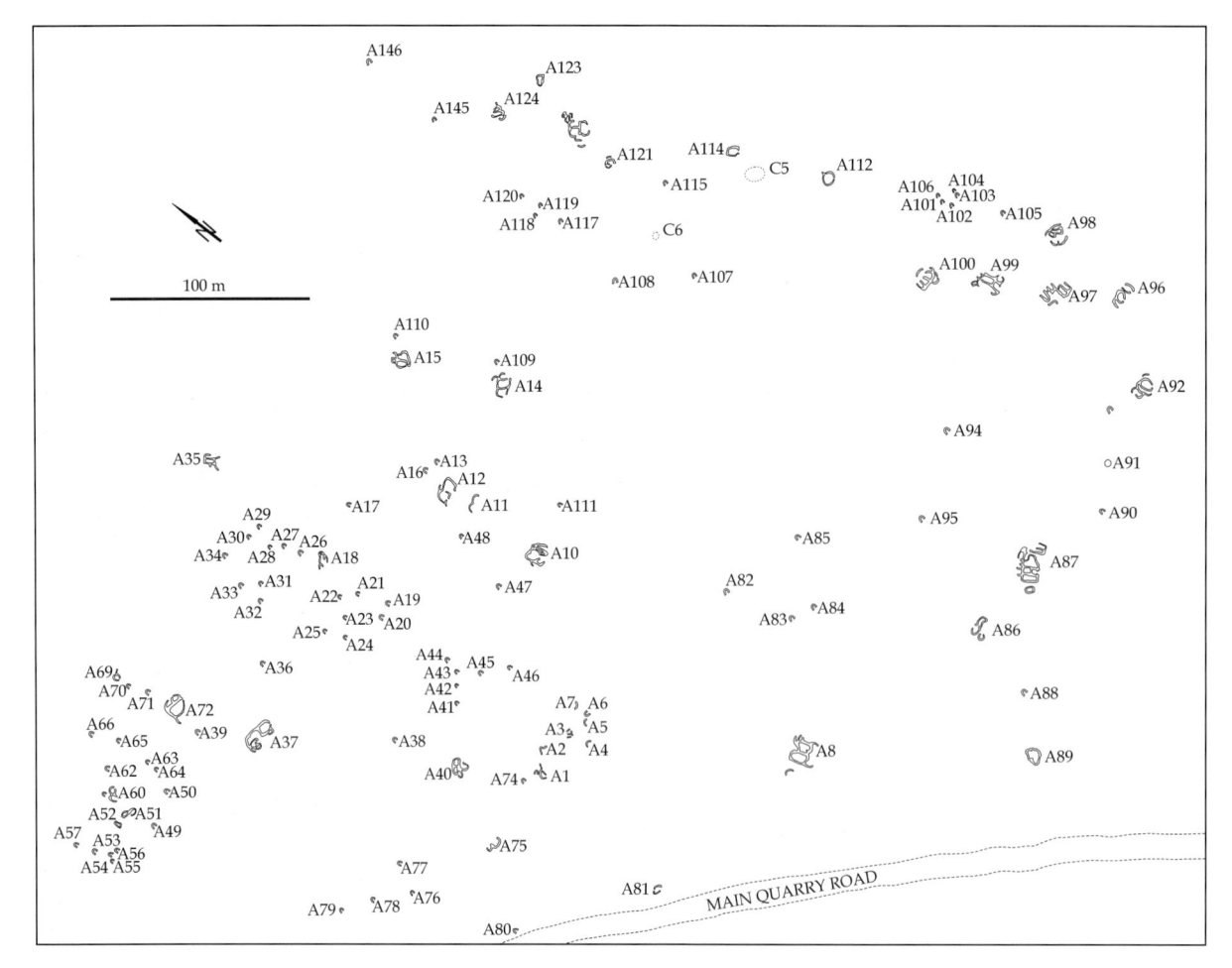

Figure 3.22. Plan showing the southwestern sector of the A1–179 group of structures.

slopes down steeply into a wadi running eastwards towards the main peak and cairn (C7 on the main site map). An ancient path leads up from the main wadi, skirting the knoll to the north of Hut SW9 and climbing northeastwards towards Hut S4. To the left of this path, just after it has emerged from the wadi, are the indistinct remains of S15, a round hut containing travertine chips and various Old Kingdom sherds, as well as a piece of animal vertebra in the northwestern section of the interior. Some 20 m in the opposite direction from SW9, i.e. southwards and down into the main wadi, is **SW10**, a large round structure with a fairly flat interior (7.8 × 7.1 m), full of tiny limestone chips and only a few small pieces of travertine. There are no potsherds inside the hut, but outside its southern end are fragments of several Old Kingdom jars as well as a small concentration of travertine chips. This structure seems to be at the southwestern edge of the entire Quarry P settlement area.

3.3.7 Structures A1–179

Many of this very large group of small stone structures (figs 3.21–2), primarily comprising windbreaks, were surveyed in February 1990. There were 179 structures altogether, most of them containing very few potsherds, and in many cases none at all; those that contained significant quantities of ceramics are described below.

Structures A1–7 form a distinct group located to the north of the dense encampment adjacent to Quarry P, beside the ancient road. Hut **A1** (7.2 × 6.5 m) consists of one oval room and an immediately adjacent windbreak to the north, and several large New Kingdom sherds immediately to the south of the entrance. **A2** (2.8 × 1.6 m), **A4** (2.7 x 2.2 m), **A5** (2.7 × 1.7 m), **A6** (1.7 × 0.9

Figure 3.23. One of the Old Kingdom beer jars discarded on the slope between hut A10 and the main wadi.

m) are fairly basic windbreaks, and **A3** (3.6 × 2.8 m) is a very roughly constructed two-room hut containing the remains of one Old Kingdom vessel. Hut **A7** (2.4 × 0.7 m) is a windbreak; it contained the neck of a bottle-type vessel, eroded but with traces of red slip on exterior, as well as body sherds of open forms, which had been red-slipped and burnished on both exterior and interior surfaces. **A8** (11.5 × 9.8 m) is a five- or six-room hut containing a few Old and New Kingdom sherds, as well as travertine chips. Hut **A9** (3.9 × 1.8 m) contained hand-made body sherds of closed forms, the rim of a beer jar, and the rim of a Meidum-type bowl. Immediately to the east of this hut the base of a beer jar was found.

Structures A10–15 were clustered together. Hut **A10** (13.2 × 10.3 m; survey point W), a large four- or five-room hut, contained a general scatter of travertine, including a number of roughly shaped pieces in the area around the outside of the hut. It also contained the shoulder of a large hand-made jar with an incised post-firing pot-mark comprising an isosceles triangle containing a square and two lines emerging from it, probably representing a stylised human figure. Several beer jars appeared to have been thrown down the slope towards the main wadi (see fig. 3.23). The rest of the pottery included the rim of a slightly flared bread-mould rim, the simple rim from a well-burnished bowl, a pointed base, a large gaming counter or lid (made from a sherd deriving from a hand-made closed form), a badly broken and eroded Meidum-type bowl, an angular fragment from the shoulder of a marl clay vessel, with the characteristic depression where the rim joins the shoulder, and the shoulder scraped to a sharp carination. As well as these Old Kingdom sherds and vessels, there was also a New Kingdom jar, wheel-made, with a short flaring rim and a knife-scraped base.

Hut **A11** (8.65 × 0.9 m) is a windbreak with some Old Kingdom potsherds inside it and a scattering of travertine fragments behind its back wall. The two-roomed Hut **A12** (10.3 × 6.2 m), with a separate entrance for each room, contained one large sherd from an Old Kingdom vessel, and had two associated orthostats, one just outside the westernmost entrance, and the other behind the back wall.

Hut **A18** (9.65 × 3.2 m), a two-roomed structure with two small windbreaks attached to it, is situated midway between Hut **A26** and a group of small windbreaks (**A19–25**). It contained sherds from beer jars and Meidum-type bowls, as well as body sherds from at least one hand-made vessel, a large fragment of a bread-mould, and the slightly out-turned rim of a bowl with red burnish both inside and out (similar to type U171, see Kaiser 1969: 65). Hut **A35** (7.5 × 7.5 m; survey point V) is a two-roomed structure with a large quantity of travertine chips in front of it, situated on a knoll just to the north of windbreaks A30–4. Inside it were found a sherd from a bread-mould, fragments of at least one Meidum-type bowl, numerous red-burnished body sherds from open forms, the in-turned rim of a bowl with red-burnished slip on the inside and upper part of the exterior. Finally, this hut also contained sherds of a Roman amphora in soft, chocolate-brown Nile silt fabric; (fig. 3.24); the sherds were all from the bottom part of the vessel, including the toe, and characteristic black resin was found on the inner surface of the base. The large group of windbreaks to the west of A35 are almost devoid of pottery, but there are occasional sherds of Meidum-type bowls and other fragments of Old Kingdom forms.

The six-roomed Hut **A37** (13.6 × 8.4 m) contains a thin scatter of travertine chips and potsherds throughout. The pottery includes rim sherds from two different types of bread-mould (one resembling form U258 and another similar to U258 but with a larger lip); the round base of a

Figure 3.24. Base of a Roman amphora, fragments of the lower part of which were found in Hut A35.

wheel-made vessel; red-burnished body sherds; the slightly inturned rim of a red-burnished bowl; the base and rim of a beer jar; the rim of a Meidum-type bowl; and the out-turned rim of a bowl with scraped base, roughly finished and unslipped.

The three- to four-room structure **A40** (8.65 × 7.0 m) contains comparatively few travertine fragments and sherds, considering its size. The pottery includes several jar rims, apparently wheel-made, and some fragments from a burnished bowl with slightly incurving rim. These potsherds are clustered in a small wadi, and thus should be considered less secure than the other pieces, but there is no actual evidence to suggest that they are washed in. Hut A40 also contained a large fragment of a bread-mould, comprising both the flaring rim and the 'carination' in the lower part of the vessel body.

Hut **A59** (7.1 × 1.6 m) is a very irregular structure, comprising only one room, and contains a single Old Kingdom sherd and only one piece of travertine, a triangular worked piece with traces of copper on one side. The neighbouring two-room structure **A60** (6.1 × 3.7 m) contained a very small quantity of travertine chips and sherds, including parts of a Meidum-type bowl.

Feature **A89** (8.6 × 6.8 m) is a very low-walled roughly circular area that, like the rather more complex nearby feature A86, was probably more of a working area than a hut. Not surprisingly, therefore, it contained a quite dense concentration of travertine fragments, both inside the walls and outside the northwestern side. There were also several sherds from large Old Kingdom vessels inside the feature, and a number of animal bones about five metres to the northwest, possibly making up the remains of a single herbivore of some kind.

Hut **A97** (12.3 × 9.6 m) is part of a group with A96 and A98–100. It consisted of four fairly solidly built rooms, and contained a number of chips of travertine including a lump that is probably a semi-worked vessel (fig. 3.25). It was strewn throughout with Old Kingdom pottery, the best-preserved items being an almost complete beer jar and half of a Meidum-type bowl.

Hut **A99** (13.3 × 8.5 m), a neatly built structure with an unusually straight wall at its northeastern end (fig. 3.26), was situated midway between two other multi-room huts, **A98** and **A100**. It contained dense concentrations of travertine fragments, including an unusually large

Figure 3.25. Semi-worked travertine artefact and sherds of an Old Kingdom vessel in *situ* in structure A97.

Figure 3.26. Structure A99, which has an unusually straight wall at its northeastern side.

roughed-out rounded lump in the southeastern corner (fig. 3.27). It also yielded a large quantity of sherds, including parts of beer jars; fragments of Meidum-type bowls; the flat base of an open form; the simple, fairly straight rim of a bread-mould; and a lid or gaming counter in silt clay, red-slipped on the outside.

Hut **A100** (11.9 × 10.9 m) contained the base of a beer jar (as well as a sherd comprising an almost complete profile of this same jar), sherds from the rim of a hand-made, red burnished closed form vessel, red-burnished bowls, and a complete beer jar in medium fine silt. The latter is an unusual type of beer jar, with a finger-modelled lower section and a rim with a groove beneath, similar to that from Hut S26 in the north-south wadi. There is also one round base of a closed form with deep rills inside it and may be New Kingdom, though this is not certain.

Figure 3.27. The large roughed-out lump of travertine found in structure A99.

Features **A114–5**, **A117–23** and **C5–6** form a particular group comprising a mixture of cairns, windbreaks and multi-room huts. Among these, a very large five- to six-room structure, **A122** (19.8 × 9.3 m) contained a number of roughed out alabaster cylinders found just outside one of the eastern walls of the hut; each of these rough cylinders was about 13 cm^3. **A123** (6.9 × 6.0 m) is an unusual hut in that it was hollowed out of a large heap of stones, rather than being built. It contained only a few Old Kingdom sherds and very few chips of travertine.

Hut **A160** (7.19 × 0.8 m), a kind of Y-shaped structure evidently comprising a pair of windbreaks sharing a common wall, also contained about twelve fairly large (c.10 cm^3) chunks of travertine, including one that had been roughed out into a cylindrical shape.

3.3.8 Structures B1–59

This group of 46 huts and windbreaks (fig. 3.28) is situated to the south of the main quarry road, between the New Kingdom encampment (to their west) and the 'N1–21' group of huts (to their east).

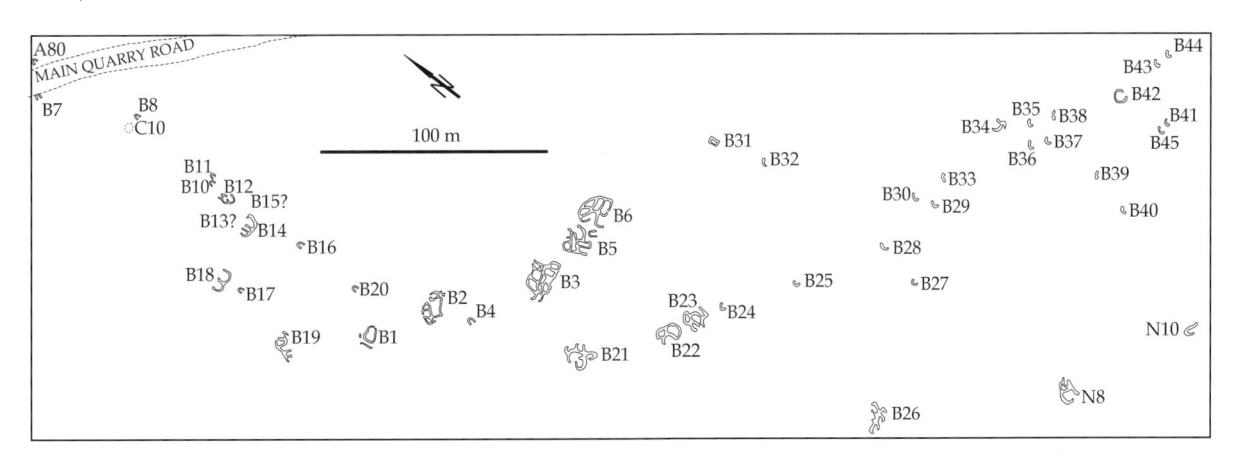

Figure 3.28. Plan showing the B1–46 group of structures.

Structures B1–6 form a reasonably coherent group in terms of their location, and all are multi-room buildings apart from Hut **B1** (6.6 × 6.2 m) which consists of a single, heart-shaped room, in which four small worked pieces of travertine (perhaps fashioned in the form of pendants) were found (see fig. 3.29). This hut also contained beer jar fragments, red-burnished open forms, an eroded jar like that at Hut B19 (see below), a simple rim from a bowl completely blackened by weathering, and the rim and body sherds from a Meidum-type bowl. The five-room Hut **B2** (11.0 × 6.3 m) also contained evidence of the working of travertine into artefacts, in the form of a disc-shaped piece, and another that had been roughed out into a cylinder and then partially hollowed out (see fig. 3.30).

Figure 3.29. Structure B1, containing four worked fragments of travertine (each approximately 30 mm in length).

Figure 3.30. The cylindrical and discoid worked fragments of travertine from Hut B2.

The exceptionally large ten-room Hut **B3** (18.5 × 10.2 m) contained quite substantial amounts of pottery, some being undiagnostic marl body sherds, but others including a hand-made silt-ware round base from a carefully worked vessel, two rims from Meidum-type bowls (one red-burnished both inside and out), a marl rim from a closed form of vessel, apparently originally burnished but now severely eroded, fragments of at least one beer jar, and the rim from a red-slipped jar with clear rilling from a potter's wheel or, at the very least, evidence of careful turn-table manufacture. Outside this hut were several clear deposits of travertine chips, particularly along the south side, evidently indicating distinct working areas.

The eight-room Hut **B5** (12.9 × 8.2 m) contained sherds from beer jars (including one base), fragments of a red-burnished closed form, sherds from a hand-made jar, two non-joining fragments of a type of bread-mould (see fig. 5.23), a gaming counter or lid made from part of a hand-made closed form, the rim of a Meidum-type bowl, and the base of a red-slipped wheel-made base of a round bottomed vessel, possibly of New Kingdom date.

Only about half a metre from Hut B5 is the six-room structure **B6** (16.9 × 9.5 m), which contained about half of a Meidum-type bowl, slipped on the exterior only, possibly broken in antiquity or perhaps weathered away by attrition (see figs 3.31 and 5.4), and fragments of another, less complete, Meidum-type bowl. Among the many other sherds in B6 were bases and body-

Figure 3.31. Meidum-type Old Kingdom bowl from structure B6.

sherds from beer jars, a gaming counter or lid made from part of a red-slipped closed form, a marl sherd of closed form showing fine lines or rills inside (as if wheel-made, although the uneven exterior clearly shows the hand-forming process), the out-turned rim of a bowl, with heavily knife-scraped outer surface, a marl sherd from the shoulder of a vessel preserving three incised lines (probably a post-firing pot-mark), and a siltware jar with an unusual rim (with much chaff visibly impressed into the interior, but the exterior less clear due to erosion). In addition, an unusual find in B6 was a red-slipped, closed-form, globular vessel preserved from the upper shoulder almost down to the base (the lower part being knife-scraped on the outside), with a 2.5 × 2.0 cm hole in side, possibly intended to serve as spout; this vessel had rills on the inside, but it was nevertheless not clear whether it was wheel-made.

This part of the site was dominated by a large cairn (**C10**), which had a reasonably substantial windbreak (**B9**) tacked onto its western side. The windbreak contained travertine chips as well as potsherds, including some fragments of a jar coated with red slip on its external surface, several gaming counters or lids, about 80% of a flat-based Meidum-type bowl, which had been very finely made (although damaged by wind-blown sand), another flat-based Meidum-type bowl, this time in fragments and much less complete, a steep sided open vessel with red burnishing both inside and out, the flaring rims of eroded, closed form jars, wheel-made body sherds in marl C, and the rim of a bread-mould.

Two small windbreaks (**B10** and **B11**), situated very close to one another, contained a few travertine chips and some Old Kingdom sherds, including the rims of Meidum-type bowls, a beer jar, and fragments of red-slipped jars.

The three-room structure **B14** (5.7 × 3.0 m), situated in a small group with Huts B12–13 and B15, had only one room that would have been sufficiently large to accommodate a sleeping worker, suggesting that the other two rooms might have only been utilised as shelters for working or storage. One of these smaller rooms contains a fragment of animal bone, and the hut as a whole contains a few chips of travertine and some Old Kingdom potsherds, including body sherds from one or more beer jars, some marl C body sherds, a Meidum-type bowl, rims from red-burnished jars, a badly eroded rim of a simple bowl, a flat base from a vessel that was probably wheel-made, an upright marl rim (fig. 3.32), a squared jar rim and about two-thirds of a jar, with very eroded red slip, of biconical type in medium fine silt ware.

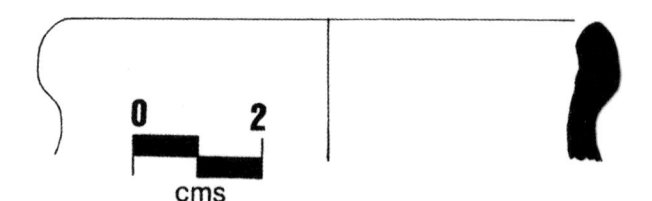

Figure 3.32. Upright rim from a marl beer jar found in structure B14.

Structure **B18** (7.15 × 3.4 m), essentially a joined pair of crescent-shaped wind-breaks, contained very few travertine chips, but a number of pottery types were present, including a virtually complete red-burnished spouted vessel (figs 3.33-4), sherds from several red-burnished closed forms, the rim of a Meidum-type bowl, and a round-based, red-burnished closed form with a 13 mm hole in the base and the remains of a second hole higher up the body at the broken edge of the sherd (probably the result of rivet repairs). A nearby small windbreak, B17, contained a few Old Kingdom sherds and some travertine chips.

The five-room structure **B19** (11.05 × 6.7 m) contained comparatively few travertine chips for its size. A small and very low-walled windbreak tacked onto the northeastern side of the building might have provided shelter for a small working area, but even here the travertine *débitage*

Figures 3.33–4. Old Kingdom spouted vessel from structure B18.

was fairly sparse. Pottery from the main building included a complete beer jar, another jar with a long neck and squarish rim, a complete bowl red-slipped inside and out with a simple rim and a scraped base, a severely weathered jar that had once been red-slipped, and the rim of a Meidum-type bowl. In the area between Huts B19 and B1 there are large sherds of *zir*-like vessels without any slip, and with numerous rope marks, probably dating to the New Kingdom.

The five-room structure **B23** (9.8 × 9.5 m) contained numerous roughly cylindrical semi-worked travertine artefacts both inside and outside. Only a few Old Kingdom sherds were found outside the building, mainly to the south and west. Just inside the northeastern room were two flint flake tools, and in the central room there was an unusual roughly rectangular block of local limestone.

A very small low-walled windbreak, **B27**, contained a few travertine chips as well as a beer jar, a fragment of a bread-mould, the rim of a jar in marl or marl/silt mixture with red burnish on the outside, the rim of a Meidum-type bowl, and a simple-rim bowl (fig. 3.35). There was also a silt jar with eroded red slip on the outside, which had wheel marks on the inside but was made from a coarse fabric (fig. 3.36).

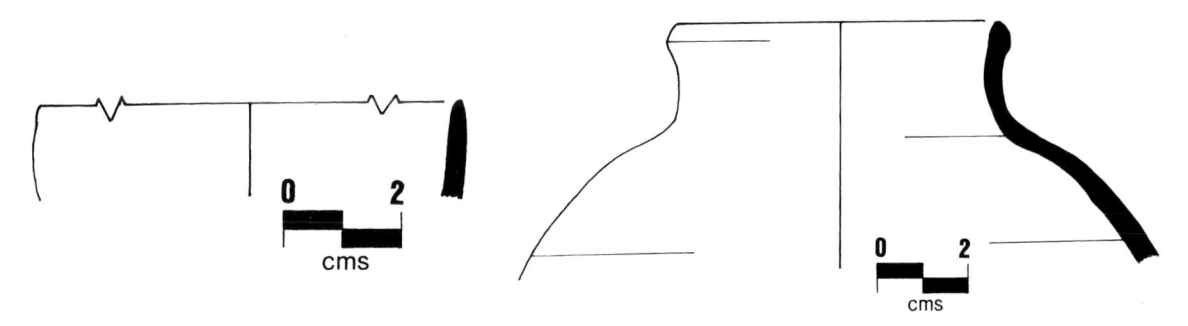

Figure 3.35. A simple-rim bowl from windbreak B27.

Figure 3.36. A Nile-silt jar with eroded red slip on the outside and wheel marks on the inside from windbreak B27.

B31 (*c*.3.0 × 2.5 m), a neatly constructed rectangular structure contained some large Old Kingdom potsherds (probably from a storage vessel) and a medium to heavy scatter of travertine chips. An unusual discovery just outside the northwestern corner of the hut was a roughly circular, centrally pierced pottery disc, *c*.60 mm in diameter.

Structure **B34** (*c*.4.0 × 2.5 m) is a kind of low-walled double windbreak, its plan almost in the shape of a letter 'y', which contained some fairly large lumps of travertine. Its location overlooks the part of the main quarry road closest to Quarry P (i.e. the section between the quarry and the first causeway).

B46, a windbreak, contained the rim of a badly weathered Meidum-type bowl, body sherds of closed forms with clear rilling lines (though the red slip and generally treatment suggested that the vessel was Old Kingdom), and the base of a red-burnished wheel-made closed form, possibly New Kingdom in date. Another windbreak in this area, B51, contained a few travertine chips and a small number of sherds, including some deriving from red-slipped, wheel-made closed forms as well as others from open bowls with out-turned rims and scraped lower parts.

Hut **B53**, a roughly circular, single-room structure, contained a thick, globular vessel with rilling lines but much chaff visible, which is probably a carefully made hand-formed piece of Old Kingdom date.

Two windbreaks, **B54** and **B55**, both containing some chips of travertine, were situated so close together that their pottery is here listed together, since it was difficult to precisely assign pottery to one or the other. There were red-slipped and burnished open forms, a beer jar, the irregular pointed base of a red-slipped closed form (with has clear spiral rills inside, and equally clear finger modelling on the outside), a bowl that had been red-slipped and burnished both inside and out, a marl-clay bowl similar to the classic Meidum-type, with a yellow/cream surface both inside and out (but weak reaction to hydrochloric acid, possibly due to local conditions or firing temperature), and a rim of an unusually carefully fashioned bread-mould, made from a heavy dense fabric typical of the type, blackened on the inside, probably secondarily.

The windbreak **B56** contained a very small quantity of travertine chips, a few beer jar fragments, and a large sherd from a marl-clay vessel of possible Coptic date. The latter produced a very strong reaction with hydrochloric acid, and was possibly slipped or burnished on the outside, but too little of the exterior has survived to be sure of this. The fabric is a soft, uniform brown without a core, and the inside is crudely made (possibly even hand-made).

The windbreak **B57** contained some Old Kingdom sherds and no chips of travertine. However, c.4m to the southwest there was a red-slipped, closed-form sherd deriving from a round base (very similar to a *sakkia* base) with clear wheel marks on the outside; this vessel appears to be either late New Kingdom or possibly even Roman or Coptic.

3.4 Structure S26 (excavated 7–9 October 1991)

Hut **S26** is a multi-chambered structure, comprising seven individual rooms, and with a scatter of pottery around it, particularly on the eastern, downward sloping, side (see fig. 3.37). Part of Room 2 of this structure was excavated in October 1991 (see fig. 3.38). Pottery from each room of S26 was collected, bagged and examined separately, and then a selection of material from the surrounding area was studied. The surface pottery from Room 2 was collected by metre squares. The material from S26, both surface and excavated is consistent with a date in the Old Kingdom. Though many sherds were eroded and/or of small size there was no material obviously from other periods, and this view is supported by the scatter of material found to the east of the hut. See section 5.3 for more detailed discussion of the pottery from S26.

Before excavation, the surface of squares A–D in Room 2 consisted of sand interspersed with tumble, pieces of travertine and potsherds (the latter removed and logged according to their metre squares, and the travertine set aside). Only squares A and B were excavated. Initially most of the tumble was removed from all four squares, and the sandy surface layer (unit 1) was removed down to a uniform and arbitrary depth of 50 mm. In square B a re-worked Old Kingdom potsherd was found (H91/1, for all small finds see table 3.3 below): this was a 30 mm-long thumbnail-shaped scraper. Otherwise there were only two significant finds of potsherds from square B, both probably deriving from open vessels, and both of Old Kingdom date. There were some flecks and tiny pieces of charcoal at a depth of about 35 mm into unit 1. Square B also yielded three small fragments of travertine. In square A, flecks of charcoal were found in unit 1, as well as a few Old Kingdom sherds and four fragments of travertine. As with square B, unit 1 consisted of loose sand interspersed with compacted sand, all being of the same colour as the surface.

Figure 3.37. The multi-room structure S26; Room 2, in the central foreground, was excavated in 1991.

Figure 3.38. Room 2 of Hut S26, after excavation of unit 3.

A further 50 mm depth of sand and tumble (unit 2) was next removed from squares A and B, exposing a pure white, almost powdery sand, just above the natural rock surface. During the removal of unit 2, some large fragments of travertine, as well as a dense patch of smaller fragments, were revealed at the western side of square B. In the northwest corner of square A, the removal of unit 2 exposed a rocky knoll covered by a roughly oval, dark grey, ashy stain (unit 3), and two other ashy marks immediately to the west. Within unit 3 in square B we unearthed several small finds: a piece of twig (H91/17), a fragment of animal bone (H91/18), a disc-shaped piece of travertine (H91/11) and a flake of flint (H91/9). In square A the thin layer of unit 3 material contained small pieces of charcoal and a pottery gaming counter (H91/10). Once unit 3 had been completely removed from squares A and B, a number of ashy features (F1–9) remained; these shallow ash-filled pits were sectioned and planned. F1 contained a flat roughly rectangular stone surrounded by powdery sand with a few very tiny ash inclusions (fig. 3.39). At the base of F6, a lens of ashy material cut into the fill of feature F1, was a flint point (H91/16).

Find no.	Description	Location	Dimensions
H91/1	Potsherd re-used as scraper	Unit 1, square B	38 × 32 × 6 mm
H91/2	Flint scraper	Surface (NE edge of zone of southern huts)	37 × 16 × 7 mm
H91/3	Hammer stone	Surface (N side of Sq.C, Room 2, S26)	100 × 82 × 63 mm
H91/9	Flint flake	Unit 3, Sq.B, Hut S26	
H91/10	'Gaming counter', roundish potsherd	Unit 3, Sq.A, Hut S26	diameter = 34 mm
H91/11	Travertine disc	Unit 3, Sq.B, Hut S26	diameter = 15 mm
H91/12	Travertine tool, long and triangular, stone smoothed by use	Unit 3, Sq.B, Hut S26	49 × 20 mm
H91/13	Chert tool, mottled colour	Surface, in wadi, c.20 m from Hut S26	65 × 18 mm
H91/14	Potsherd re-used as scraper	Unit 2, Sq.B, Hut S26	83 × 54 × 9 mm
H91/15	Fragment of potsherd re-used either as a scraper or 'gaming counter'	Unit 2, Sq.B, Hut S26	40 × 23 × 9 mm
H91/16	Flint tool, with very well-made leaf point and with retouch along both edges	Fill of feature F1, resting just at base of ashy lens	66 × 16 × 2.5 mm
H91/17	Fragment of wood	Unit 3, Sq.B, Hut S26	
H91/18	Fragment of animal bone	Unit 3, Sq.B, Hut S26	

Table 3.3. Small finds from S26, squares A and B, and surrounding area.

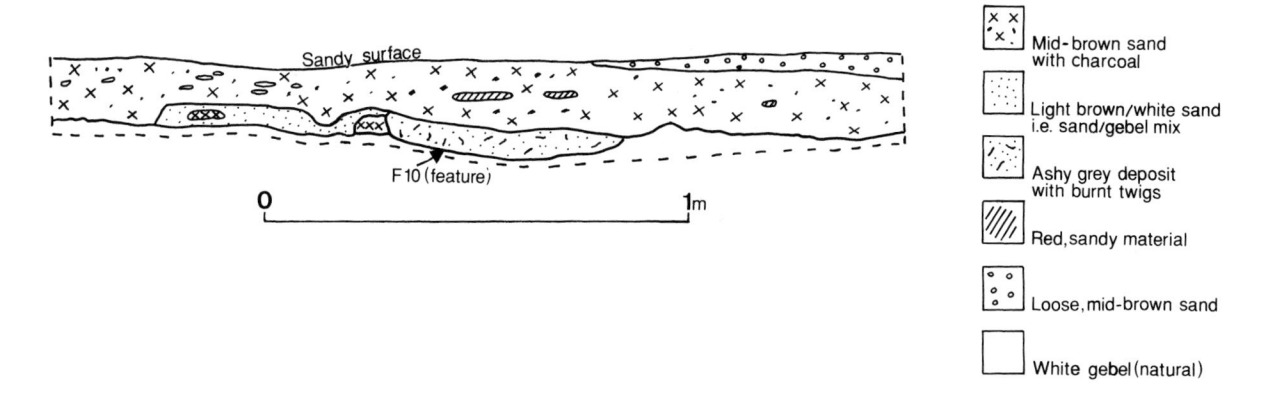

Figure 3.39. Section along the western edge of squares A–B in Hut S26.

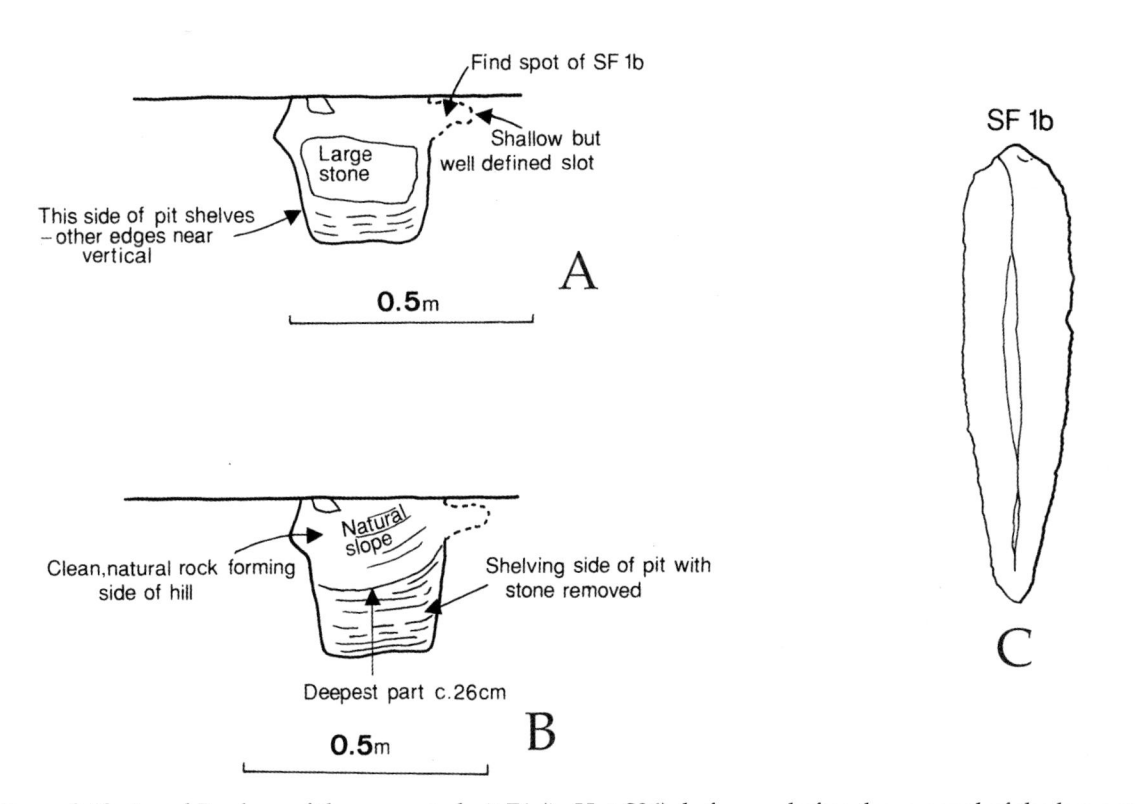

Figure 3.40. A and B: plans of the excavated pit F1 (in Hut S26), before and after the removal of the large stone. C: drawing of small-find H91/16 (a leaf-shaped flint tool), the find-spot of which is indicated in plan A.

3.5 Structure NW23 (excavated 12–13 February 1990)

Hut **NW23** (figs 3.41-2) may have served as an administrative centre at a crucial point where the quarried blocks of travertine were beginning their long journey away from the main quarrying region and across the desert towards the Nile. The likely importance of the structure is reinforced by the existence of a small shrine-like structure (see Chapter 6 below) just to the north of NW23. The shrine (labelled NW24, see fig. 6.11) consists of an upright pointed stone, 28 cm high, and a short pathway (120 × 50 cm) leading up to it, marked by two parallel rows of small stones laid on the desert surface. One extra factor distinguishes this feature from many of the other likely shrines in the Quarry P region: there is a stone-built emplacement behind the pointed stone which may have contained offerings, thus perhaps serving the same purpose as

Figure 3.41. Structure NW23.

the roofed building forming the main component of the large shrine S2, just to the north of the peak with cairns which is the high point of the Quarry P region (see section 6.3 below).

Structure NW23 was excavated between 12 and 13 February 1990, beginning by removing surface sherds from a 3 × 3 m square, and taking spot heights at all points on the grid (see fig. 3.43). The excavation area was divided into squares A–C. Square C was excavated first, working east to west and peeling off wind-blown sand (unit 1) to reveal a compact sandy surface studded with sherds (far more than in squares A and B). Both units 1 and 2 were sieved. Unit 1, with an average depth of 20 mm (apart from a small depression in the northeastern corner of square C), was removed across squares A, B and C. The surface of unit 2 was then planned.

Unit 2 was next removed across square C, taking the level down by a further 100 mm at the northern end of the square and by about 80 mm at the southern end. The layer below unit 2 consisted of a few rather decayed sherds, charcoal flecks, patches of soft white gypsum-like material and a few pieces of shaped and apparently slightly polished travertine. Unit 2 was also removed across square B, again revealing a relatively small number of sherds. As with square C, gypsum-like material appeared in patches again, and it gradually became apparent that this was the natural gebel surface. A test-hole excavated into the undisturbed gebel revealed an upper layer of surface sand and pebbles, a 200 mm-thick layer of fine sand and fine white powdery material and finally a layer of pure white powdery material. The material in unit 2 of square B did not contain any pieces of polished travertine. There was less than half of the amount of sherds compared with unit 2 in square C (i.e. same pattern as in unit 1).

When unit 2 was removed from square A, the surface was again taken down to the point where white powdery material began to appear. A small piece of slightly rounded, (possibly shaped) travertine was found when this unit 2 material was sieved. Slightly more sherds were collected here than in unit 2 in square B, but still considerably fewer than in square C. At the northern end of square A, a small concentration of charcoal appeared. Apart from the pieces left in the surface for planning, about ten fragments of charcoal were collected. Only a few flecks of charcoal had been present in square B and a few small pieces in square C. The charcoal in square A was confined to two areas of darker soil/sand cut into the gebel; these small, vaguely circular areas may be features, such as emplacements from pottery vessels, or perhaps even post-holes.

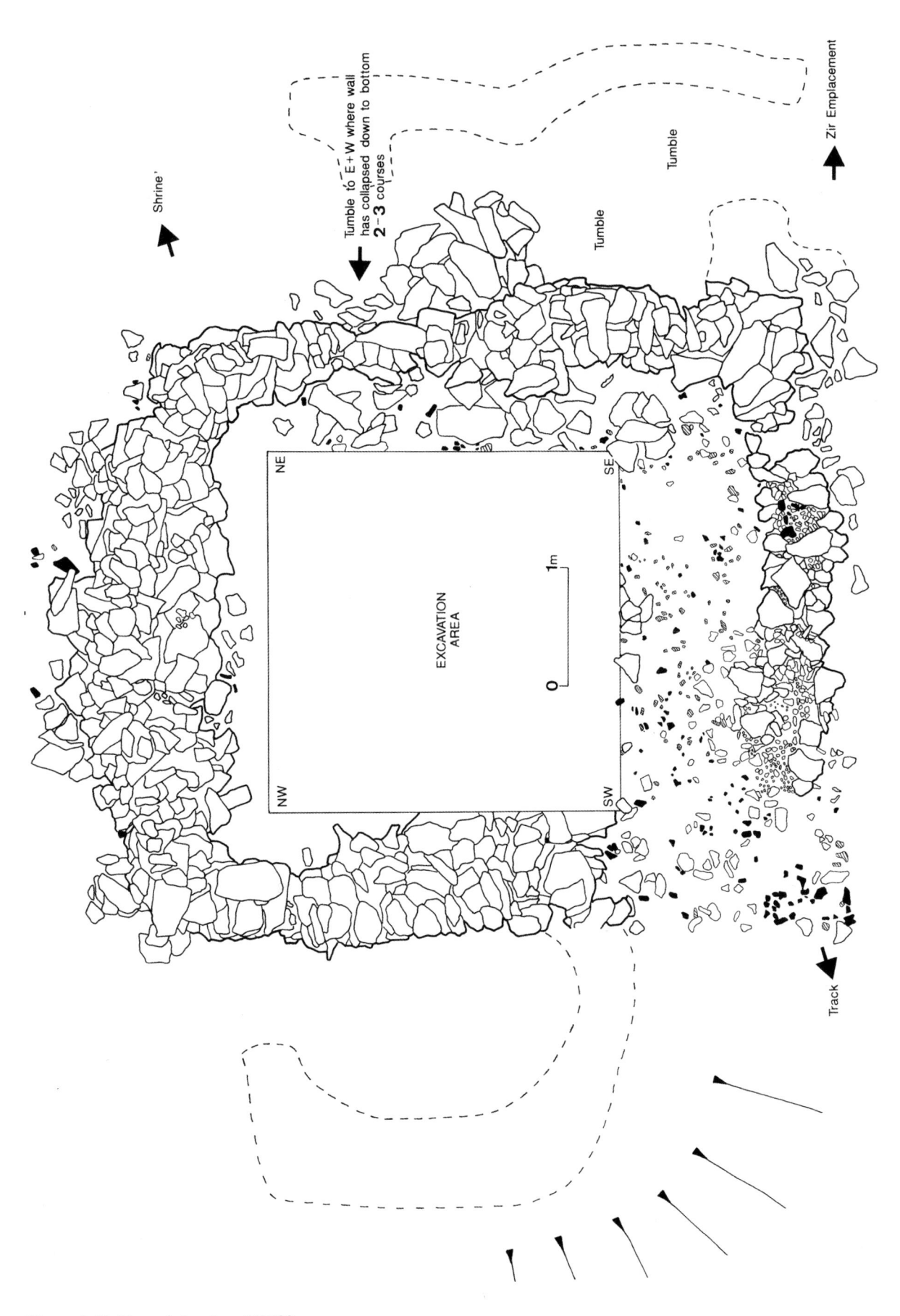

Figure 3.42. Plan of structure NW23.

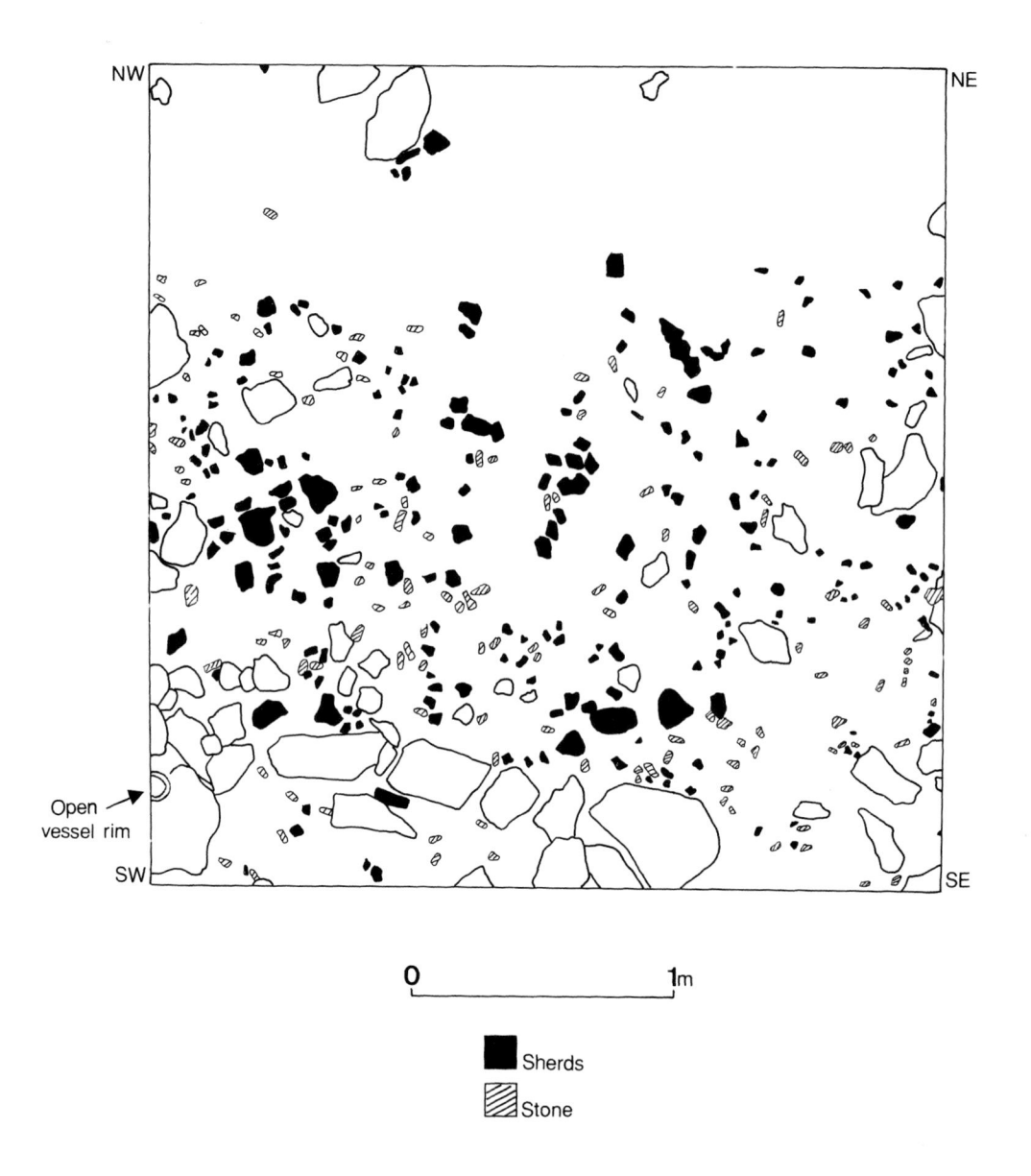

Figure 3.43. Structure NW23 before the removal of unit 1.

The surface below unit 2 was planned, including the fragments of worked travertine and organic features, and further spot heights were taken. Finally, we removed the remnants of unit 2, revealing the original gebel surface beneath (see fig. 3.46 for the northern section drawing, showing units 1 and 2 and the gebel). Surprisingly little travertine was excavated from squares A–C (see figs. 3.44–5) The travertine fragments largely consisted of pieces measuring $c.20$–50 mm^3, and virtually no small chips were found when the material was sieved. Overall there were 11 fragments of travertine in square A, 7 in square B, and 13 in square C.

The heavily charcoal-filled feature in square A turned out to be no more than 35 mm deep but remained clearly visible as a distinct feature. The more lightly charcoaled feature in square B (see fig. 3.47) was about 160 mm deep and 130 mm in diameter at the top. It was a hollow feature filled with a light brown deposit flecked lightly with charcoal. A stake hole (diameter 80 mm at top and 40 mm at bottom, 120 mm deep) was found at the eastern edge of square C, clearly visible in the eastern section face.

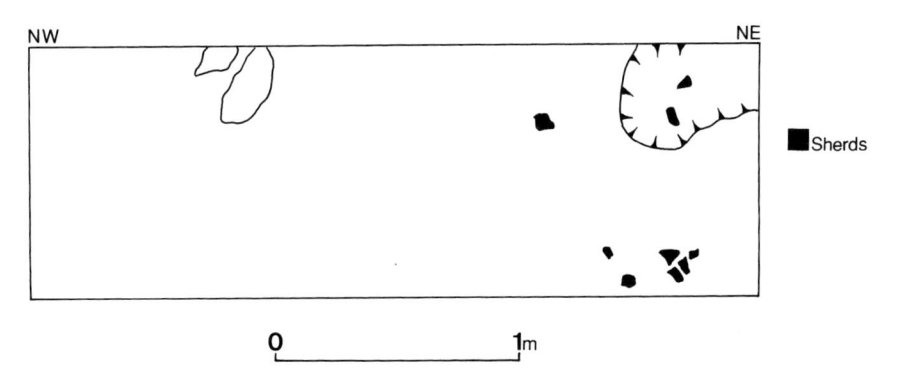

Figure 3.44. Squares A–C in the excavated area of structure NW23, after the removal of unit 1, showing a small pit in the northeast corner and a scatter of sub-surface sherds across square C. [Squares A–C correspond to the upper part of the plan in figure 3.43].

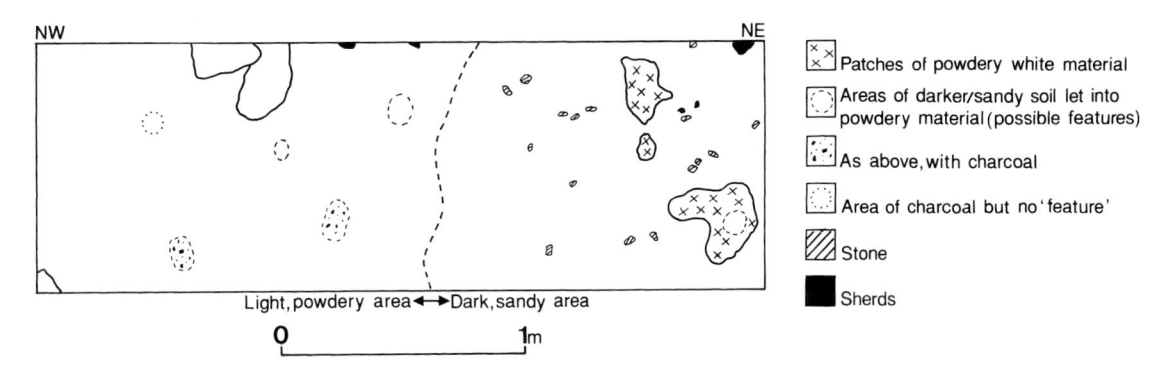

Figure 3.45. Squares A–C in the excavated area of structure NW23, after the removal of unit 2.

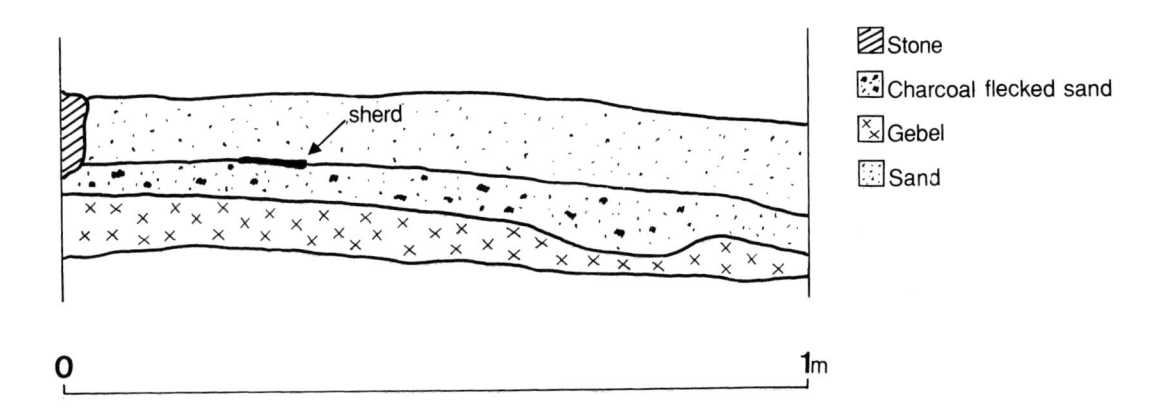

Figure 3.46. Section drawing along the northern edge of square B in the excavated area of structure NW23.

The pottery from structure NW23 was consistent with an Old Kingdom date and much of it could be related to the *Userkaf* corpus (Kaiser 1969), but there were also sherds dating to the New Kingdom. This structure was therefore evidently built and initially used in the Old Kingdom, but also re-used by the New Kingdom quarry-workers, thus presumably indicating its long-term strategic importance. A detailed description of the pottery from structure NW23 is given in section 5.4 below, but the specific types identified were:

1) Red slipped jar, wheel-made but probably Old Kingdom in date (see fig. 5.2).

2) Beer jar base and body sherds.

Figure 3.47. Charcoal-dominated feature in square B of Hut NW23.

3) Simple-rim bowl with scraped base, eroded and of uncertain date.

4) Bread-mould or platter rim, not found in the Amarna New Kingdom corpus therefore assigned to the Old Kingdom.

5) Complete profile, in 3 sherds, of a Meidum-type bowl.

6) Post-firing owner's mark on a red-slipped siltware body sherd deriving from a closed-form vessel of uncertain date.

7) Jar of uncertain date.

8) Large red-slipped pointed base, the technology of which is Old Kingdom, confirmed by the presence of a rim nearby, which is almost certainly from the same vessel.

9) Eroded rim of an out-turned bowl of uncertain date.

10) New Kingdom 'hearth bowl' (a wide bowl of fairly coarse silt clay, in this case type I:1 in the Amarna system, with string impressions below the rim).

11) New Kingdom red-slipped jar sherds.

12) Possible New Kingdom red-slipped bowl, but with a roughly finished base (although the finishing on the base is rougher than most New Kingdom examples, suggesting that this may actually be an Old Kingdom vessel).

3.6 Discussion

The survey of the Quarry P workers' encampments presents us with a number of types of information, firstly concerning the numbers and patterning of the workforce, secondly concerning the artefacts they brought with them (or at least those that have survived *in situ*), and thirdly concerning the nature of the stone shelters that they constructed.

The numbers of rooms in the structures at Hatnub suggest that the gangs of workmen in the Old and Middle Kingdoms may perhaps have been organized in multiples of three (although there is no reliable way of telling whether all of the rooms were necessarily used as sleeping compartments). In the New Kingdom settlement, on the other hand, there are only single-room shelters, perhaps indicating that the basic method of organization had changed over time.

The way in which the stone huts in the Quarry P region cluster together in certain parts of the landscape (i.e. hills, wadis, slopes etc.) meant that they could be conveniently treated as a number of different groups for the purposes of our survey, although in reality they should presumably be regarded as a fairly continuous sequence of shelters stretching across the terrain with relatively little interruption. Some were built in wadis and basins, so as to take advantage of the shelter provided by the terrain; others were positioned on the crests of ridges and beside prominent cairns, presumably acting as guard-posts against attack from the surrounding desert. One major area of uncertainty concerning the settlement as a whole centres on the degree to which any substantial part of it was occupied simultaneously. Should the Old Kingdom dated occupation be interpreted as one single quarrying community, or was it instead a long and dispersed sequence of smaller communities corresponding to the long sequence of different expeditions recorded in the texts on the walls of the main quarry?

Chapter 4

Quarries R and T at Hatnub

The Hatnub quarrying region is dominated by the major workings and extensive settlement remains at Quarry P, which is also clearly the most prolific source of inscriptions and graffiti, but there were several other quarries in the vicinity, of which the two major sites were R and T. The basic features of these quarries and the surrounding remains are discussed below.

4.1 Quarry R

The area labelled Quarry R by Petrie actually consists of two quarries, about 2 km to the southwest of Quarry P, at the southwestern end of a large basin leading towards the Darb el-Amarani (see fig. 4.1). These are the workings described by Möller and Anthes as 'kleine Steinbrüche'. The southernmost of the two (Quarry Ra) is largely subterranean and contains a few inscriptions and graffiti, whereas the one to the northeast (Rb) is a very shallow surface excavation, in the floor of the valley, with no surviving texts.

Quarry Ra probably provides an indication of the original appearance of Quarry P before its roof fell in, although even Quarry Ra has a very large hole in the roof roughly in the centre, about 25 m from the entrance and about 30 m from the rear wall (see figs 4.2 and 4.3). It is clear from all three of the late 19th to early 20th century descriptions of the quarry (Fraser, Möller/Anthes and Timme) that the partial collapse of the ceiling had happened in ancient times, probably during its peak time of use in the pharaonic period, as with Quarry P. The entrance passage to Quarry Ra is oriented roughly north-south, and its width varies between about 7 and 12 m. After a distance of about 25 m (at the point where the roof has fallen in) the gallery changes direction through an angle of about 23°, heading southwestwards for a further 30 m. The rubble from the collapsed section of roof covers a substantial area of the floor of the quarry.

Fraser (1894: 77) mentions over 28 examples of texts and painted images in Quarry Ra, nearly all of which are said to be painted or inscribed in black ink/paint (as with the graffiti at Quarry P). These, however, must have been virtually all illegible by the end of the 19th century, since Möller only produced copies of two inscriptions (XII–XIII) and three graffiti (50-2). Thus Anthes (1928: 5) points out that 'Fraser zählt 28 Stück, die, mit vier Ausnahmen (Gr.50-2, Inschr. XIII), gleichmäßig nichts als je einem Mann vor dem Gabentisch zeigen', i.e. all of them, except those incorporating the texts recorded by Möller, consisted simply of a human figure in front of an offering table. As far as dating of the legible texts was concerned, two (Gr.50 and Inscription XIII) incorporated Middle Kingdom royal names (Amenemhat II and Senusret III), two (Gr.51 and Inscription XII) were dated by context and palaeography to the Middle Kingdom, and the fifth (Gr.52) was dated palaeographically by Möller to the Second Intermediate Period ('Die

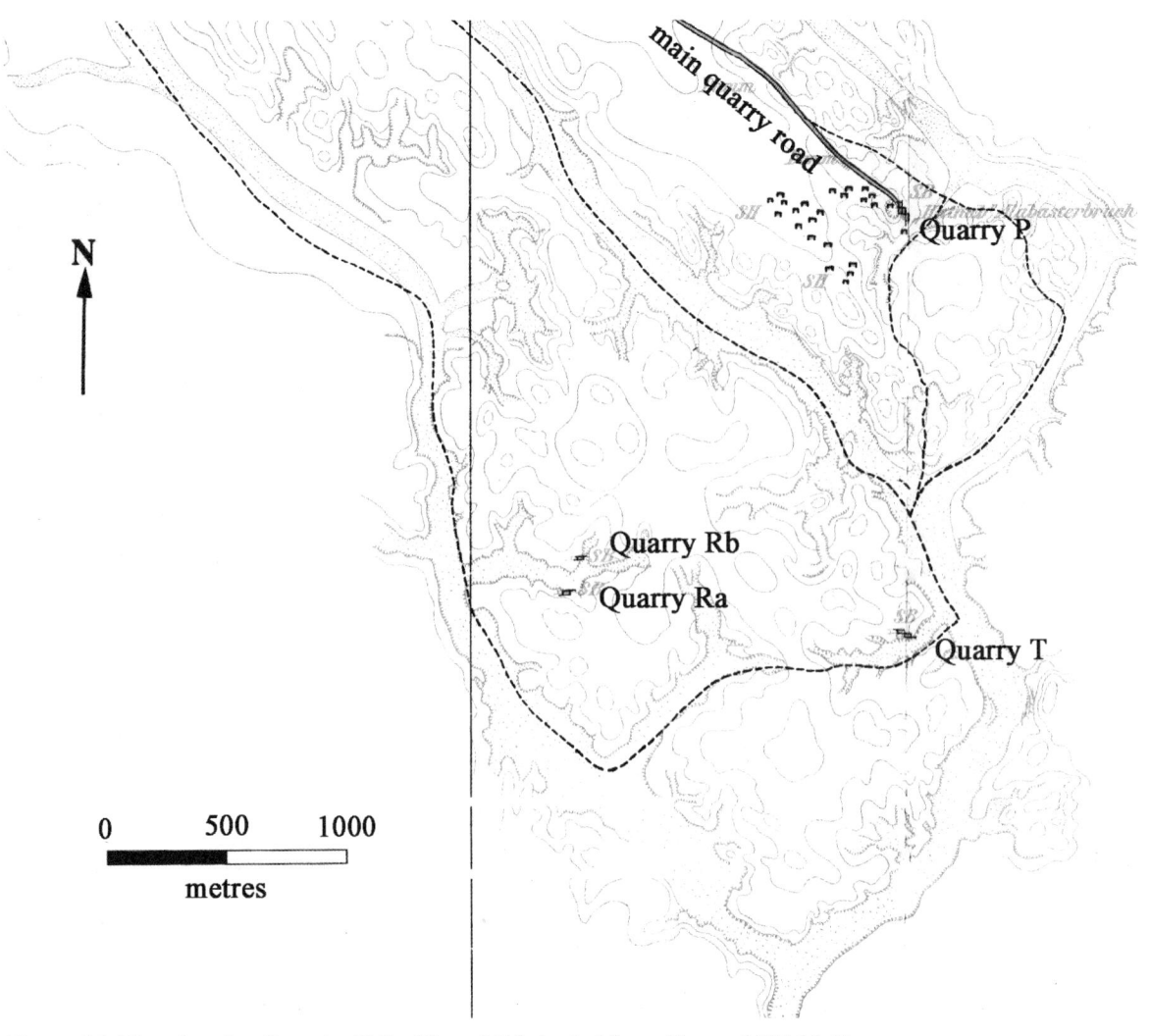

Figure 4.1. Plan showing Quarries P, Ra, Rb and T (adapted from Timme 1917: bl. 7).

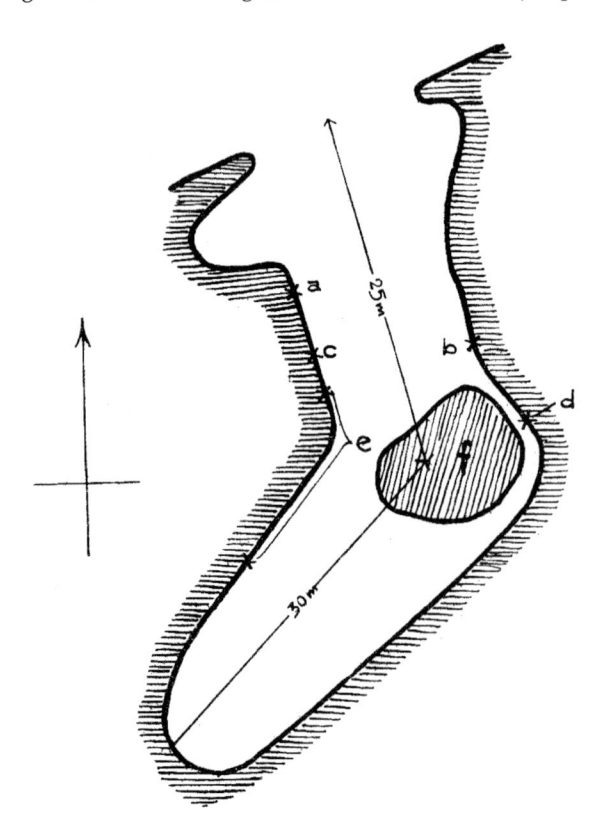

Figure 4.2. Plan of Quarry Ra, showing the locations of Inscription XIII and Graffiti 50-2 (adapted from Anthes 1928: tf. 2, skizze 6).

Figure 4.3 View of the entrance to Quarry Ra at Hatnub.

schrift deutet auf die Zeit zwischen M.R. und N.R.; sie ähnelt der des Westcar – ein klein wenig altertümlicher vielleicht', Anthes 1928: 78, quoting Möller). The 28 hieratic graffiti/'stelae' are distributed across both western and eastern walls of the quarry, on either side of the hole in the roof, while Inscription XIII was situated close to the hole, in the central part of the eastern wall, and Inscription XII was located on the rock-face above the entrance to the quarry.

During the 1991 season of the Hatnub Survey we examined the current condition of the Quarry R texts and found that they had deteriorated significantly compared with their condition when recorded by Möller 84 years earlier. There were many freshly pecked marks on most of the texts and images suggesting that visitors – presumably modern quarry-workers in the 1980s – had deliberately thrown small stones at them (see fig. 4.4).

Figure 4.4. Part of the damaged graffiti in Quarry Ra.

Figure 4.5. One of the group of semi-subterranean huts about 220 m to the northeast of Quarries Ra and Rb.

Contrary to the situation at Quarry P, there is no encampment or settlement immediately adjacent to Quarry Ra. The closest stone shelter is a single dry-stone hut situated about 200 m to the northeast. A few metres further to the north is a row of four similar huts containing some New Kingdom and Late Period sherds. These five huts were all constructed in a similar unusual way, each consisting of a hollow scooped out of the ground with its rim built up of gravel and boulders. On the southern side of the Quarry R 'basin' are about thirty huts of a more conventional nature, mostly being the simple dry-stone crescent-shaped type, with predominantly Old Kingdom sherds in association (fig. 4.5). Adjacent to one group of these huts is a travertine working area situated on a fairly exposed slope; judging from the surviving chips of travertine, the workers here were extracting an unusually translucent, almost quartz-like, form of the rock. This observation was confirmed by Barbara G. Aston when she visited Quarries P and R in 1985, and noted that the travertine samples collected from Quarry P included 'plain white travertine, white travertine with red bands, and one sample of yellow-banded travertine – though not the distinctive variety with alternating translucent yellow and opaque white bands so commonly used for stone vessels', whereas Quarry Ra yielded only 'white travertine lacking any colored bands' (Aston 1994: 46; see also discussion of provenancing studies in section 2.5 above).

Fraser (1894: 78) has a few brief comments on the pottery at Quarry R: 'The pottery fragments scattered about inside and out consist chiefly of rough red dishes and jars, the shapes of which are identical or similar with the forms which Professor Petrie found in the XIIth dynasty town of Kehun [sic], in the Fayum. There are however a limited number of white faced fragments similar to those common on the plain of Tell-el-Amarna, and a very few bits of late Roman or Coptic pottery'. The Hatnub Survey study of the pottery in the 1985 season confirmed that Quarry R was in use in a number of different periods. Within the subterranean quarry itself there were several Old and Middle Kingdom sherds but also fragments of a few New Kingdom amphorae. The stone huts in the vicinity contained sherds dating to the Old, Middle and New Kingdoms, as well as a few dating to the Late Period. The pottery surface survey therefore suggests that Quarry R was the part of the site that was exploited over the longest period of time.

4.2 Quarry T

About 1 km to the east of Quarry R is a fourth quarry, which was visited by Petrie in 1892, and designated Quarry T in his survey of the area (Petrie 1894: pl. 20). It was also included in Paul Timme's survey of the Amarna region, and described by him as 'der große Alabaster-Höhlensteinbruch'. According to Petrie's report it was simply another set of quarries without any inscriptions or graffiti (Petrie 1894: 4), but Timme publishes a photograph and description of a relief and inscription on the quarry wall, which he suggests, probably correctly, to be Roman in date (Timme 1917: 46, abb. 50; see fig. 4.6). The relief is said to be situated near the entrance to the quarry in the bottom left-hand corner of the wall to the left; it comprises, from left to right, a row of four deities facing towards an altar bearing a trussed sacrificial ox, while a male figure to the right extends a hand towards the animal. The deity nearest to the altar is a hawk-headed figure, possibly some version of Horus, while the next deity to the left wears the double crown. Above the head of the hawk deity is a roughly circular or oval shape which may either be a sun disc or an empty cartouche. Each of the deities carries an *wsr*-sceptre.

There was, however, no longer any sign of the relief described by Timme when we examined the area in 1985 and 1991. The main T quarry is a circular pit smaller and deeper than the uninscribed R quarry. It still contains a massive unquarried nodule of travertine, and a small quantity of New Kingdom potsherds survived on the surface in its immediate vicinity. A smaller

Figure 4.6. The relief and inscription, perhaps dating to the Roman period, incised on the wall of Quarry T (after Timme 1917: abb. 50).

quarry nearby was located in association with a cluster of stone huts and some Old Kingdom pottery. Unfortunately this whole section of the Hatnub region was the focus of a modern quarrying operation during the 1980s and 1990s, with many of the larger fragments of travertine in the ancient spoil heaps gradually being transported away, badly damaging the ancient remains at the site in the process.

Chapter 5

The Pottery
Paul T. Nicholson and Pamela J. Rose

The main purpose of the pottery survey at Hatnub was to determine the general periods of occupation of specific areas by a necessarily rapid inspection of the range of material found around huts within those areas. It should also be noted that the following report was created in the early 1990s, therefore it does not incorporate any more recent work on Old Kingdom ceramics.

No specific dry-stone huts were targeted, though there was a concentration on multi-roomed structures which offered the greatest quantity of pottery and might be assumed to be better built and perhaps more attractive for later re-occupation. The priorities were therefore:

1) the study of windbreaks and huts within those areas surveyed between 1985 and 1994, with a view to verifying the provisional dating of the structures plotted on the survey maps;
2) the examination of surface and subsurface pottery from the excavated structures NW23 and S26.

5.1 The Old Kingdom pottery

The short time available to conduct this work, and the relatively large area to be covered, meant that it was not possible to examine every sherd at each location in terms of form and fabric. Instead, the pottery in selected parts of the site was examined and notes were taken of diagnostic pieces. Fabrics were divided simply into silt and marl, since to develop a fabric typology for the Old Kingdom material was beyond the scope of the work. Both in this chapter and also in Chapter 3 we use numbers prefixed by 'U' to refer to vessel type numbers in the *Userkaf* corpus (Kaiser 1969), which is used simply as a shape typology. The presence of a given shape need not imply that the fabric was the same as those recognised by Kaiser, nor that the dimensions of the piece were exactly those of the vessel illustrated (see fig. 5.1 for part of the *Userkaf* corpus: U107–14). However, the shapes are only assigned to pieces of closely similar size and in most cases the fabric is also as described in the *Userkaf* corpus. Since the Hatnub pottery is generally eroded or discoloured, the typing to these forms should be regarded as a general guide rather than a precise type designation, although the matching between sherds and illustrations was, on the whole, good.

Many vessels could not be typed to the *Userkaf* corpus (Kaiser 1969), but were simply described, and when possible, dated. Pottery forms that could be given general dates were not moved from their locations, since it became clear at a very early stage that much of the settle-

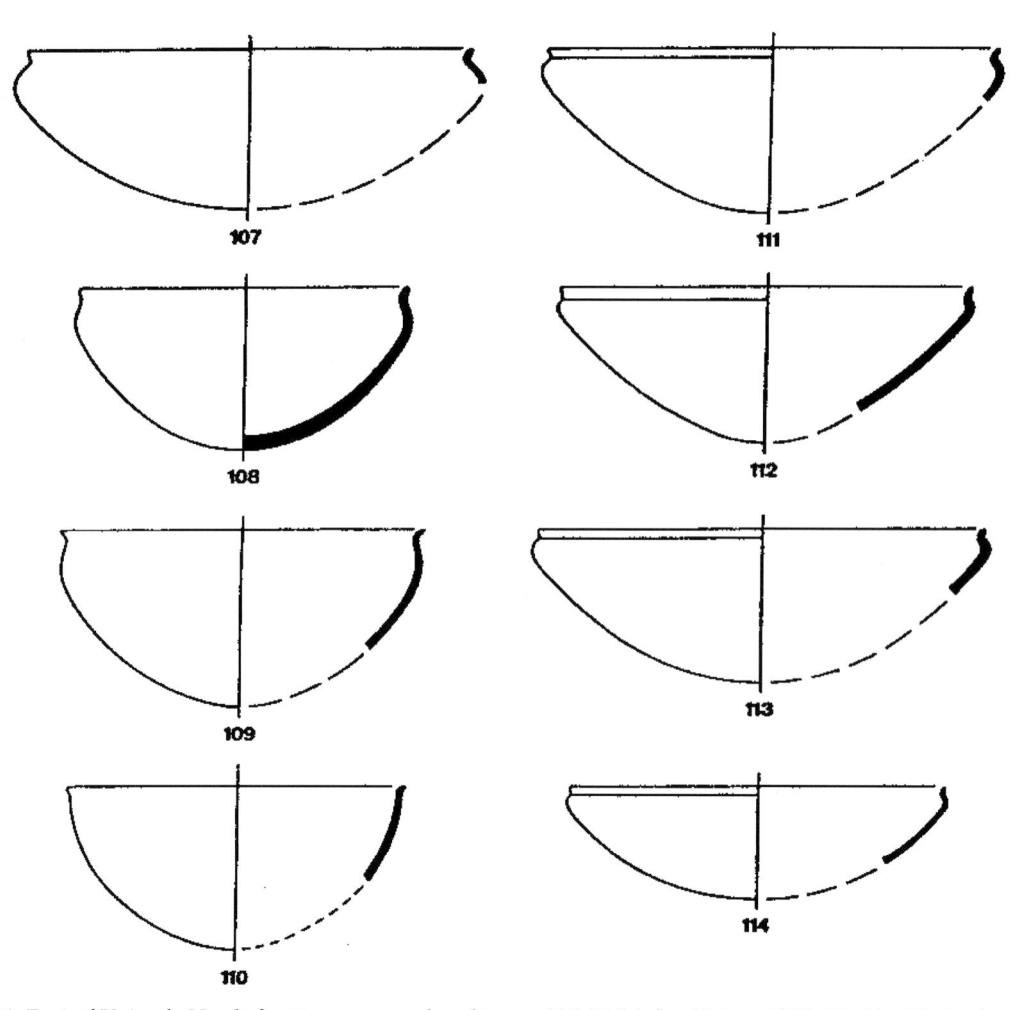

Figure 5.1. Part of Kaiser's *Userkaf* pottery corpus: bowl types 107–114 (after Kaiser 1969: 59 abb. 17). Scale = 1:4.

ment offered the opportunity to undertake, at some point in the future, a more sophisticated object distribution survey and to have moved the position of objects unnecessarily would have been damaging to this. In any case, to have unnecessarily altered the distribution on such a well-preserved site would have been pointless. Since it was possible only to make a very general survey, and since this was all that was required at this time, it seemed better to leave the site unaltered until future work could be carried out.

The following notes on the Old Kingdom pottery from Hatnub may be helpful in reviewing the results:

Beer jars

Old Kingdom beer jars have a very distinctive, coarse silt ware fabric and show clear evidence of hand manufacture (NB - hand-made vessels are those produced without the aid of a true potter's wheel, although a turntable device of some kind may sometimes have been used; see Bourriau *et al.* 2000: 125–6), notably deep finger markings on the outside and often around the rim. The bases are heavy and pointed (see fig. 5.2, showing an intact jar from Hut NW23). In this they are clearly distinguished from the less coarse, wheel-thrown fabric of New Kingdom beer jars, which at Amarna also commonly have knife-scraped bases, often marked by a cut into the thick fabric. The fabric feels rougher than that of the rather powdery Old Kingdom examples.

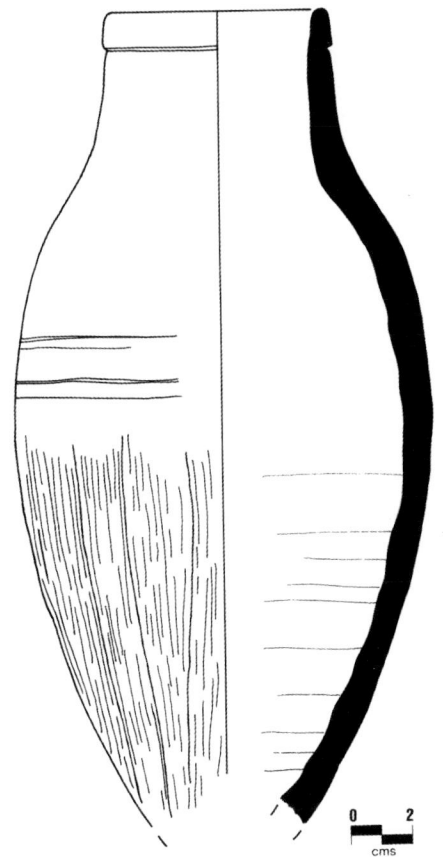

Figure 5.2. A complete Old Kingdom red-slipped, wheel-made beer jar found on the surface within structure NW23 in the Quarry P settlement.

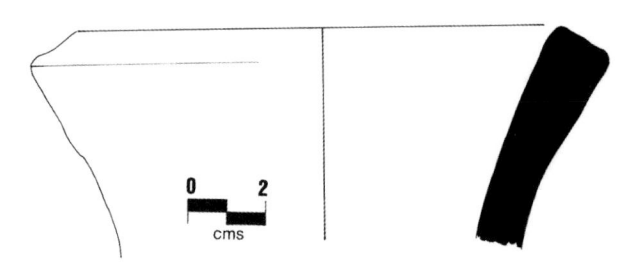

Figure 5.3. An Old Kingdom bread-mould from structure B5 in the Quarry P settlement.

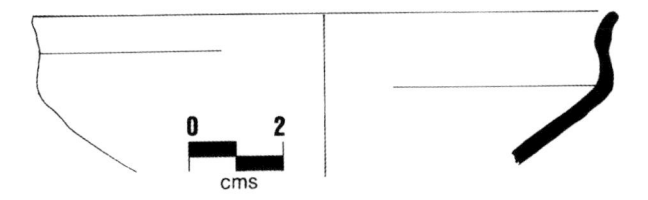

Figure 5.4. An Old Kingdom Meidum-type bowl from Hut B6 in the Quarry P settlement.

Bread-moulds

Old Kingdom bread-moulds are usually large, roughly made vessels of a bell-like or somewhat chalice-like shape (that is, having a form like a coarsely proportioned wine glass). They are larger than the rare examples of New Kingdom chalice-shaped moulds found at Amarna. The fabric is a light grey and powdery silt, often very dense and heavy. The exterior shows their clear hand modelling, and they may flare outwards before being inturned toward the base. The insides are very smooth where they have been formed around a core, and may show vertical 'cracks' or compressed folds where they have been pressed around this. The fabric is similar to bread-moulds of the New Kingdom but the diameter of the Old Kingdom pieces clearly separates the two, as does the greater thickness of the more ancient examples (see fig. 5.3).

Meidum bowl

The term 'Meidum-type bowl' is used here to refer to an open vessel with a sharp carination at the waist and an outcurving rim. They are usually, but not invariably, red slipped and burnished on both surfaces (see fig. 5.4, a Meidum-type bowl from Hut B6 in the Quarry P settlement).

Slip

The Old Kingdom red slips tend to be thickly, but evenly, applied and are often extremely well burnished. The red colour tends to be a dark cherry red, or red-brown, and it often crazes with weathering, though this is not invariable. The New Kingdom red slips are less often burnished and are more thinly applied. Generally they do not weather to a dark colour, but the unusual conditions at Hatnub make this possible. More commonly they flake off as a result of weathering.

Hand-made versus wheel-made technology

The wheel-made vessels often show clear, fairly evenly spaced 'rilling' lines on the inside of closed forms where the potters' hands have left marks while drawing the vessel up by centrifugal force. However, good quality hand-made vessels, shaped on a tournette or turntable (sometimes misleadingly called a 'slow-wheel'), can also show rilling, and in small body sherds the two technologies can be very difficult to differentiate. Wheel-made rims are sometimes applied to hand-made bodies, and if the join is a good one, the clear differentiation of the different technologies can be difficult. The hand-made bread-moulds have been formed around a core or *patrix*.

5.2 The New Kingdom pottery

During two days spent at the Quarry P region of Hatnub examining surface pottery, in the 1986 season, 27 groups of post-Old Kingdom sherds were noted. These were recognised initially by the presence of an entirely wheel-made body and base sherds among them, and closer examination showed that some of the pieces were comparable to those excavated at the Amarna Workmen's Village. In many cases, however, the sherds were so weathered that it was not possible either to make any definite identification as to shape and date (except to assign them to the New Kingdom or later) or to tell whether all the sherds in a single cluster were from the same vessel. The heavy weathering of the pottery also made it difficult to determine how far sherds from the same individual vessels had spread.

The first two clusters of surface sherds noted came from structures within the wadi (Huts W1–17), and consisted of silt ware body sherds in one group, and the neck, shoulder and handle of a cream-slipped amphora in the other. The rest of the clusters of sherds came from the structures surrounding an area of limestone quarrying near a large knoll (i.e. W18–38 and NW1–5). The most common identifiable form among these was a silt ware jar, unslipped, with a short, flaring rim (i.e. Amarna 'Group 18', see Kemp 1984: 137), fragments of which were found in seven of the clusters (see fig. 5.5 A and B). Presumably many of the unslipped body sherds were from these vessels. Red-slipped silt ware body sherds, and fragments of rims, necks and shoulders in four groups indicate the presence of biconical jars (Group 17 in Kemp 1984: 137). Blue-painted silt ware sherds were present in six clusters, but there was no indication as to the original vessel form(s). The remaining vessel types are all of marl clay, and almost all of Amarna fabric type III.2 or related fabrics (Kemp 1985: 136). All these sherds are cream-slipped, and may originally have been burnished; they derive from amphorae of various shapes, since both vertical and horizontal handles are represented, and one large rim sherd is from a vessel of Amarna type XVII.10 (Peet and Woolley 1923: pl. 53, no. 76/228).

A single decorated sherd found close to the entrance of Quarry P (fig. 5.5 C) is also of New Kingdom date, and can be compared with a type known from Deir el-Medina (Nagel 1938: pl. 6;

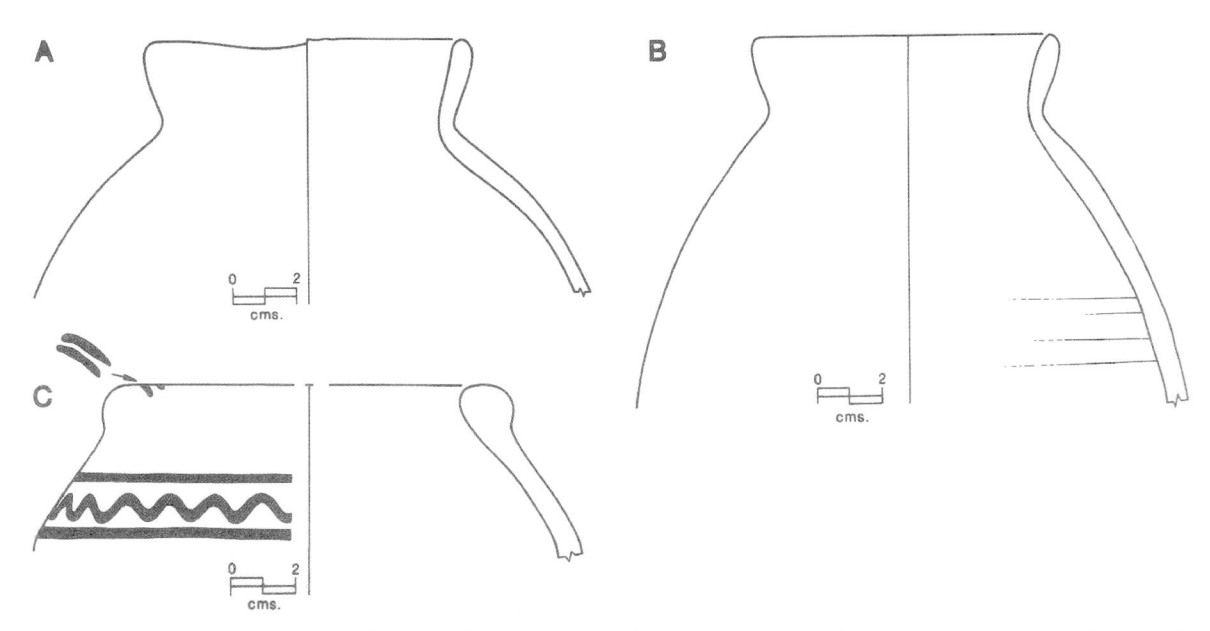

Figure 5.5. New Kingdom vessels found in the Quarry P settlement. Types A and B are 18th Dynasty unslipped silt-ware jars, with short, flaring rims (i.e. Amarna 'Group 18', see Kemp 1984: 137), while type C is a rim sherd from a painted 19th Dynasty jar, of a style known from Deir el-Medina (Nagel 1938: pl. 6).

type VIII, nos K.2.93 and 94), which was found in a context dated to the 19th Dynasty, suggesting that some of the New Kingdom quarrying activity belongs to the post-Amarna period.

It is interesting to note that no New Kingdom open forms were recognised among the sherds at Hatnub; the vessels in use consisted of small and medium-sized silt ware jars, and amphorae. This emphasis on closed forms can probably be explained by the need for water containers in such an inhospitable environment. The 'Group 18' jars are especially interesting, since this form is by no means common in the Workmen's Village at Amarna (although concentrations of these jars have been found around the Great Temple during pottery surface surveys carried out during the 1985 season at Amarna, see Rose 1987); they may perhaps be considered as 'standard issue' for the New Kingdom workmen employed at Hatnub.

5.3 Pottery from structure S26

Collection of potsherds from Hut S26, and over the site as a whole, required particularly close examination of the ground surface and of the sherds collected, because of the peculiar weathering characteristics encountered at Hatnub. Sherds tend to weather to a very dark red or glossy black colour, the latter colour being shared by the surface limestone, which presumably has a high impurity content. Because of exfoliation of the limestone surface rock, sherds can be difficult to distinguish from rock fragments on the surface and close observation of the ground surface must be made before declaring any area devoid of pottery.

It was apparent at S26 as well as at most other locations at the site, that the larger sherds tended to be outside the structures or pushed into cracks in their walls, while small pieces remained in the rooms (and this phenomenon is also apparent from ethnoarchaeological studies). The greater quantity of pottery tended to be found outside the structures, suggesting periodic cleaning out of the rooms.

5.3.1 Surface

Room 1: This room, with its entrance-way, yielded the bulk of the pottery, including the larger fragments from within the house. However, it should be noted that the larger pieces came from the entrance-way, rather than from the room itself, perhaps suggesting a desultory attempt at clearing the room of debris. All of the material was consistent with an Old Kingdom date and consisted of 75 body sherds, three rims from open forms, five rims from closed forms, and one base from a closed form.

Open form rims:

1) Two examples. Silt fabric with burned out limestone, red slipped inside and out, slightly thickened rim (fig. 5.6). One example was too eroded to give a diameter, while the other piece had a diameter of 14 cm, 7% of which was preserved. These two examples were typed to the *Userkaf* form 110, hereafter cited in the form U110.

2) Silt fabric with burned out organic matter, perhaps dung. The vessel is red-slipped both inside and out; it has a 22 cm diameter of which 4% was preserved. It was typed to U171.

Closed form rims:

1) Coarse silt fabric with numerous burned out straw inclusions. This piece was hand-made, with a sharply angled shoulder; it has a diameter of *c.*12 cm, of which 11% is preserved (see fig. 5.7). It has no exact parallel in the *Userkaf* corpus but was close enough to be typed to U10.

2) Two examples. Coarse silt fabric with some burnt-out straw inclusions. Apparently better smoothed than type 1 but the finish has crazed and weathered badly. One piece is too badly preserved to yield a diameter, and the other has a diameter of 10 cm, of which 6% is preserved. The pieces conform to type U10.

3) Possibly marl clay. Weathered outside but with white-grey/greenish slip, as described by Kaiser (1969: 53) for this class of vessel, similar to type U47. The diameter is 10 cm of which 8% is preserved.

4) A possible silt/marl mixture. Badly weathered but apparently having a cream-pink slip (such differences frequently being a result of firing in marl clays). The diameter is 12 cm, of which 10% is preserved. This sherd was too broken to identify the form with certainty, but it is apparently similar to type U24.

Closed form bases:

Coarse silt with burnt-out straw. Vertical or steeply angled finger drags on the outside, with spiral marks running around the inside. This was clearly the base of a beer jar of form U67.

Body sherds:

Most of these were at least partly eroded on one side, and often on both. However, it was possible to put all of them into open or closed categories, as follows:

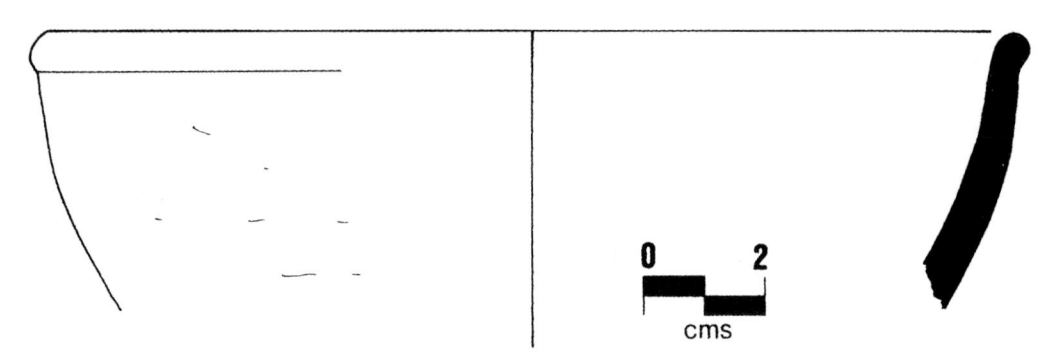

Figure 5.6. Red-slipped Nile silt open-form vessel from the surface in Room 1 of structure S26 in the Quarry P settlement (*Userkaf* form U110).

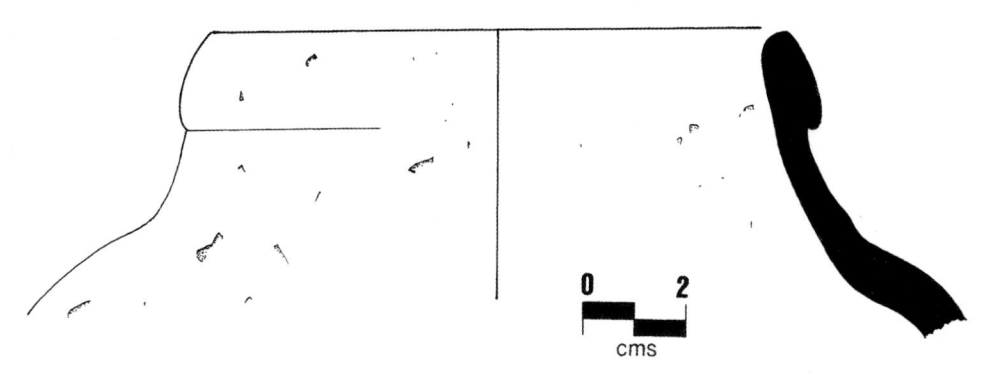

Figure 5.7. Nile silt closed-form vessel from the surface in Room 1 of structure S26 in the Quarry P settlement (similar to *Userkaf* form U10).

- 5 open forms preserving a smooth red slipped surface (four of them red-slipped on both inside and outside), all of which were silt,
- 45 uncoated or eroded body sherds of silt,
- 17 closed form silt body sherds,
- 6 closed form marl sherds, two of which are apparently of 'marl C' fabric, according to the Vienna System of pottery classification (see Nordström and Bourriau 1993: 168–82; Bourriau *et al*. 2000: 130–2).

Room 2: The surface material in this room was examined by metre square, following the sequence in which it was excavated (see section 3.4 above). The surface of square A yielded four body sherds, three of which were silt ware, and the other marl. The three silt sherds are very coarse and come from a beer jar or jars, deriving from somewhere near the base(s), as indicated by the finger marks and curve of the pieces, though they cannot be typed. The marl sherd (from the shoulder of a closed form vessel) is cream-slipped outside and has very regular lines inside it from either wheel manufacture or careful hand modelling. On the surface of square B there was no pottery.

Square C contained ten body sherds, nine of them Nile silt clay, and the other of marl. Three sherds are from small, open forms that could not be assigned to any specific vessel type. Four sherds are from a coarse, badly eroded beer jar. There are also two sherds from bowls slipped inside and outside, one showing a sharp angle change similar to that of U139, though it is not exactly the same as this type. The single marl sherd is probably from a closed form. It is well smoothed on both sides. The interior shows more marks than usual for a wheel-made piece, and it may be deduced that the piece is Old Kingdom hand-made work.

Square D contained seven sherds. These comprised two rims of open forms. The first of these was out-turned and covered in a matt red slip both inside and outside. The uneven shape is consistent with hand manufacture. It is made from silt ware and is comparable to type U187. The second piece is a badly eroded fragment of a thin-walled silt ware vessel, not able to be precisely correlated with a specific type, due to its bad preservation (nevertheless similar to U85). There is one body sherd from an open form, which is of silt ware with red-burnished slip both inside and out. The remaining four sherds are fragments of a roughly made beer jar in a coarse silt ware fabric typical of this vessel type.

Room 3: No pottery.

Room 4: This room as a whole yielded six sherds, comprising three from open forms, two of which were of marl or mixed clay, one being unslipped and badly smoothed, the other being smoothed on both sides. The third open-form sherd is made from silt ware and is well smoothed on the outside, though the inside surface has been lost through erosion. There are two closed forms, one of which is silt ware of a coarse type intermediate between the very coarse beer jar fabric and the finer clay used for bowls etc. (probably part of a slipped jar, though the surface is lost). The other closed-form piece is hand-made from fine marl clay, very blackened by weathering but showing traces of cream slip. One sherd is too eroded to assign to open or closed form, but its fabric is silt ware.

Room 5: This room yielded five sherds, comprising three from marl open forms, of which one was a rim. The latter was too small to allow a diameter to be measured, but had a fairly vertical stance. The outer surface bore traces of a red/cream slip, but the inner surface was lost. The type appears to be similar to U200. The body sherds are cream on the outside, and one shows traces of hand manufacture. The closed forms are coarse fragments of silt ware beer jars.

Room 6: This room contained five sherds, all of which were of silt ware. There were two open forms including one rim, though this was too small to measure the diameter. It was covered in a burnished red slip inside and out, and though it cannot be precisely typed it is very similar to U112 or U113. The body sherd is similarly red-burnished on both surfaces. The closed forms comprised two body sherds and one rim. The rim had a diameter of 12 cm of which 11% was preserved. It has an unpolished red slip outside and is of a medium-fine silt ware. The form is similar to U7. The body sherds are from coarse clay beer jars.

Room 7: This room contained seven sherds, including two fragments of open forms, both of them silt, of which one was a rim. The rim was too small to measure the diameter but preserved a good profile; it was unslipped but well smoothed, though the exterior shows many traces of burned out organic matter. The form is matched to U94. There are also two marl body sherds that may derive from open forms, though this is not certain. The closed forms are all body sherds of coarse beer jar fabric.

Area to the east of S26 as a whole: The material in this area was not fully collected, but rather selectively sampled, diagnostic pieces being collected and examined. The area consists of a fan of debris made up of pottery and blackened stones, many of them comprising either wall tumble, travertine chippings (especially in the area immediately east of Room 7) or pounder stones. S26 is bounded on the north and south by wadi channels, that to the south apparently being the most active; most of the pottery described here seems to be attributable to the occupants of the hut itself rather than to wadi action. The sherds are generally larger and more numerous than those found inside the house, but are broadly of the same types.

Area immediately to the east of Room 7: This area yielded the following:

- A small lid or gaming counter with a *c.*5 cm diameter, made from a red-slipped silt sherd deriving from a hand-made closed-form vessel. This lid/counter was found beside the thickest concentration of travertine chippings.
- A rim sherd from a Meidum bowl (diameter 14 cm), red-burnished both inside and out, of which 11% was preserved, similar to U94, but with a more bulbous belly and with a rim diameter less than that of the maximum diameter.
- The uncoated rim and shoulder of a vessel similar to U24, the two sherds being separated by an old break, and comprising, between them, 35% of a *c.*10 cm-diameter vessel.
- The coarse hand-made rim of an uncoated silt ware beer jar with a 9 cm-diameter rim, of which 15% was preserved.
- The rim of a vessel similar to U6, eroded but with traces of possible red slip, a diameter of *c.*10 cm, about 6% of which was preserved.
- A base from a thick-walled, heavy, silt ware beer jar, and a joining sherd.
- About 26% of a beer jar of similarly coarse material, corresponding to U65, with a diameter of *c.*10 cm, 26% of which was preserved.
- A possible marl or mixed clay base from a round form that was eroded but seems to be very similar to U17.
- A marl C gaming counter or lid with diameter of *c.*3 cm.
- The rim of a vessel similar to U6, with weathered red slip on the outside surface and a diameter of *c.*10 cm, about 8% of which was preserved.

Area immediately to the east of Room 5: This area contained the following:

- A heavy hand-made base in silt ware fabric, very reddened inside but blackened from weathering outside, from a vessel corresponding to type U16.
- The virtually flat base of an open-form vessel, red-slipped inside and possibly burnished, but the outside surface lost. It probably corresponds to type U150.
- The rim of a closed-form vessel in silt ware, with a diameter of 10 cm, 20% of which is preserved. A cross is incised on its rim (probably post-firing, but too weathered to tell). Corresponding to type U8, this form was also recognised in a further sherd from this area, which preserved traces of a possible red slip.
- A badly eroded sherd from a vessel of type U59, with a 9 cm diameter, 10% of which was preserved.

- The rim of a finely made silt ware bottle, reddish-white on the outside, and carefully smoothed (fig. 5.8). It was probably either wheel-made or carefully formed on a turntable. The diameter of the rim was 9 cm and 24% of the vessel was preserved.

Area immediately to the east of Room 6 of Hut S26: This area yielded an over-fired body sherd, with fabric reduced to vesicular mass, apparently deriving from a thick-walled Meidum type bowl (U9). There was also a rim sherd from a red slipped and burnished open form similar to U148 (15 cm diameter and 11% preservation). Finally, there were two silt ware rims from closed forms, both with a *c.*10 cm diameter, one corresponding to U42 and 35% preserved, and the other corresponding to U6 and 15% preserved.

Wadi to the south of Hut S26: Although this wadi seems to have been the 'busiest' of those in the immediate vicinity of Hut S26, the amount of pottery found here is relatively small and is generally restricted to the area nearest to the hut itself. There is no evidence to suggest that this pottery has been washed from higher up the slope. The sherds include the rim of a bowl that had been red-slipped and burnished on the outside, but the surface on the inside had been eroded; it corresponds to type U24 but its diameter is impossible to ascertain. Several fragments of bases and body sherds from beer jars were also found, all made from a coarse silt ware fabric with organic filler.

Small wadi running north-south as a tributary of the southern wadi beside Hut S26: This small wadi yielded the rim of a beer jar, showing clear traces of hand manufacture, and with a very uneven outer surface; this type does not seem to correspond to any of those in the *Userkaf* corpus (Kaiser 1969), and the vessel is characterised by a distinctive groove under the rim (fig. 5.9). In this wadi we also found an over-fired sherd deriving from vessel type U9; this is almost certainly a diagnostic sherd from the same specific over-fired vessel noted above, in the area immediately to the east of Room 6 of Hut S26.

5.3.2 Subsurface of Room 2: excavated squares A and B

Only squares A and B were excavated in Room 2 of S26, and not all of the stratigraphic units produced pottery. These sherds are described below, except when they had received secondary working, in which case they were treated as small-finds (see H91/1, H91/10, H91/14, and H91/15 in table 3.3 above).

Unit 1 in square A yielded two silt ware sherds, both of medium fine clay, one from an open form vessel and the other from a closed form (the surface treatment having been lost through erosion). This unit also yielded two marl clay sherds from a closed form. Unit 2 in square A produced ten marl body sherds deriving from closed forms, each with a cream surface. The fabric of these ten sherds is gritty, probably making it an early instance of marl C. There were also seven coarse silt ware body sherds from beer jars, although all of these were relatively small and badly eroded.

Unit 1 in square B produced three silt ware sherds, all from beer jars, although two of these were very tiny, badly weathered pieces. The third piece is relatively well-made and shows careful smoothing over part of its surface. There was also one marl body sherd from a closed-form vessel. Unit 2 yielded five more body sherds from closed form vessels, of a similar type to those

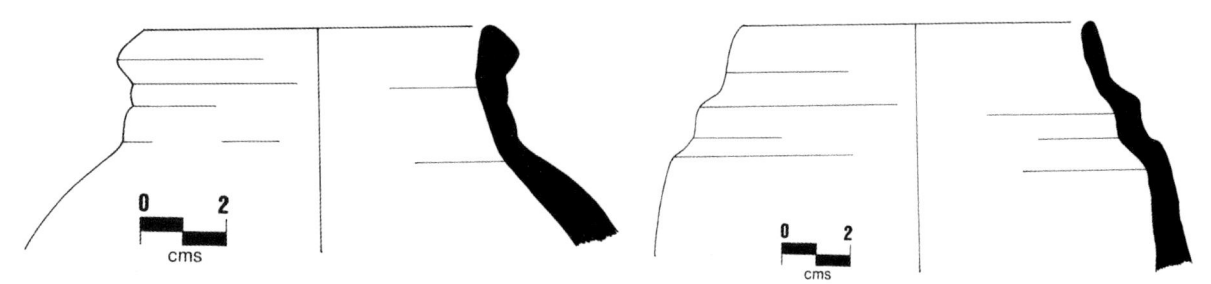

Figure 5.8. Finely made Old Kingdom silt ware jar, probably either wheel-made or carefully formed on a turntable (diameter of the rim: 9 cm) from the area immediately to the east of Room 5 of structure S26 in the Quarry P settlement.

Figure 5.9. Beer jar, showing clear traces of hand manufacture, and with a very uneven outer surface; this type, with a distinctive groove under the rim, does not seem to correspond to any of those in the *Userkaf* corpus.

described above. There were also three silt ware sherds from closed form vessels, and one from an open form, probably a Meidum type bowl with red slip on both inner and outer surfaces (possibly originally burnished but now eroded). Unit 3 in square B produced two silt ware sherds from a very coarse, badly eroded beer jar, three sherds of finer silt ware with traces of red slip outside, probably from jars or bottles, and three silt ware rim sherds deriving from open forms, all of which were very badly eroded. Four very tiny and badly eroded sherds of marl clay were also found, though the type of vessel they came from could not be ascertained.

5.4 Pottery from structure NW23

Virtually all of the pottery from structure NW23 is consistent with forms common in the Old Kingdom, with only occasional and dubious sherds of an apparently later date. The range of forms is very restricted, almost all of them being bowls and jars. Much of the pottery is badly eroded or has weathered to a very dark colour over the years, particularly in the case of the sherds found on the surface, which had apparently hardened and turned to a black colour. As with structure S26 above, the descriptions deal first with surface material collected before excavation, and then with excavated subsurface material. Most pieces were typed to the *Userkaf* corpus (Kaiser 1969).

5.4.1 Surface

Northern strip within the 3 × 3m square (squares A–C): This context contained 13 fragments of open bowls, of which five were diagnostic sherds; all were of silt clay and showed scraping on the bases. The vessels were red-slipped on the inside, with the slip extending over the rim (this applies to virtually all the fragments of red-slipped bowls found at Hatnub). Forms U189 and U190 were identified. A beer jar base was also found, and has been typed to U65 (fig. 5.10).

There were 15 undiagnostic sherds, which could not be assigned to any of the forms in the *Userkaf* corpus. All of the pieces so far mentioned date to the Old Kingdom, although there were three very badly eroded sherds from a jar with a short flaring rim, which may possibly belong to the New Kingdom (since this form is commonly represented at Amarna). It should be noted, however, that these particular sherds were in such poor condition that no absolutely certain identification could be made.

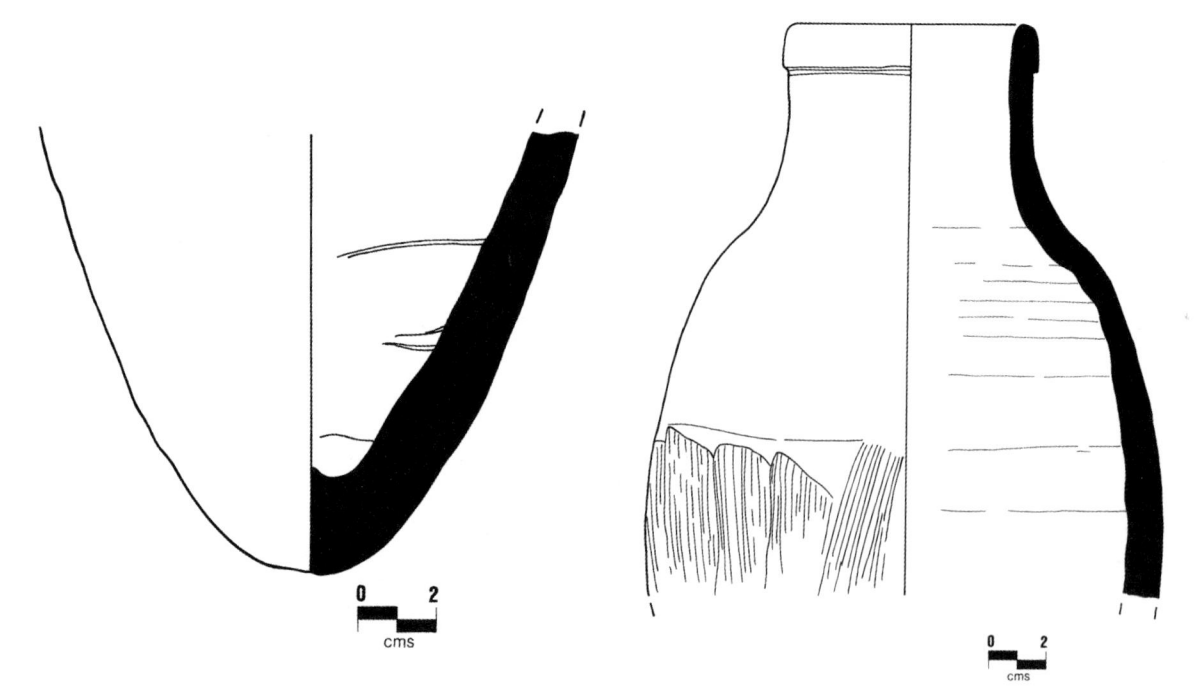

Figure 5.10. Old Kingdom beer jar of *Userkaf* form U65, from structure NW23 in the Quarry P settlement.

Figure 5.11. An Old Kingdom bottle of a type that could not be identified in the *Userkaf* corpus, from the surface of squares D–F in structure NW23 in the Quarry P settlement.

Middle strip within 3 × 3m square (squares D–F): This area incorporated 25 bowl rims, mainly red-slipped on the interior. Those pieces whose diameters could be readily measured were 18–19 cm, and were identified with U190. Included among these 25 pieces were two rims of Meidum bowls similar to U90/U112 and four rims of bowls resembling U187. There were also 36 body sherds from open bowls.

The closed forms comprised 86 body sherds plus a further 12 that joined rim fragments to make up two bottles of a type not identified in the *Userkaf* corpus (fig. 5.11). There were also two bases of type U1.

There were four marl sherds of which two were rims of type U42. These are noted in the corpus as occurring in, for instance, Ballas clays. The two sherds join and have a red band under the rim, possibly all that remains of a red slip, although the shape of the preserved section of this red area has clear outlines suggesting a deliberate band. The rest of the deposit comprised eroded body sherds that may be from either closed or open forms.

Southern strip within 3 × 3m square (squares G–I): This context included five rims and two body sherds of Meidum bowls. There were twelve rims of open bowls, eight being red-slipped inside, two unslipped, and two having completely lost their surfaces. There were 13 body sherds from these bowls, which are of form U189 (fig. 5.12).

Of the closed forms there were four rims, typed to U61, and two bases, one of which could be typed to the group of forms represented by U64–7. The second base, which has a very rough external surface, probably belongs to the same class, but this is uncertain from the description given in the *Userkaf* corpus (fig. 5.13).

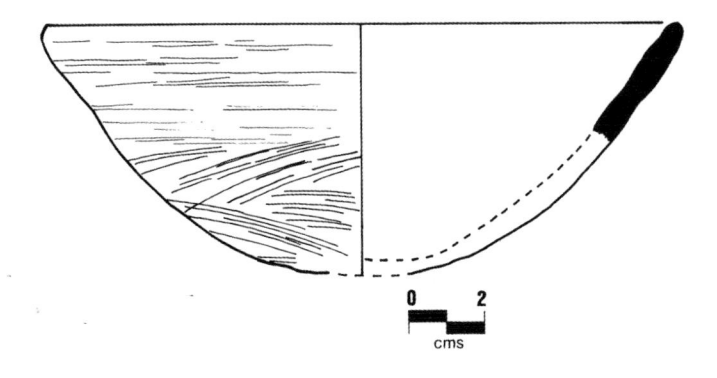

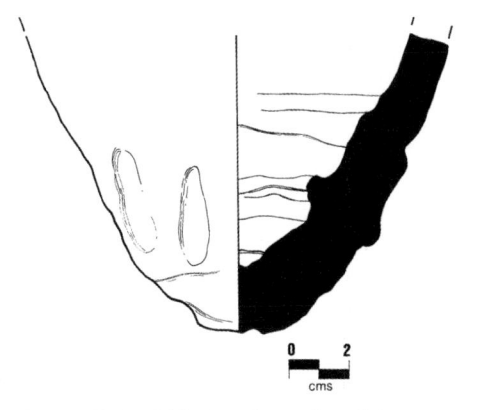

Figure 5.12. Meidum-type bowl (*Userkaf* form U189) from the surface of squares G–I in structure NW23 in the Quarry P settlement.

Figure 5.13. Old Kingdom closed-form vessel, possibly to be typed to the *Userkaf* group U64–7, of which only the base survived, on the surface of squares G–I in structure NW23 in the Quarry P settlement.

There were ten definite marl clay body sherds (all giving a positive reaction with 10% hydrochloric acid), but many sherds believed to be silt wares also gave a positive reaction when acid-tested, suggesting that the clays are in fact a marl-silt mixture, or that calcareous material has somehow contaminated the samples. There are also 52 supposedly silt ware body sherds.

Western windbreak: This context contained two rim sherds of open bowls of form U189, and two sherds of a badly eroded rim that could not be typed. There were also fifteen undiagnostic sherds, most of which seem to have belonged to open forms.

Eastern windbreak: This context contained 17 diagnostic open-form bowl rims, which have all been typed to U189, except for one out-turned bowl rim that falls into the group U186–8. A single rim from a Meidum bowl was classified as form U99. There were also six body sherds from open bowls.

Closed forms were represented by two so-called beer-jar bases, which fall into the group of forms U64–7. A total of 11 undiagnostic sherds are also believed to have come from beer jars, while a further 11 are of uncertain origin.

Area immediately to south of the 3-metre square (i.e. entrance of NW23): This deposit contained four Meidum bowl rims. Of these, one was U88, another U111, and the remaining two could not be correlated with any of the types in the *Userkaf* corpus (Kaiser 1969). Of five open-bowl fragments, four were red and one was too eroded to ascertain its surface treatment. A single rim from an open bowl could not be typed. Of 10 marl sherds, two may come from open forms.

There were six rims and two bases of closed forms. One of the rims was a red-slipped example of U4, four were in the general group of U64–7, and one could not be typed. One base is probably U21, but the other could not be typed. Of the closed forms, six sherds were red-slipped diagnostics, 23 were unslipped diagnostics, and a further 30 were completely undiagnostic.

Area immediately to the south of south wall of NW23: This context contained two rim sherds of bowl form U189. Closed forms included one red-slipped beer jar diagnostic and 15 body sherds from this type of vessel, most of which were also red-slipped. The sherds have been assigned to the general range of types U64–7. One sherd was completely undiagnostic.

Area immediately to the north of north wall of NW23: The pottery from this context consisted mainly of closed forms. There were only two sherds from open forms, and these were of uncertain type. Of the closed forms, there was one rim of a large red-slipped jar that is similar to, though not uniform with, U1 and U22. There were also 22 coarse sherds from closed forms, three of which preserved traces of red slip – these sherds are probably from beer jars. A total of six definite marl sherds were also identified, although all were undiagnostic.

5.4.2 Subsurface

Square A, unit 1 (wind-blown sand): This small context included one rim from a Meidum bowl, typed to U88, four open-form body sherds, and two sherds too badly eroded to be assigned to either closed or open forms.

Square B, unit 1 (wind-blown sand): This deposit contained two rims of open bowls, which were provisionally assigned to U189 and U193. There were also two undiagnostic body sherds.

Square C, unit 1 (wind-blown sand): This deposit contained four rims from open bowls, two of which were out-turned types of form U187, and two others are U193. There are also 12 open-form body sherds and one undiagnostic fragment.

Square A, unit 2 (occupation layer): This context contained nine rims of open forms, five of which are definitely red-slipped, while the others are too badly eroded to properly identify. Four of the rims have been assigned to U189 and one to U187. One Meidum bowl rim was also found; this was of a heavy type not represented in the *Userkaf* volume. There are 11 undiagnostic red-slipped sherds from open forms, and one red-slipped undiagnostic sherd from a closed form. The remaining 16 pieces are from closed forms of indeterminate types. A single marl body sherd was also found.

Square B, unit 2: The pottery from this context comprises nine bowl rims, eight of which were red-slipped, while the other was too worn to properly identify. It was possible to assign six of the rims to type U189, and three to the out-turned U187. The 10 body sherds of open vessels are all red-slipped on the interior, and one is heavily ribbed on the exterior. We found three closed-form body sherds, and a further three sherds were too eroded to assign to either open or closed forms with any certainty. As with Square A, a single marl sherd was found.

Square C, unit 2: This context included two rims from Meidum bowls, one of which could be assigned to type U7. Of the other 18 bowl rims, 16 could be typed to U189, one to U187, and one to U188. These were accompanied by 25 red-slipped sherds from open forms, and 20 sherds from open forms, the surfaces of which were completely eroded. The excavations yielded three body sherds from closed forms, as well as three marl sherds.

5.5 Discussion

It will be apparent from this brief study that the potential offered by the pottery from Hatnub is very great, and that the present work can do no more than illustrate these possibilities and give

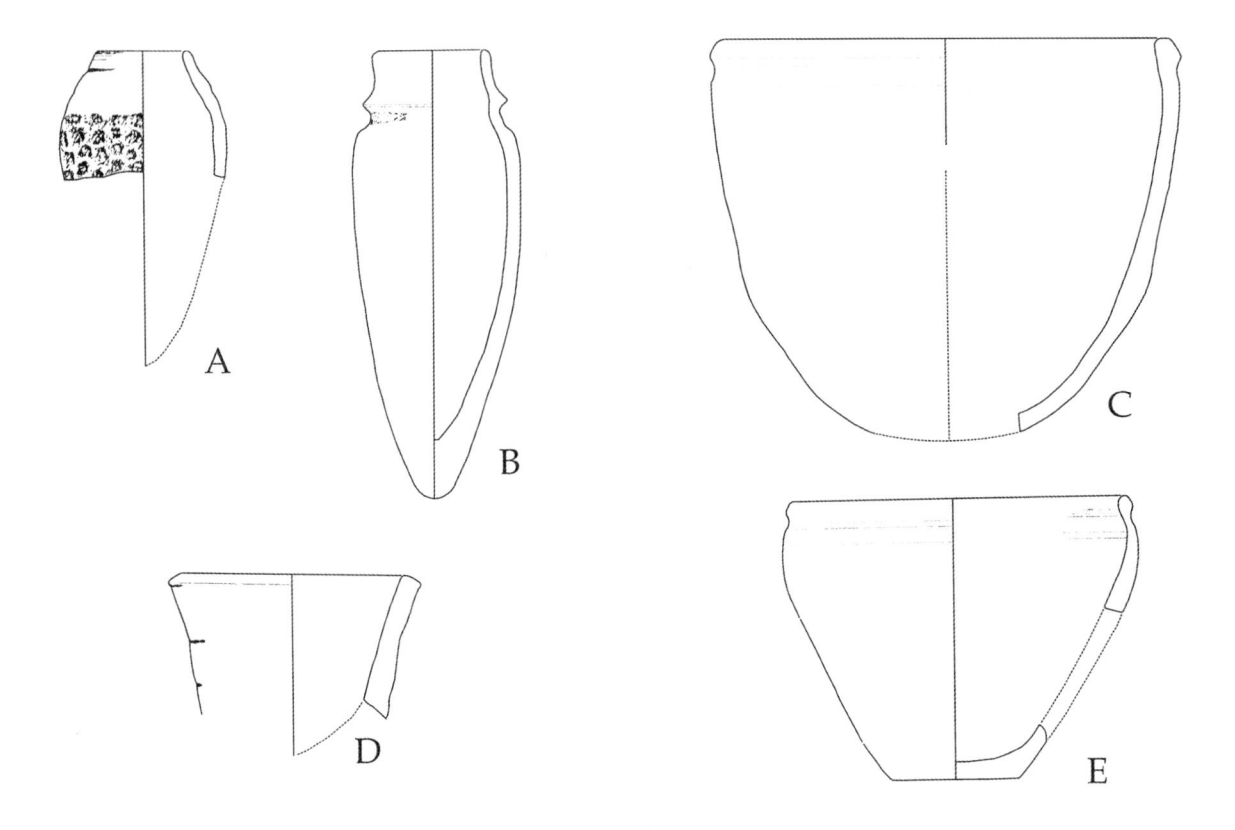

Figure 5.14. Old Kingdom pottery from the Wadi Gerrawi travertine quarries: A–B: beer jars, C: bread-mould, and D–E: bowls (adapted from Dreyer and Jaritz 1983: abb.7).

general indications of the date of the various areas investigated. It is to be hoped that it will be possible at some future time to return to the site and make a selection of Old Kingdom material for drawing as a corpus, and to obtain a wider selection of the available fabric types.

The almost unique preservation of some of the huts and their environs should be studied for object distribution and then related to ethno-archaeological studies of discard. In relation to the pottery it might even be possible to recognise successive phases of occupation in this way. Unless the occupation areas are subjected to even greater threat than that which they currently face, at least some of the huts should ideally be untouched, with their objects left *in situ*. The principal New Kingdom encampment (W1–38 and NW1–5) seems to be slightly more disturbed in some areas than the bulk of the Old Kingdom occupation. Most of the forms and fabrics seen there are already known and form part of the Amarna corpus of fabrics and forms (see Rose 2007).

In summary it is possible to confirm the general view that the majority of the ceramics associated with the stone huts and windbreaks at Hatnub date to the Old Kingdom (see fig. 5.14 for a small selection of Old Kingdom types from the Wadi Gerrawi travertine quarries, for comparison with those from Hatnub discussed above), but with isolated Roman and Coptic occupation of some of the Old Kingdom areas, and some possible New Kingdom sherds, though these are generally at such a low level of density as to suggest only casual discard. The situation in the New Kingdom encampment may be more complicated and more interesting, with some huts being constructed in the New Kingdom while others are likely to have been re-used structures of the earlier phase.

Chapter 6

Religion and Ritual at Hatnub: Petroglyphs, Priests and Standing Stones

Although at first glance it might appear that Hatnub incorporates very little in the way of remains of religious or ritualistic activities, there are in fact a number of surviving archaeological and textual traces that suggest the practice of some forms of religious ritual at the site. There is little to compare with the unique temples at the Serabit el-Khadim turquoise mines and the Timna/Wadi Arabah copper mines, or indeed the cult shrines at the Gebel el-Zeit galena mines, but various aspects of the Hatnub archaeological remains recall some of the other religious 'monuments' at these three sites. There are three basic types of archaeological feature at Hatnub that might be interpreted as forms of religious or ritualistic expression: petroglyphs, 'shrines' and stone alignments. Although the petroglyphs (described below) have survived in only one part of the site, the 'shrines' and alignments occur sufficiently frequently to suggest that they reflect certain patterns of behaviour.

6.1 Petroglyphs

The highest point in the immediate vicinity of Quarry P is a low hill, at one end of which a small cairn (C7, see fig. 6.1) was raised, almost certainly at the time of the Old Kingdom quarrying. Fraser (1894: 76) mentions another cairn (C8) at the far end of this low hill, but few traces of this had survived by the time that the 1985–91 surveys and excavation were undertaken. Just below the main cairn, a number of features are carved into the limestone rock-face, most of them taking the form of sets of carved horizontal lines resembling miniature steps, a few of them being outlined in roughly oval shapes that can perhaps be interpreted as representations of the soles of feet (fig. 6.2). These petroglyphs were first noted by Flinders Petrie (1894: 4), who described them as 'model flights of steps, only a few inches wide, cut by the ancient workmen'. The practice of carving votive symbols in the form of feet has been studied in some detail by Laszlo Castiglione (1967; 1971; 1974) at a variety of other sites. Castiglione usually identifies them as the feet of Serapis, with reference to the cult of 'göttliche Fußspur' in Ptolemaic and Roman Egypt. Indeed, rock-carved feet are found at many sites throughout the Mediterranean in the Hellenistic and Roman periods, but examples from earlier periods are much rarer. In the case of Hatnub, the foot-symbols seem more likely to date to the pharaonic period, given the dearth of Ptolemaic or Roman material at the site.

Other pharaonic-period examples of petrogyphs representing feet and sandals have been documented in Dakhla Oasis (Kaper *et al.* 2002: 81–9), the Wadi el-Hol (Darnell 2002: 121), and Nubia (Hellström 1970: 70, 85, 163; Verner 1973; Wilson 1996: figs 3.2–7 and 3.3–42). Winkler

Figure 6.1. Cairn C7 and the petroglyphs comprising sets of carved horizontal lines within 'foot' shapes.

Figure 6.2. The petroglyphs below cairn C7.

(1939: 5, 8, 9, 13, pl. 9.2) points out that, in the Western Desert, foot-shaped petroglyphs tend to occur in association with material clearly dating to the Old Kingdom, and the examples documented on several hilltops in Dakhla Oasis by Kaper *et al.* (2002) also seem to date to this period. These examples suggest that the Hatnub petroglyphs may date to the Old Kingdom phase of quarrying.

6.2 Stone alignments and orthostats

The use of stone alignments in Egypt and Nubia stretches back into prehistory, notably at the late Neolithic site of Nabta Playa (*c*.4900 BC) in the Western Desert, about 100 km to the west of Abu Simbel, where a unique miniature 'megalithic' complex was discovered in 1992 in the vicinity of seasonally occupied cattle-herders' encampments (Wendorf *et al.* 1996). This complex consisted of an alignment of 10 large (2 × 3 m) stones, a circle of small upright slabs (almost 4 m in diameter), and two slab-covered tumuli, beneath one of which were the buried remains of a long-horned bull. Similar small alignments of megaliths have also been observed at other sites in the Nabta basin. As Hendrickx and Vermeersch (2000: 33–4) have noted, 'although their function is not obvious, these megalithic constructions clearly represent public 'architecture' and therefore refer to increasing social complexity'.

There are several main groups of stone alignments at Hatnub. One set of single stone slabs (supported by other stones at their bases) is situated in a level area between Hut S15 and the southernmost group of huts (see main map: fig. 3.6). A second and more extensive group of standing stones is located on the other side of the main wadi, on high ground, to the south of the Quarry P region, but also some distance to the north of the two R quarries. Figure 6.3 shows

Figure 6.3. A view of part of the W50 group of aligned standing stones.

Figure 6.4. A carefully carved standing stone found among the W50 group of alignments.

Figure 6.5. One of the largest standing stones at Hatnub (S42), which was 1.38 m in height.

part of the W50 group of standing stones, and fig. 6.4 appears to be a very carefully carved example of one of these orthostats, found among the W50 group of alignments. One of the largest orthostats at Hatnub is S42 (fig. 6.5).

When Petrie undertook his surveys of the Sinai turquoise mining sites in 1904–5, he noted that there were many patterns of standing stones near the mines at Serabit el-Khadim, frequently positioned 'along the ridges of the hills, or an edge of a precipice, or any other striking position' (Petrie and Currelly 1906: 63-4). In view of Charles Currelly's discovery of large numbers of upright stones near Mount Sinai, Petrie suggests that their use at these sites is perhaps a cultic 'borrowing' from Syria-Palestine, either through use of Syro-Palestinian labourers, or the adoption of such monuments by Egyptian workers. However, the presence of such upright stones at Hatnub and other quarrying and mining sites in the Eastern Desert suggests that they might actually be a characteristic of Egyptian religious provision outside the Nile valley, or perhaps even a form of religious practice particularly characteristic of quarrying and mining expeditions. When quarry-workers were deposited temporarily in a barren landscape, they might have adopted this minimalist means of worship in much the same way as the Neolithic inhabitants of Nabta Playa.

6.3 Shrines

Scattered throughout the region surrounding Quarry P at Hatnub, there are a series of limestone dry-stone structures that might be interpreted as 'shrines'. These shrine-like buildings could perhaps be regarded as elaborate versions of the configurations of upright stones described above.

Structure S2, the largest of the Hatnub shrines, is located less than 100 metres from the peak carved with petroglyphs, described above. It consists of a small dome-shaped structure (height:

Figure 6.6. Shrine S2 from the south, with its stone lined 'avenue' running horizontally across the image, from west to east.

Figure 6.7. Shrine S2 from the east.

Figure 6.8. Shrine N3 from the north.

1.07 m, area: 5.2 × 4.9 m) with a rectangular interior space, approached along a stone-lined track stretching for a distance of 15 m (see fig. 6.6). Two large stones mark the opposite end of this track, one on either side, and from this point a rough footpath has been worn away, leading northwards to Quarry P. There is too little space inside the dome-shaped structure to have accommodated a human occupant, as in the case of the surrounding dry-stone habitations, suggesting that this building had some other purpose. It was first noted by Timme (1917: 36, abb. 40), who described it as a kind of 'dolmen' like those described by Petrie (1907: pl. 38a) at the site of Rifeh. S2 and other similar constructions, are probably briefly described by Fraser (1894: 76), when he refers to 'curious constructions built of boulders with little paths worn up to them, (?ovens)'. However, Fraser's suggestion that they are ovens seems unlikely, given that none of them has any associated charcoal or traces of burning (nor any of the fragments of bread-moulds that we might expect). A more likely option is that S2 was some kind of shrine within which offerings could have been placed.

Another possible shrine is structure N3, which consists of a small cairn of stones, making up a hemispherical shape almost two metres in diameter (somewhat smaller than S2), with an approach path leading up to it (fig. 6.8). As with S2, there is also a footpath worn away, leading from the approach path to a standard crescent-shaped hut to the northeast, about one hundred metres from the large area of dense settlement immediately beside Quarry P.

A third possible shrine is structure N7 (fig. 6.9), a simple dolmen-shaped construction of boulders and slabs (*c*.1.25 m wide) located in a large open area about 100 m from the peak with petroglyphs. There are no indications of an approach path leading up to N7, but, since it appears to be neither a standard cairn nor a hut, it fits best into the same category as S2 and N3.

At the southwestern edge of the S group of structures is a set of three shrine-like structures designated S11a–c (fig. 6.10). This feature is again in a relatively isolated location, lying about 150m south of the southern edge of the encampment adjacent to Quarry P. In terms of the Hatnub landscape, the context is halfway down a slope leading down into the valley between the

Figure 6.9. Shrine N7.

Figure 6.10. Shrine S11a.

Figure 6.11. Shrine NW24.

P and R quarrying regions, at the foot of a knoll surmounted by a large cairn (another instance of association between shrines and major cairns). The S11 shrines radiate out from the cairn, and a footpath leads up along the edge of the slope, skirting the northernmost edge of Hut S7 and heading off northwards (passing to the east of S2) towards the dense encampment beside Quarry P.

A further shrine-like structure is NW24 (fig. 6.11), which is situated at the western edge of the Quarry P plateau, not far from the group of three large cairns (A–C). It has already been briefly described in section 3.3.4 above, where it was pointed out that the combination of a pointed stone and a 1.2 m approach track is augmented by a small emplacement behind the stone that may have held offerings, making this a possible miniature version of the S2 structure. A short distance to the north of feature NW24 are two other shrine-like structures (NN9–10), both of which seem to be in roughly the same relationship with one cairn in the group of large cairns, as we have already observed with shrines S11a–c described above.

6.4 Textual references to religion and ritual at Hatnub

In the depiction of lines of men dragging Thuthotep's statue in his tomb at Deir el-Bersha, three of the four groups of men (each numbering 43) are described as either 'youths' or 'warriors', but the fourth is described in the accompanying inscription as *s3w n w'bw* ('a phyle of *wab*-priests').

Among the graffiti at the Hatnub quarries there are 18 that include references to priests. Mostly these are simply indicating the priestly titles held by governors of the Hare nome, to whom many of the monuments are dedicated. Thus, Graffito 9 is commissioned by the nomarch Iha who also held the title of 'chief priest of Thoth, lord of *ḫmnw* (Hermopolis Magna)'. Graffiti 11 and 12 were commissioned by Ahanakht, another nomarch (of the Hare nome) who is described in both graffiti as a chief priest, and in addition Graffito 12 was inscribed by the scribe Thutnakht, who calls himself an 'excellent lector-priest'. Graffito 7 was inscribed by Ankhy whose titles include 'lector-priest, chief of the priests of living Khnum'; in the same graffito, reference is made to Ankhy's father Khnumankh, also a lector-priest and chief priest. Graffiti 14, 20, 22, 25 and 26 were dedicated to the nomarch, Nehery, who also held the titles of 'chief priest' and 'overseer of priests', while Graffito 16 refers to his son Kay, also nomarch and chief priest. Graffiti 17, 23 and 31 were created for the nomarch Thutnakht, whose titles included 'overseer of the priests', 'high priest of Thoth', and 'great *wab*-priest of Thoth'. Graffito 17 goes into some detail as to the various religious acts performed for Thoth by Thutnakht. Graffito 49 is dedicated to the nomarch Amenemhat, who governed the Hare nome in the reign of Senusret I, and whose titles include 'chief priest'.

Graffito 15 is unusual in that it provides the names and attributes of two priests of the goddess Sekhmet: one called Heryshefnakht, who is also identified as an 'overseer of magicians' and 'king's chief physician', and another called Ahanakht, also apparently having medical skills, by whom Graffito 21 was inscribed. A priest of Thoth called Khnumhotep is the subject of Graffito 27. A clear distinction should be made here between the inclusion of priestly titles in the overall titulary of governors of the Hare nome, as opposed to priests such as those mentioned in graffiti 15, 21 and 27, who actually seem to have been physically present at Hatnub.

Sekhmet and Thoth are both mentioned in Graffito 25: 'as before Sekhmet on the day of battle'; 'whose end Thoth has ordered… whose property Thoth has made large'. Thoth is also mentioned several times in Graffito 26, and in Graffito 42 he is specifically cited as the god that will punish anyone who destroys this graffito and the adjacent image of the nomarch Thutnakht IV. Similarly, in Graffito UT3 (from the reign of Senusret III) both Thoth and a more local deity (Anty, lord of *ṯrtỉ*) are invoked as punishers of anyone who defaces the text and images.

6.5 Discussion

Other Egyptian quarrying and mining sites incorporate parallels for all three of the types of archaeological features found at Hatnub (e.g. orthostats at Serabit el-Khadim, shrines of various tpes at Gebel Zeit, Timna and Serabit el-Khadim, and petroglyphs at Wadi el-Hudi and Wadi Maghara). This suggests that the cultic needs of the members of quarrying and mining expeditions at Hatnub were by no means unique. It is interesting to note, however, the ways in which the combination of features differs from one quarrying location to another. In other words, the particular mixture of features at Hatnub (shrines, groups of orthostats, and a very small number of petroglyphs) is not really replicated in its entirety elsewhere.

There may well be a number of factors that would explain such differences in religious arrangements. Firstly, some sites (such as Gebel el-Asr, Gebel el-Zeit, Timna and Serabit el-Khadim) are far more remote than others, thus perhaps necessitating some attempt to create temples or major votive areas, rather than the more casual ritualistic environments that characterise sites such as Hatnub and Wadi el-Hudi that were located closer to the Nile valley. On the other hand, the fact that 'remoteness/proximity' is by no means the only factor involved is clearly demonstrated by the significant cult installations at the Gebel el-Silsila sandstone quarries, for instance, which lie within the Nile valley itself. It is also worth bearing in mind that some quarries, such as those at Wadi el-Hudi, Gebel el-Asr and Serabit el-Khadim, seem to have been worked by ethnically and racially mixed groups of workers (for non-Egyptians at Wadi el-Hudi see Sadek 1980: 100; for those at Gebel el-Asr see Rowe 1938: 391-4; for Serabit see Valbelle and Bonnet 1996: 34-5), thus perhaps resulting in different religious arrangements.

A final aspect of the religious data at Hatnub that is worth noting is the fact that, unusually, the goddess Hathor is never mentioned, despite the fact that she is the deity overwhelmingly associated with other major quarrying regions, such as the turquoise mines in the Sinai (see Valbelle and Bonnet 1996), the carnelian mines at Gebel el-Asr, the amethyst mines at Wadi el-Hudi, the copper mines at Timna and Wadi Arabah, and the galena mines at Gebel el-Zeit. Bloxam (2006: 282) notes, for instance, that 76% of the 123 recorded inscriptions at Serabit el-Khadim mention Hathor, while only 10% refer to Horus, 8% Soped and 6% other deities (including Ptah and Ba'alath). The epithet *nb ḫ3swt* ('lord of the desert') is held by the gods Horus, Min and Soped from at least the Old Kingdom onwards, thus associating these deities both with expeditions into 'foreign' territory and with the control of the geographical areas where mines and quarries are mostly located. The 4th Dynasty ruler Sneferu, for instance, is represented in the form of Soped smiting enemies at the Wadi Maghara turquoise mines (Valbelle 1998: 50-1, fig. 34). But it seems to be Hathor, and, to a lesser extent, Horus, who are the most prominent deities in the depictions and texts at the quarries themselves. The votive objects found at Stele Ridge carnelian mines in Gebel el-Asr include three small images of falcons probably representing Horus (JE59497-8; Engelbach 1933: 72), and royal Horus names are portrayed as the recipients of offerings from Hathor on two of the Middle Kingdom stelae from Stele Ridge (JE59483 and JE59485; Engelbach 1938: 387).

In these different contexts, Hathor is frequently identified as the patroness of the material being exploited, thus *nbt mfk3t* ('mistress of turquoise') at Serabit el-Khadim and Wadi Maghara (Seyfried 1981: 237-8.), *nbt msdmt* ('mistress of galena') at Gebel Zeit (Castel and Soukiassian 1985: 291), and *nbt ḫnmt* ('mistress of carnelian') at Gebel el-Asr (Englebach 1938: 72), but there is never any instance at Hatnub or elsewhere of the goddess being identified as *nbt bit* or *nbt šs* ('mistress of travertine'): there is the very slight possibility that the *ḥwt* element in *ḥwt-nbw* (Hatnub) refers obliquely to Hathor, as Simpson (1977: 1043) has suggested. It is notable, however, that instances of minerals identified with Hathor all seem to be gemstones or cosmetic materials rather than rock types used for sculptural or architectural purposes – thus at Gebel el-Asr the Middle Kingdom stelae refer to Hathor as mistress of carnelian, but none of the stelae describe her as *nbt mntt* ('mistress of gneiss'), despite gneiss being the principal material quarried in the region, probably since Neolithic times. It is therefore possible that stones such as gneiss and travertine, which were used primarily for such purposes as funerary vessels and sculpture, were treated differently in terms of their divine associations.

The deities that are most frequently mentioned in the graffiti at Hatnub are Thoth and Khnum, the gods closely associated with the Hermopolitan nome from which virtually all of the official 'state-sponsored' expeditions seem to have been launched. The Hatnub quarries were undoubtedly primarily exploited by the local governors and nomarchs of Middle Egypt, sometimes working on behalf of the king, therefore it is perhaps not surprising that the religious cults represented in their inscriptions were primarily those with relatively local associations.

Chapter 7

The Hatnub Quarry Roads and the Transportation of Travertine

There are several roads linking the Hatnub region with the Nile valley, and connecting the various quarrying areas at Hatnub itself; these are known collectively as the Darb el-Agl. Although Fraser (1894: 77) only describes two ancient roads in his brief report on the first epigraphic season at Hatnub, there were perhaps as many as six roads altogether, and Paul Timme mapped most of these in 1911 in his survey of Amarna and the surrounding area (Timme 1917: see fig. 4.1 above).

The principal 16 km route between Hatnub and the Nile valley at el-Amarna is undoubtedly the best-preserved Egyptian road from the pharaonic period as a whole (see Timme 1917; Shaw 1986: 195-8; Shaw 1987: 160-2; and Shaw 2006). The course of the main road, which probably dates back to the peak of the Hatnub quarries' use in the middle of the 3rd millennium BC, is still relatively well-preserved, although there are increasing signs of deterioration through the use of heavy vehicles by modern travertine quarry-workers. A number of very large cairns are located at the quarry end itself and would have served to guide the quarrying teams along the last part of their journey.

One of the 'minor' roads runs virtually parallel with the main road (described below) for about a third of its length and then heads northwards to terminate at a site identified by Timme as a travertine quarry later in date than the main workings of the Old and Middle Kingdoms (Timme 1917: bl. 6). This secondary quarry road is simply a track cleared in the desert rather than being a dry-stone construction punctuated by substantial causeways like the main road. Certainly an obvious implication of this difference is that the later travertine quarry at Hatnub was not producing the same quantity or weight of stone, but it is equally possible that the secondary road is much more characteristic of the initial 'prospecting' stages of quarrying rather than full-scale exploitation.

7.1 The main Hatnub road

The northwestern, Nile valley end of the main Hatnub road is first clearly visible near Kom el-Nana, the site of an 18th Dynasty temple complex at el-Amarna excavated by the Egypt Exploration Society during the 1990s (Kemp 1995: 433-8). The road must originally have run further to the west, presumably ending in a small harbour, the remains of which would now be buried beneath the cultivated land adjacent to the modern villages of Hagg Qandil and Hawata. Inscriptions at Deir el-Bersha and Hatnub during the Middle Kingdom include references to a

Figure 7.1. View of a typical section of the main Hatnub road, crossing level terrain.

Figure 7.2. The major stone-built causeway bridging a steep wadi about halway between Hatnub and the Amarna cliffs.

hilly region on the east bank of the Nile known as *trtỉ*, which may well have been the original name of a small settlement and/or harbour at the western terminus of the road (see Kessler 1981: 98, and see also section 1.3 above, on ancient toponyms for the Hatnub/Amarna region).

After Kom el-Nana, the road passes for 3 km across the Amarna desert, then ascends the scarp face of the eastern high desert, passing eastward across undulating terrain, punctuated by oc-

Figure 7.3. One of the dry-stone wayside huts to the north of the main Hatnub road.

casional embankments/causeways (fig. 7.1). At a little more than 7 km from Kom el-Nana, not far from the midpoint of the journey, the ancient route encounters a deep, wide wadi, crossing it by means of a very large causeway consisting of rocks and boulders heaped up to a maximum height of 5 m (fig. 7.2). It is clear from the cross-section of this causeway that it was built in two separate stages – Fraser (1894) points out that 'there are two finished batters, one within the other' – suggesting that it had been enlarged at some point in the past, either as a repair or in order to accommodate a larger or heavier load of travertine.

The total journey from Amarna to Hatnub takes about three hours on foot, but the time taken by quarrying expeditions carrying tools, provisions and water (on their outward journeys) and blocks of travertine (on their return journeys) was no doubt longer. It is therefore not surprising that there are many groups of wayside huts along the 7 km stretch between the embankment and the Quarry P region. It should be noted, however, that the texts from Serabit el-Khadim and Wadi el-Hudi (Seyfried 1981: 219–20), as well as the archaeological evidence from Gebel el-Asr/Tushka (Murray 1939: 110, and see also section 7.3.3 below) indicate that donkeys were frequently used for quarrying and mining expeditions. If they were used at Hatnub (despite not being mentioned in any of the Hatnub inscriptions or graffiti), the journey-time might have been slightly shorter.

The first group of wayside huts, situated to the north of the road, is encountered soon after the large embankment, and consists of about 20 windbreaks (see fig. 7.3), with associated scatters of travertine fragments and Old Kingdom sherds. About 2 km further on there is a second group, this time on both sides of the road, consisting of around 20 huts to the south (including two very well-preserved huts, one with two rooms and the other with three) and twelve to the north, all once more with scatters of travertine and Old Kingdom pottery.

The third, and largest, group of huts occurs just before the point at which the main road branches, one fork heading eastwards for about 4 km, towards Quarry P, and the other being

Figure 7.4. The unifinished(?) causeway leading southwards from the main plateau surrounding Quarry P.

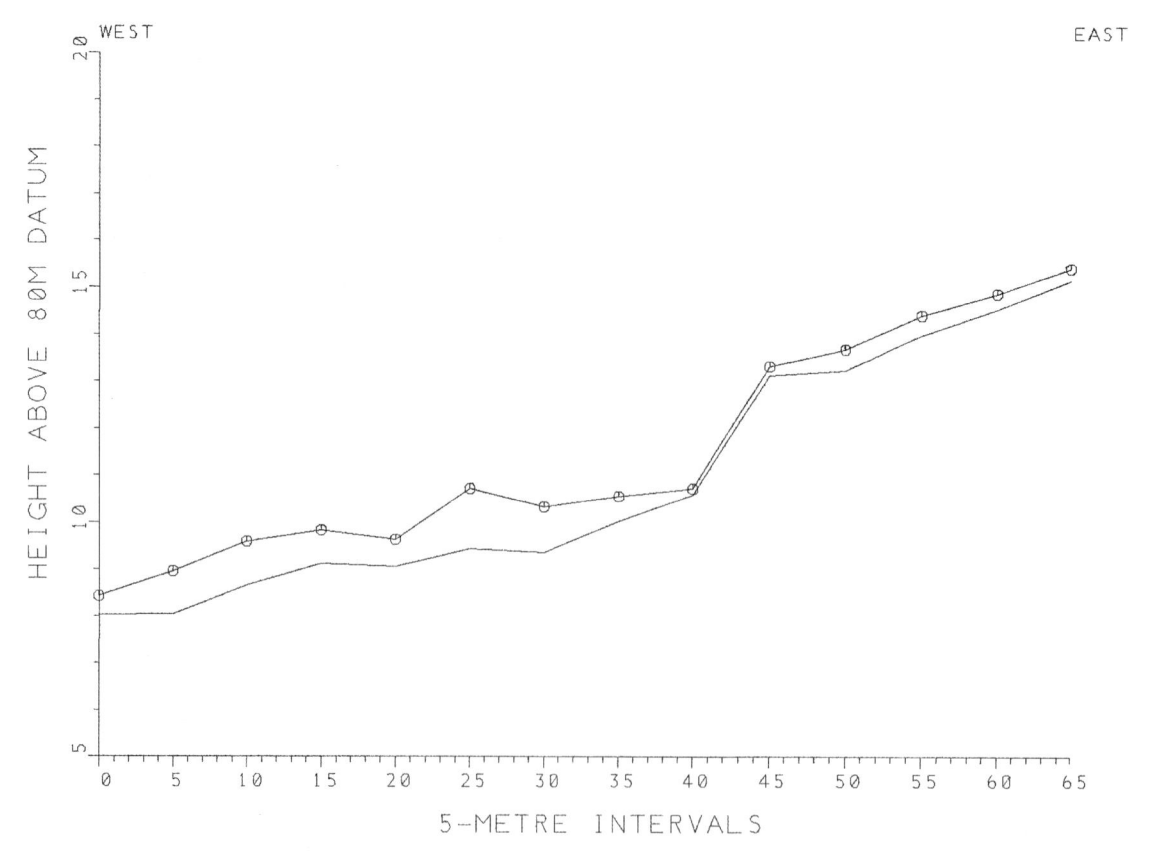

Figure 7.5. A diagrammatic cross-section of the causeway shown in fig. 7.4, at the southwestern edge of the Quarry P plateau.

a secondary route following the wide wadi between quarries P and R, leading eventually to Quarry T. The latter route is described by Petrie (1894: pl. 34) as an 'Arab road', whereas Timme (1917: 41, Bl.8) includes the road on his map and describes it as 'ein Fußpfad…nach den kleinen Steinbrüchen'. At this forking of the main road there are 56 wayside huts, 36 to the north of the road (mostly simply crescent-shaped windbreaks) and 20 to the south. It is possible that this proliferation of huts might be due to the fact that the main road not only forks here, but also approaches closest to another road to the north, which is labelled 'Südlicher Steinbruchweg' on Timme's map (Timme 1917: Bl.8). The space between the two roads would perhaps have been a convenient resting place for all three sets of road-users/quarry-workers.

Altogether, the three groups of wayside huts along the main road would probably have sheltered around a hundred workmen, if all occupied simultaneously, although it seems more likely that they indicate individual expeditions of around twenty or thirty workers. Such figures would be well below those cited in several of the Hatnub inscriptions and graffiti, or in the depiction of the hauling of the Thuthotep colossal statue. On the other hand, it is worth remembering not only that many expedition members might have slept without any shelter, but also that the textual evidence relates no doubt to the more ambitious expeditions, whereas the archaeological remains may provide evidence of the more frequent smaller-scale forays procuring fragments of stone for vessels, shabtis or statuettes.

A few metres further on to the southeast, the outlying huts of the main Quarry P settlement begin to appear, gradually becoming more numerous in the final approach to the quarrying region. The road slowly ascends towards the high ground surrounding Quarry P, finally reaching a small plateau overlooking the large wadi to the southwest (beyond which quarries Ra and Rb are situated), not far from the area of New Kingdom settlement. At this point the road is visible only as a cleared strip of ground scattered with limestone fragments and travertine chips, since the level landscape here needed little modification by the workers; there are, however, also traces of a *zir*-emplacement close to the edge of the road. At the southwestern edge of this plateau the ground rises a little, before plunging down into the wadi. Along this ridge is a cluster of three very large cairns (marked C1-3 on the map in fig. 3.6), with a group of around fifteen huts dispersed around them. Between two of these cairns a pair of parallel alignments of stones indicate another fork in the road, comprising a route heading off southwestwards. This route is built up by embankments as it descends the side of the main wadi, but seems to peter out after about 300 m, before it reaches the wadi floor (fig. 7.4). It may represent the beginning of an unfinished road leading directly from the Quarry P settlement to Quarry R, or it may simply be a link with the southern branch of the main quarry road (i.e. with the section that branched off from the main road about 3 km earlier). Figure 7.5 presents a diagrammatic cross-section of the road, which might have been abandoned because of the sheer steepness of the slope (see Stocks 2003b for a discussion of the optimal gradients along which ancient Egyptians dragged stone).

The southeastern end of the main road is situated about 100 m to the north of the entrance to Quarry P, and it is at this point that the presence of a cluster of small dry-stone windbreaks and large piles of stone chippings indicate that the larger blocks were probably being roughed out before they began their journey to the Nile. The road encounters its last topographic obstacle in the form of a shallow wadi running at right angles to the most direct north-south route. A long dry-stone causeway, 130 m long and 11 m wide, with a maximum height of 2.5 m, was constructed to bridge the gap (figs 7.6–7). A close examination of the upper surface of the embankment revealed the existence of two parallel track ways that may have been worn away by pairs of work-gangs hauling travertine blocks, like those depicted in the tomb of Thuthotep at Deir el-Bersha (Newberry 1893: pls 12 and 15, see section 7.2 below). A series of spot heights measured along the side of the main road and causeway at this stage have demonstrated that the aim of the causeway was not only to cross the wadi but also to ease the progress of the blocks of stone, avoiding sharp gradients by cutting down below the ground surface at the edges of the wadi (fig. 7.8).

Figure 7.6. The main stone-built causeway near the Hatnub travertine quarries.

Figure 7.7. A view of the side of the dry-stone causeway close to Quarry P, showing its composition.

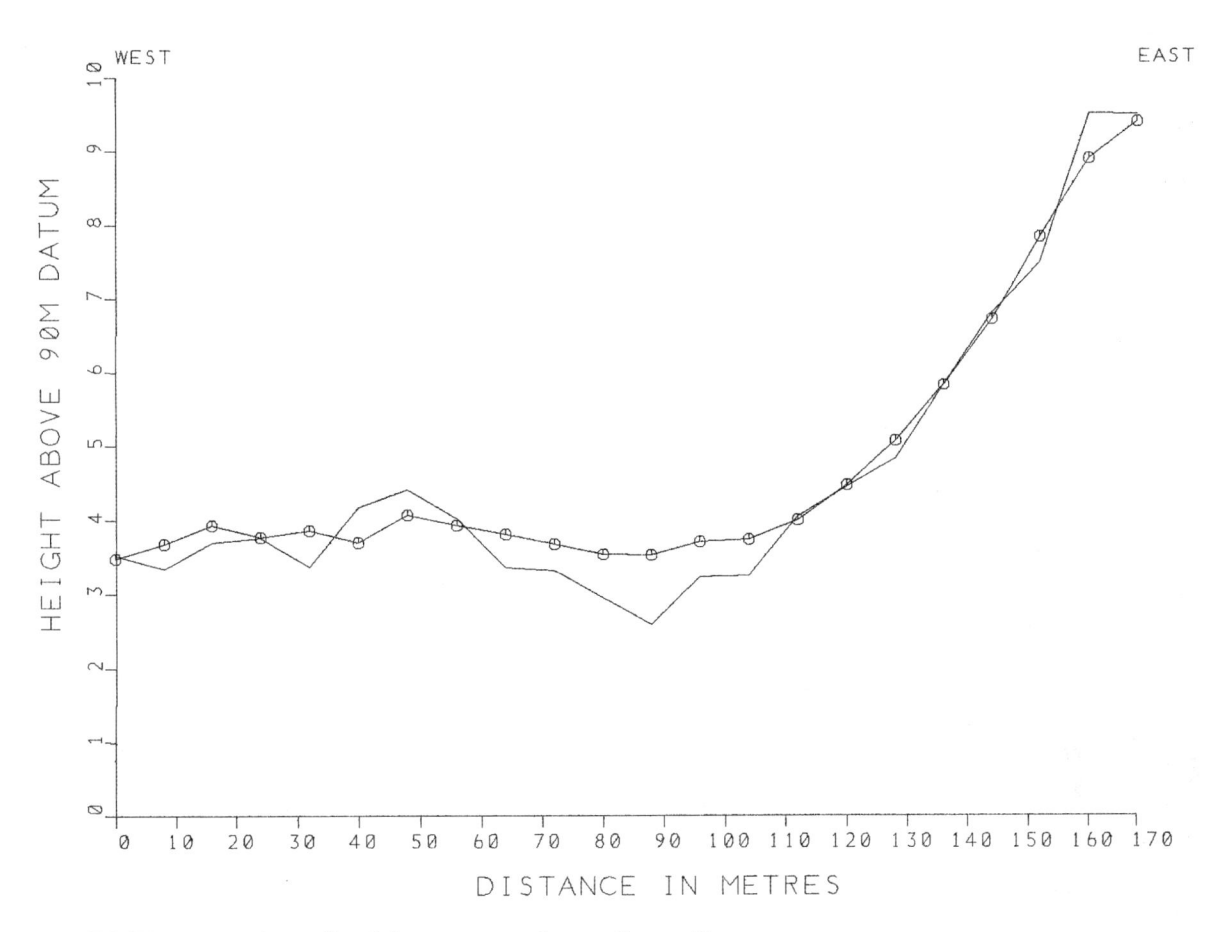

Figure 7.8. Diagrammatic profile of the causeway close to Quarry P.

7.2 Evidence on stone transportation derived from the tombs of Weni and Thuthotep, and the Ma'sara quarries

Several visual and textual sources from locations elsewhere in Egypt can also shed light on the question of stone transportation during the pharaonic period. One of the earliest is a 6th Dynasty monolithic limestone stele (Cairo, Egyptian Museum, CG1435), which was discovered by Auguste Mariette in 1860 in the tomb of Weni, in the 'northern cemetery' at Abydos, between the Old Kingdom town of Abydos and the Early Dynastic royal cemetery. The stele formed one wall of Weni's single-room mastaba-tomb chapel, which was re-excavated in 1999–2000 by Janet Richards, demonstrating beyond doubt that this was an actual burial place rather than a cenotaph (Richards 2000; 2001). The 'biographical' inscription on the stele describes the principal events in Weni's life, broken down into typical Old Kingdom themes: his career as a bureaucrat in the palace administration; his procurement of stone funerary equipment for his burial; his military campaigns in the Eastern Desert and Palestine; a hymn of victory including a stereotypical description of an Asiatic country; his organization of quarrying expeditions to Hatnub and Aswan; and his creation of a new river channel through the first cataract at Aswan.

One section describes Weni's Hatnub expedition:

His person [Merenra] sent me to Hatnub to bring down a large offering table of Hatnub-travertine. I brought down for him this offering table in 17 days. I quarried [it] in Hatnub and I ensured that it sailed downstream (i.e. northwards) in this wsḫt-*boat, which I hewed for it, a* wsḫt-*boat of acacia wood of 60 cubits in length and 30 cubits in width. I assembled [it] in 17 days in the third*

month of summer when there was no water on the sandbanks. I moored at the pyramid 'Merenra appears beautifully' in safety. It happened through me entirely in accordance with the order which the person of the lord gave.
(Sethe 1933a: §108).

The same verb, 'to bring down' (sḥꜣ), used in the above section of Weni's biography is also used in line 10 of Graffito 9 at Hatnub (Anthes 1928: 23, tf. 13: 'I brought down 700 stone blocks and 803 'ꜣt-blocks'). The 6th Dynasty funerary texts of Sabni, at Aswan, also describe the building of 'wsḫt-boats' specifically commissioned for the transportation of stone.

The famous scene in the 12th Dynasty tomb of Thuthotep at Deir el-Bersha (c.1900 BC) shows a colossal statue of the deceased (or perhaps of one of the 12th Dynasty rulers) being dragged along on a sledge by groups of workmen, their path lubricated by water poured in front of the runners (Newberry 1893: 16–26, pls 12–19; Arnold 1991: 277–8; see also the section on flooring in Chapter 3 of Arnold 1991). The frequent use of wooden sledges to convey large stone blocks or sculptures appears to be confirmed by several funerary reliefs and paintings from different periods, such as those in the tomb of Ti at Saqqara (c.2430 BC). There is evidence from the early 8th century BC of a very similar method being used by Assyrians to transport colossal statues from quarries (Reade 1983: 36–9).

Hans Goedicke (1959: 58) has raised the possibility that an unprovenanced Middle Kingdom travertine stele almost certainly deriving from Hatnub (UT3 in Appendix 4 below), might be an account left by one of the officials connected with this quarrying expedition sent by Thuthotep: 'The wording of the text seems to point to the execution of a particular project, which apparently was a major one, and not a permanent enterprise. In how far this can be linked with the colossal statue made at Hatnub described in the tomb of Dhwty.nht [*sic*] at El-Bersheh is questionable. The latter tomb dates to the reign of Sesostris III and it is at least tempting to envisage such a connection.' (see Appendix 4 below for full translation of the text).

An early 18th Dynasty rock carving (dated to year 22 of the reign of Ahmose, c.1528 BC) was found at the base of one of a pair of stelae in the entrance to the limestone quarries at Ma'sara, near Cairo; it shows (fig. 7.9) a block carried on a sledge pulled by oxen, driven along by three foreigners holding batons. The carving is now in the Egyptian Museum, Cairo (JE62949; see Saleh and Sourouzian 1987: No.119).

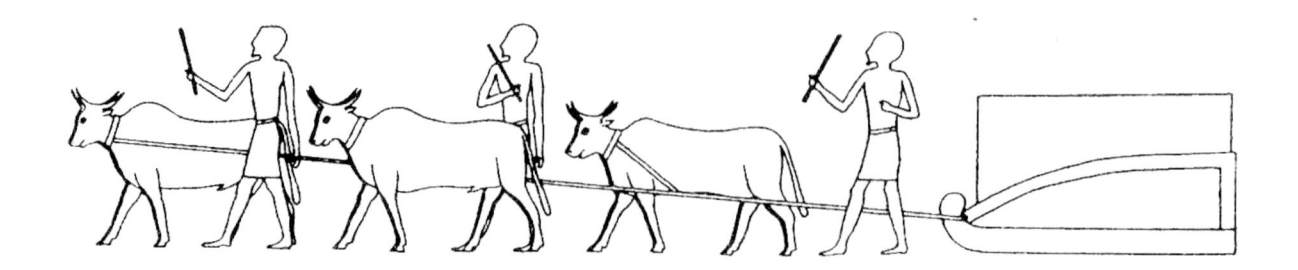

Figure 7.9. Rock-drawing in the limestone quarries at Ma'sara showing a stone block on a sledge being hauled by oxen (c.1528 BC).

7.3 Other quarrying and mining roads of the pharaonic period

The processes of road building and route-making must have been particularly crucial aspects of the Egyptian technological infrastructure, and evidence for quarry roads has survived at a number of sites other than Hatnub, providing a good context within which the Hatnub roads can be better understood. A number of papers have been published concerning the desert roads of the Ptolemaic and Roman periods (e.g. Murray 1925; Sidebotham *et al.* 1991, Sidebotham 1996), but the study of the roads of the pharaonic period has been surprisingly neglected, despite the fact that some of them are among the earliest surviving roads in the world (see Forbes 1964; Partridge 1996; Darnell 2002; Riemer and Förster forthcoming, and for comparison with roads of ancient Israel see Dorsey 1991).

7.3.1 The Widan el-Faras road

The Widan el-Faras (or Gebel Qatrani) basalt quarries at the northern edge of the Faiyum are linked with the so-called 'workmen's settlement' and temple at Qasr el-Sagha by a 10 km road described by Harrell and Bown (1995) as the world's 'first paved road', pre-dating the roads of the Minoan civilization (see also Caton-Thompson and Gardner 1934: 136–7; Arnold and Arnold 1979: fig. 13, Sliwa 1992: 177–91; Bloxam and Storemyr 2002; Bloxam and Heldal 2007).

Figure 7.10. The basalt-quarriers' road at Gebel Qatrani/Widan el-Faras.

The characteristics of this road (fig. 7.10), which is 2.4 m wide and paved with sandstone slabs and logs of tertiary fossil wood, derive from several factors: firstly, as with the main Hatnub road, local materials are used (i.e. sandstone slabs, as opposed to the limestone pebbles and boulders at Hatnub); secondly, the need for a built road, as opposed to a simple cleared track, must have been dictated by the bulk and quantity of the basalt blocks being quarried; thirdly, the economic investment and manpower involved in the construction of a long and substantial road must have benefited from the same highly-organised infrastructure as the planned settlement at Qasr el-Sagha (although the road seems to date primarily to the Old Kingdom, pottery at its southern terminus, near the Qasr el-Sagha settlement, is both Old and Middle Kingdom in date, see Bloxam and Storemyr 2002: 31). Both the road and the planned community are also typical of quarrying sites located in comparative proximity to the Nile floodplain, as opposed to more isolated locations such as the gneiss quarries at Gebel el-Asr or the turquoise mines at Wadi Maghara.

7.3.2 The Dahschurstrasse

Another, somewhat less substantial, road, which was first documented by Flinders Petrie (1888: 33–6), stretches southwestwards for about 20 km from the region immediately to the north of Dahshur, beside the Mastabat Fara'un, to the northern edge of the Faiyum. This Dahshur-Faiyum route – the so-called *Dahschurstrasse* – is said to be roughly 23 m wide for most of its length. It is simply a cleared strip of ground rather than a causeway or paved structure – the surface gravel has been swept to either side, and according to Caton-Thompson and Gardner 'these margins, which alone betray the execution of the road, consist of a broad band of gravel sweepings' (see Caton-Thompson and Gardner 1934: 109). Because of a proliferation of drainage channels in the area between the desert and the Faiyum, it seems likely that the archaeological traces of the road have been obscured before it reaches its western destination, leaving a degree of uncertainty as to whether it was the road to the Widan el-Faras basalt quarries, the Umm-es-Sawwan gypsum quarries, or both. Even an enterprising aerial examination of the site by Caton-Thompson in 1931 was insufficient to resolve this problem (Caton-Thompson and Gardner 1934).

It is possible that the *Dahschurstrasse* constituted a land-route for work-forces sent to the basalt quarries from the Middle Kingdom pyramids at Dahshur, but the Widan el-Faras basalt itself would have been most conveniently transported from Qasr el-Sagha by river rather than road – indeed the basalt quarriers' paved road terminates in an L-shaped stone ramp adjacent to the Middle Kingdom quayside at Qasr el-Sagha (Arnold and Arnold 1979: 26). It is therefore perhaps more likely that the track from Dahshur was the ancient route between the Memphite region and the gypsum quarries of Umm el-Sawwan. A rough desert track also appears to have linked the Umm el-Sawwan quarries with those at Widan el-Faras.

Petrie identified eight uninscribed limestone way marks along the route of the *Dahschurstrasse*, but since 1957 a number of stone stelae dating to the 25th and 26th Dynasties (*c*.712–525 BC) have also been discovered. Six of these appear to have served as way marks, since they were placed at rough intervals of about 3.3 km along the route (see Goedicke 1962; Altenmüller and Moussa 1981; Moussa 1981). The other two stelae are more commemorative in nature, and the text on one describes how it was erected by the 25th Dynasty King Taharqa in order to commemorate the speed of his army in covering the distance of 50 km from Memphis to the Faiyum in about five hours. It concludes with the information: 'The name of this area of the desert on which the stele has been erected is "Road of the Camp"'.

The reference to the Road of the Camp has led to suggestions that the road actually led to a military camp or *bȝ*, but Goedicke's excavations at the western end of the road appear to have revealed little other than a surface scatter of potsherds. Altenmüller and Moussa (1981: 81–2) suggest that the word *bȝ*, translated as 'camp', may actually be referring to the quarries. The best solution to the problem may be that the *Dahschurstrasse* served one or both of the quarries during the Old and Middle Kingdoms, but had begun to be used primarily as a military road by the Late Period. Petrie also identified a second road, similar in appearance and dimensions to the *Dahschurstrasse* and running due westwards from the same origin, apparently crossing 200 km of desert to Siwa Oasis – presumably this too was a military road.

7.3.3 *The Gebel el-Asr gneiss-quarriers' road*

The longest surviving Egyptian quarry 'road' is the 80 km route linking the anorthosite gneiss quarries of the Old and Middle Kingdoms (*c*.2650–1650 BC) at Gebel el-Asr with the nearest Nile embarkation point at modern Tushka. The gneiss quarrying area, consisting of a cluster of sites in the Western Desert midway between the Naqlai Oasis and the Dunqul Oasis, was rediscovered in 1932. Reginald Engelbach and George Murray undertook two seasons of survey and excavation at the site in 1933 and 1938, including a detailed examination of the ancient road leading to Tushka (Engelbach 1938: 388–9; Murray 1939: 108–11). The Gebel el-Asr/Tushka quarry road demonstrates above all that there was more to roads than the creation of cleared tracks and causeways – roads also need some kind of infrastructure to sustain the groups of people using them.

The Gebel el-Asr road was not a built structure, as the roads to Hatnub and Widan el-Faras were; instead it appears to have been simply a cleared track (rather than a paved or dry-stone structure), the course of which was clearly identifiable through a variety of evidence: pieces of discarded gneiss and potsherds, numerous cairns (including one large example marking the point almost exactly midway between the Nile and the quarries), occasional dry-stone encampments, and, on the harder ground, well-preserved donkey-tracks along the road itself. Murray describes the hoof-marks as 'countless parallel trails, too thin and straight for camel tracks, that showed where the donkey caravans had taken provisions up to the quarries and brought smaller pieces of gneiss down' (Murray 1939: 110).

Further clues concerning the methods of transportation from the gneiss quarries were provided by Murray's discovery of three large dry-stone 'ramps' near the quarries, which are presumed to have been used to load the stone onto sledges or carts. The best-preserved of the three is 8 m long and 1.2 m high, and stretching in front of it are an enigmatic pair of parallel trenches, each gouged out of the desert to a depth of 80 cm (see fig. 7.11). One of the trenches contained potsherds, apparently of early Old Kingdom date (Engelbach 1938: 372), which suggests that the ramps relate to the mode of transportation employed in the earliest years of the quarries' use (see Shaw and Bloxam 1999 for recent excavation of the ramps and discussion of their possible significance in the process of transporting the gneiss from the quarries to the Nile valley).

Figure 7.11. One of the dry-stone ramps in the Gebel el-Asr gneiss quarries.

The Tushka end of the gneiss quarriers' road proved the most difficult section to discern, but according to Murray 'it led down firstly to a lozenge-shaped structure about 2 miles out of Tushka, next to the remains of a considerable camp, and finally to a large heap of stones adorned with flags' (Murray 1939: 110). Since four Egyptian artefacts dating to the dynastic period (a 1st Dynasty jar-sealing in a C-group grave, a sandstone block bearing an Old Kingdom inscription, and two Middle Kingdom stelae) were discovered in the vicinity of the modern village of Duki Dawur, Simpson (1963: 53) suggests that this area of Tushka West may have been the quarriers' embarkation point. The road as a whole can be dated at least as early as the Middle Kingdom, on the basis of potsherds described by Engelbach (1938: 388). It is possible that the Old Kingdom gneiss quarriers were using some other road, such as the ancient Darb el-Arba'in caravan-route from Sudan to Middle Egypt, which passes a few kilometres to the west of the main gneiss quarries.

In 2003 an Anglo-Norwegian team undertook a fresh programme of survey and excavation along the 10 km section of the track nearest to the quarrying region (the rest of the ancient route having been largely destroyed or obscured by modern road-building and settlements, as well as the Tushka Hydrological Project, which has had a severe impact on the region, see Shaw and Heldal 2003; for further discussion of the Gebel el-Asr quarry road and accompanying roadside camps, see Shaw et al. in press). The principal results of this Anglo-Norwegian work were the discovery and excavation of several very shallow, but large ground-water wells along the ancient track to the Nile, providing evidence of the former, much wetter climate in the area,

Figure 7.12. One of the encampments beside the road leading from Gebel el-Asr to Tushka.

which is an important clue to the understanding of how this area was formerly inhabited (note however that at least one of the 'wells' near the track, and several in the quarrying region itself, may actually be structures created for priestly ritual ablutions, perhaps in connection with the consecration of blocks of stone intended for royal statues). These wells also confirmed the presence of Nubian aquifers, whereby the groundwater was close to the ancient surface (Shaw and Heldal 2003: 16). Many cairns along the ancient track were recorded, providing evidence concerning the ways in which ancient routes were marked. Finally two dry-stone built camps were excavated near the track-side wells, revealing that their main purpose was for the preparation and consumption of food, including the baking of bread (fig. 7.12).

7.3.4 Local paths and ramps

As well as long-distance quarry-roads there are numerous surviving shorter paths and ramps that were constructed both at the beginning and end of the transportation process. Some have been preserved in the immediate vicinity of the structures for which the raw material was destined. Dieter Arnold describes the employment of short dry-stone, mud-brick and timber roads in the construction of tombs and temples at such funerary sites as Saqqara, Sinki (southeast of Abydos), Dahshur, Meidum, Giza, el-Lisht and el-Lahun. Arnold also discusses the evidence for the use of such tools as levers, rockers, sledges and rollers to facilitate the movement of heavy objects (see Arnold 1991).

Short roads and ramps were often constructed directly beside mines and quarries, as at Wadi el-Hudi, the Gebel el-Asr gneiss quarries, and the sandstone and granite quarries on the west and east banks of the Nile at Aswan. At Wadi el-Hudi, immediately to the northwest of a 12th Dynasty amethyst-miners' fortress, there is a small strip of desert cleared of stones and gravel. This may be interpreted either as the southeastern terminus of a major road linking the mining area and the Aswan region (35 km to the northwest) or simply as a formal approach to the fortress. According to Ahmed Fakhry there were once further traces of the road in the vicinity (Fakhry 1952: 12), but in 1992 the only other stretch of road still discernible at Wadi el-Hudi is another cleared track heading eastwards away from a mica mine about 2 km southeast of the fortress (Shaw and Jameson 1993: 92). The fact that the surviving road immediately beside the fortress is only a cleared track rather than a paved structure no doubt relates to the processing of amethysts and gold *in situ* – the resulting raw material would have been easily transported, compared with the large slabs and blocks of stone from Hatnub or Widan el-Faras. At Wadi el-Hudi there are no surviving indications of the modes of transport used by the miners, although one of the texts appears to describe the use of sledges to transport the amethysts (WH143, JE71901); 'I brought (it) from there in great quantity, when I collected (it) just like at the door of a granary, (it) being dragged away by sledge, loaded into pallets' (Sadek 1980: 85 - the word translated here as 'sledge' is *wnš*).

An impressive surviving network of roads at Aswan was designed to transport the stone as efficiently as possible to the river-bank, both from the granite quarries on the east bank and the silicified sandstone quarries to the west. On the east bank there was a long north-south road running parallel to the river, which would have allowed the blocks from the granite quarries to be transported easily along the edge of the floodplain to suitable harbours (see Jaritz 1993, for discussion of the mud-brick wall that appears to have protected the main transportation route between Aswan and Philae).

On the west bank, at the quarry-sites of Gebel Gulab and Gebel Tingar, there are numerous short dry-stone causeways by means of which the quarried silicified sandstone could be dragged through the undulating and boulder-strewn terrain in which the quarries were located (see Klemm and Klemm 2008: 219–28; Storemyr *et al*. in press). The shorter stretches of road average 3–4 m in width and 10–30 cm in height, but the most substantial surviving stretch of

Figure 7.13. One of the Gebel Gulab/Tingar roads used by quartzite quarriers.

road, leading away southwestwards from the best-preserved ancient quarry-face on the west bank (fig. 7.13), is about 8 m wide and – at its highest point – about 1.5 m high, making it comparable in dimensions with the causeway near the main quarries at Hatnub, as described above (fig. 7.7).

7.4 Discussion

Quarrying and mining settlements had to be linked with the Nile valley by roads and tracks stretching across the desert landscape, thus enabling the materials to be conveyed to the nearest embarkation points. The routes usually taken by Egyptian commercial and military expeditions outside the Nile valley often correspond to such naturally occurring topographical phenomena as the Wadi Hammamat and the Wadi Gasus. Louise Bradbury (1988) has discussed some of the most important arteries of communication between the Nile and the Red Sea. There were also recognised caravan routes such as the 'oasis road' mentioned by Harkhuf in the Old Kingdom. However, not all pharaonic routes were entirely 'natural' in origin.

The commemorative texts carved by the leaders of Egyptian mining and quarrying expeditions frequently mention that routes through the desert were 'opened up' for the workers, and many surviving traces of specially constructed roads have been found in the surrounding areas of mines, quarries and major structures. Indeed Henry Fischer (1991) identified various instances of the Old Kingdom titles 'master of the roads' and 'official of the masters of the roads', both in the Memphite necropolis and in the mining areas of the Wadi Hammamat and Wadi Abbad (in the Eastern Desert), suggesting that the coordination and maintenance of land routes was a high priority for the Egyptian administration. In the case of the more extensive mineral sources, which were revisited year after year, considerable resources of time and energy were clearly expended on road construction. The travertine quarries at Wadi Gerrawi, although less remote than those at Hatnub, are said to have been linked with the Nile by a long road, which still partially survived in the late 19th century (Erman 1885: 623).

The Egyptians' official accounts of quarrying and mining expeditions routinely emphasise the difficulties and hardships endured by the workmen, perhaps partly in order to increase the prestige of the materials themselves, but, just as the surviving texts largely ignore such practical questions as the process of building pyramids, so they rarely make reference either to the building of roads or to the ways in which cargoes and stone blocks were conveyed along them (although see Quirke 1990: 71, for discussion of papyri from Lahun that may describe specialised work-forces responsible for the dragging of stone blocks). However, some idea of the construction methods of Egyptian roads can be deduced on the basis of the various preserved stretches of ancient road, causeways and ramps discussed above. The occasional survival of such equipment as wooden rollers and sledges helps to fill in the crucial gaps left by the texts.

There are also some textual references to the use of donkeys - sometimes numbering several hundred – in quarrying expeditions to Sinai, Gebel el-Asr, and Wadi el-Hudi (Gardiner *et al.* 1955: 11, 114; Simpson 1963: 52–3; Seyfried 1981: 219–20). As mentioned above, the upper surface of the large embankment in the main road close to Quarry P at Hatnub still bears traces of a pair of trackways perhaps deriving from the use of sledges (Shaw 1987: 162). In contrast, there is a puzzling lack of wear on the paved road leading from the Widan el-Faras basalt quarries, which, according to Harrell and Bown (1995: 82–3), might be explained by the use of wooden planks laid across the width of the road, between the sledge and the stone paving. Bloxam and Storemyr (2002: 30), however, point out that 'the use of unfixed rollers or crossbeams with sledges to move heavy weights over large distances has been proven impractical'.

The nature of each Egyptian quarrying and mining road appears to have been dictated mainly by three factors: the bulk and quantities of the minerals being procured, the character of the topography, and the types of materials locally available for road building. When the surfaces crossed by the roads are relatively flat, as in the case of the Gebel el-Asr gneiss-quarriers' road, it is clear that the surviving archaeological traces may often be highly ephemeral, and thus particularly vulnerable to destruction through modern quarrying, irrigation and road-building in the desert. Certainly such current building works as the Tushka Hydrological Project and the activities in the area of the Widan el-Faras basalt quarries suggest that these delicate traces of land travel during the pharaonic period are liable to deteriorate rapidly unless urgent steps are taken to record and protect them (see Bloxam and Heldal 2007).

Chapter 8

The Organisation of Pharaonic Quarry-Workers at Hatnub: a Synthesis of the Archaeological and Textual Data

From the late Predynastic period onwards, the procurement of stone and metals was an integral part of the social and economic relationships between the pharaoh and his high officials (and also between such officials and their subordinates). Since the products of mining and quarrying were the natural resources from which essential items of religious and funerary architecture and equipment were made, the large-scale quarrying of stone in ancient Egypt has often been interpreted as a rough index of fluctuations in royal power and social stability at different dates (Hikade 2001: 131–50; Shaw 2002).

Royal officials appear to have relied on the king to provide them with the necessary labour and raw materials for their funerary equipment. Thus the 6th Dynasty inscription of Weni at Abydos not only describes the quarrying expeditions to Hatnub and Aswan/Ibhat that he organised for the king, but also states that the king presented him with a fine limestone sarcophagus, a false door, and a libation-basin from the quarries at Tura (Sethe 1933a: 98–110; Lichtheim 1973: 18–23). This, like many other examples, emphasises the crucial role that the procurement of stone played in society as a whole during the pharaonic period.

8.1 Sources of evidence for the organisation of quarrying expeditions

Although many major expeditions were evidently sent by kings or nomarchs (both types are attested at Hatnub), there is good evidence for the involvement of temples in the procurement of stone and metal. Mineral deposits are often listed among the assets of funerary estates or temples. Thus, an inscription on the walls of the Kanais rock-temple in the Wadi Miya/Wadi Abbad, about 35 km east of Edfu, announces that the gold mines in the vicinity were owned by the temple of Seti I at Abydos (Gunn and Gardiner 1917: 242; Gauthier 1920: 7). The text makes it clear that this endowment included not only the mineral rights but also the means to exploit them, comprising a team of miners, their settlement, and a well dug on the king's orders:

> *The special interest which King Setoy, or Sethos I, as we usually call him, certainly took in this district seems to have arisen out of the building of his superb funerary temple, 'The House of Menmare' at Abydos. Large quantities of gold were required for the embellishment of this construction, and Sethos took the opportunity to appoint in perpetuity a 'staff of gold-washers' at the mines east of Edfu, under the direction of a military officer, the 'Captain (literally, chief of a troop) of the Gold', for the exclusive purpose of furnishing the House of Menmare directly with the metal. In the*

inscriptions it is indicated that the supply of gold thus secured to the Abydos temple is to be used for decorative purposes there for all time; doubtless, however, it was further intended to be a source of great profit to Sethos' funerary endowment, but on this feature of the matter the king would naturally not wish to dwell in his addresses to posterity.
(Gunn and Gardiner 1917: 242).

Archaeologists can often distinguish between instances of low-level exploitation of mineral resources by individuals and the more intensive level of organization (and greater visibility) associated with large-scale expeditions sent to acquire stone or metals for the king and/or his high officials (Shaw 1986: 197; Kemp 2006: 317–9). Thus some sites, such as Hatnub, the Umm el-Sawwan alabaster-gypsum quarries, and the Gebel el-Zeit galena mines, suggest that certain raw materials were the object of intermittent private exploitation throughout the pharaonic period (perhaps sometimes following in the footsteps of the major state expeditions - see Bloxam 2006 for discussion of some of the evidence for use of local labour forces and the exploitation of stone by individuals as opposed to the state), while others, such as the turquoise mines in the Sinai and the amethyst mines at Wadi el-Hudi, were almost certainly visited primarily by royal workmen (see discussion of settlement types in section 8.3 below). It is not clear precisely which raw materials were subject to royal monopoly (if any), but the awkward and expensive logistics of many quarrying and mining expeditions would in practice have made it very difficult for private individuals to undertake them without royal support.

The ability to send expeditions out to the remote mining areas in the deserts rested principally on kings' (or nomarchs') capacity to marshal together the necessary workforce. The numbers of workers sent on quarrying and mining expeditions were probably comparable with those sent on military campaigns. An inscription in the Wadi Hammamat quarries in the Eastern Desert describes the dispatching of an expedition comprising over 18,000 workers in the 38th year of the reign of Senusret I, apparently with the aim of bringing back sufficient *bḫn*-stone (siltstone/greywacke) for the carving of 60 sphinxes and 150 statues (although it should be noted that only two greywacke statues of Senusret I have so far been discovered - see Vandersleyen 1995: 66; Seyfried 1981: 248–53 for discussion of the year 38 inscriptions of Senusret I at the Wadi Hammamat). If we take the number of workers at face value, therefore, the scale of Senusret I's expedition was comparable with the 20,000 Egyptian troops who are said to have fought at the Battle of Qadesh in the reign of Ramesses II (see Spalinger 2005: 229-30 for a discussion of the likely size of the Egyptian army at Qadesh). The archaeological remains at quarry sites themselves often suggest that much smaller workforces were actually sent (see, for example, Bloxam and Storemyr 2002: 28–9).

There are few surviving indications, either textual or archaeological, of the extent to which the various expedition members were given training for their specific tasks (although see Bloxam 2003 for discussion of the likelihood that all quarrying expeditions included skilled specialised workmen). Many of the workers appear to have been simply press-ganged into quarrying by means of a corvée system operating in the various regions of Egypt and Nubia, just in the same way that workers were obtained for large-scale, state-organized agricultural, hydrological or architectural projects (see Eyre 1987). The more detailed descriptions of personnel carved on the walls of quarries often list the geographical origins of various groups of recruits, who would have made up the bulk of the workforce, engaged in such laborious non-skilled duties as digging and transportation (as well as related tasks such as the provision of military escorts in dangerous terrain). These manual labourers are often described as *ḥrtyw-nṯr* (stone-cutters), and stelae 106 and 117 in the Sinai mines each record the presence of 200 workers of this type (Gardiner *et al.* 1955: 17).

Each mining or quarrying expedition must also have included at least a small group of professionals (see Bloxam 2003 for discussion of the archaeological evidence for these), and we can occasionally catch glimpses of these in the inscriptions. It is possible that such men as *smntyw* ('prospectors' - see Yoyotte 1975 and Fischer 1985 for a discussion of the evidence for roles played by *smntyw* in the Old Kingdom) and *ỉkwyw* (possibly professional miners/quarries, see discussion of inscription UT3 in Appendix 4 below) might have been more permanent state employees. One prospector, a 'reckoner of gold' called Thuthotep, left a graffito in the vicinity of the Abrak well, in the Nubian Eastern Desert about 240 km southeast of Aswan (de Bruyn 1955). Gardiner *et al.* (1955: 17) note that the ratio of *ỉkwyw* to other workers is in a fairly consistent ratio, thus in Sinai stele 106 there are three *ỉkwyw* listed, as opposed to 200 general workers, and in Sinai stele 114 there are eight, compared with 80 workers, although, in contrast inscription UT3 mentions 1080 *ỉkwyw*.

Some of the most detailed descriptions of expeditions have survived in the form of inscriptions at the Wadi el-Hudi amethyst mines, the Wadi Hammamat *bḫn*-stone quarries, and the Sinai copper/turquoise/malachite mines (for the texts from Wadi el-Hudi see Sadek 1980; for Hammamat see Couyat and Montet 1912-13; for Sinai see Gardiner *et al.* 1955); these provide a good opportunity to study the composition of the mining workforces. Early Dynastic and early Old Kingdom quarry inscriptions tend to concentrate on the recitation of royal names and titles, but from the 6th Dynasty onwards the texts provide more of the names and titles of the actual leaders and members of the expedition. For most of the pharaonic period, the overall controller of the expedition usually held the title *sḏꜣwty nṯr* ('god's treasurer'), although the less specific rank of *ỉmy-r mšʿ* ('commander of the expedition/army') is also sometimes used. In one early 12th Dynasty stele of Hotepu at Wadi el-Hudi (text WH6), it is clear that the lower ranks were recruited mainly from local towns, some 1400 of them being supervised by about 100 officials from the north (Sadek 1980: 16-19). Similarly, the 11th Dynasty stele of Intef at Wadi el-Hudi (text WH4) describes the expedition members as 'thousand after thousand' of local Nubians (Sadek 1980: 10-14). Smaller numbers of workmen are recorded at the Serabit el-Khadim turquoise mines, where, according to the texts, the Middle Kingdom expeditions ranged from 168 to 734, usually accompanied by a similar number of donkeys, the average expedition comprising approximately 300 men and 400 animals (Gardiner *et al.* 1955: 14-20; Valbelle and Bonnet 1996: 32-3).

The names of about a tenth of the officials organizing quarrying and mining expeditions tend to recur over certain periods of time, and a considerable amount of analysis can be undertaken into the changing ranks of officialdom. During the late 12th Dynasty reign of Amenemhat III, for instance, most of the repetitions of names of high officials involved in expeditions to the Sinai take place with periods of less than ten years, and it is noticeable that the individuals have usually been promoted to some extent by the time their name reappears (see Murnane 1975).

Lower-ranking quarrying officials (e.g. doctors, foremen and workmen) not only seem to have been sent on a larger number of successive expeditions than their superiors but they were also less likely to be promoted, whereas higher officials, such as treasury representatives and scribes, were less likely to return, but more likely to have been promoted if they did so. This continuous process of change in personnel, especially in the higher ranking jobs, must have been due both to the unpopularity of the task and the fact that the king may have been deliberately preventing any officials from gaining control of quarries. The control over precious raw materials could be as powerful a tool for ambitious officials as it was for the king.

The Hatnub inscriptions and graffiti (see Appendices 2–6 below) contain many references to high officials and the common labourers and recruits, but most of the textual evidence relates to the expedition leaders and officials rather than to the actual workforce. Some texts present an impression of the basic numbers of quarry workers involved. Graffito 1 (dated to the time of Teti) describes the sending of 300 'men [of the best] who are in the palace' and 60 'men of the *smḫ*-ship', while the unprovenanced travertine stele UT3, thought to be from Hatnub and dating to the time of Senusret III, mentions 1,080 *ikwyw* ('quarry-men'), 360 'artists', and an unknown number of 'necropolis workers' (see Appendix 4 below, and Goedicke 1959). Hatnub Graffiti 4 and 5 (both from the time of Pepi II) refer to expeditions of 1,000 and 100 *rmṯ* ('people') respectively.

8.2 A typology of settlements and encampments associated with mining and quarrying

The three basic types of mining/quarrying accommodation at sites such as Hatnub are: rectangular walled settlements built of dry-stone or mud brick, and with varying degrees of fortification (e.g. Qasr el-Sagha and Wadi el-Hudi Site 9 - for Qasr el-Sagha see Sliwa 1992; for Wadi el-Hudi see Shaw and Jameson 1993), dense concentrations of dry-stone huts, often located on a high point and sometimes surrounded by an enclosure wall (e.g. Wadi Maghara, Wadi el-Hudi Site 5, Hatnub settlement immediately beside Quarry P), and, most frequently, wide scatters of rough stone shelters and wind-breaks (e.g. Hatnub, Umm el-Sawwan, Gebel el-Zeit).

Most sites, such as Wadi Maghara, Wadi el-Hudi and Hatnub (Shaw 1986; 1987), incorporate two or three of these different types of accommodation. At the Serabit el-Khadim turquoise mines there is dispersed settlement across the plateau as well as a walled concentration of dry-stone huts just to the east of the miners' temple (Valbelle and Bonnet 1996: 65–6). Not unexpectedly, some of the least significant ancient workers' settlements have been found at mineral sources close to existing substantial towns or villages, as in the case of Aswan (granite and sandstone), Gebel el-Silsila (sandstone) and Tura (limestone). At these sites only minimal accommodation was required, since the quarry-workers were close to permanent settlements.

The Old and Middle Kingdom structures at Hatnub are usually sprawling multi-roomed huts evidently housing organized gangs of workmen. The dry-stone construction in these buildings is of a fairly high standard, using closely packed pebbles and medium-sized stones. The overall settlement pattern in the Old and Middle Kingdoms is open to a number of interpretations: the widely dispersed structures and the apparent lack of communal protective measures at Hatnub suggests a low level of concern regarding attacks from the desert, as well as relatively low-key organization and administrative hierarchy, particularly in comparison with the Old Kingdom hilltop settlement at Wadi Maghara and the Middle Kingdom settlements at Wadi el-Hudi and Qasr el-Sagha (discussed below).

The alabaster-gypsum quarries of Umm el-Sawwan, at the northern edge of the Faiyum region and about 35 km southwest of Cairo, date primarily to the Old Kingdom (*c.*2575–2134 BC); in 1928 they were surveyed and excavated by Caton-Thompson and Gardner (1934). The workers were accommodated in a large sprawling settlement of at least 250 small stone-built structures similar to those at Hatnub. Caton-Thompson also found considerable evidence for the local production of flint tools for quarrying and vessel-making. Some of the gypsum appears to have been carved into small funerary items for private tombs, but it also seems that considerable quantities were ground into mortar for large-scale state-sponsored building purposes.

The Gebel el-Zeit galena mines, located on the Gulf of Suez coast about 50 km to the south of Ras Gharib, date from the Middle Kingdom to the Ramessid period, i.e. most of the 2nd millennium BC (Castel and Soukiassian 1989). The settlement pattern, again essentially dispersed, shows two main regions of ancient activity. Site 1 is a network of more than thirty gallery-mines and associated dry-stone encampments spread over the northwestern slope of Wadi Kabrit: at the centre is a small sanctuary, evidently dating from the Middle Kingdom to the 19th Dynasty (*c.*2040–1200 BC). Site 2, covering a larger area in the southern part of Wadi Kabrit, consists of hundreds of mine-shafts, as well as numerous dry-stone shelters and votive structures.

There are no surviving large-scale commemorative inscriptions and carvings at Gebel el-Zeit, but survey and excavations in the 1980s revealed a cache of votive objects in the sanctuary at Site 1, including small stone and faience portable stelae (Castel and Soukiassian 1985). Some stelae bear depictions of kings making offerings to 'Horus master of the deserts' and 'Hathor mistress of galena', suggesting a degree of official involvement in the galena mining. One stele was left by Minemhat, a 17th Dynasty governor of the province of Coptos, traditionally the nerve-centre for quarrying and mining in the Eastern Desert. Gebel el-Zeit would have been the northernmost outpost for expeditions sponsored by 17th Dynasty kings (*c.*1674–1567 BC), whose power-base was at Thebes.

Castel and Soukiassian (1985: 293) suggest that the lack of large rock-carved memorials at Gebel el-Zeit may partly result from the quality of the local rocks, which are too poor for such grandiose gestures. They note that the modest scale of the mines and encampments combine with the small stelae to suggest the sending of repeated small-scale expeditions to Gebel el-Zeit, as opposed to the more impressive – but also more sporadic – royal expeditions sent for travertine or turquoise. The acquisition of galena may have lain somewhere between that of gypsum and travertine in the degree of government involvement, the constancy of demand, and the prestige associated with its procurement.

8.3 Planned and fortified quarrying settlements: organizational and defensive factors

Expeditions to sites such as Wadi Maghara and Wadi el-Hudi, at the very edges of Egypt proper, were necessarily tightly organized, small-scale and military operations, without the mass of unskilled workers whose rough stone shelters dot the landscapes of Hatnub, Wadi Gerrawi or Umm el-Sawwan. Commemorative texts list smaller numbers of workers on the expeditions to Sinai and Wadi el-Hudi than in the Wadi Hammamat or Hatnub (Sadek 1980: 104), where major expeditions and heavy, awkward loads to the two latter sites would have required large numbers of unskilled corvée-labourers.

Figure 8.1. View of part of the fortified Old Kingdom settlement at Wadi Maghara.

The Sinai Peninsula was the major Egyptian source of turquoise and copper throughout the pharaonic period. The mines at Wadi Maghara, 225 km southeast of Cairo, were particularly exploited during the Old and Middle Kingdoms. Petrie, examining the site in 1904–5, found a hill-top miners' settlement, primarily used during the Old Kingdom and consisting of about 125 stone-built structures (Petrie and Currelly 1906; Chartier-Raymond 1988; see fig. 8.1). There were also two unfortified groups of slightly larger and more regular Old Kingdom structures – one next to the remains of an enigmatic wall or dam built across the northern end of the wadi and the other built on a shoal at the southwestern end of the wadi (largely destroyed by flash-floods and modern quarrying activity). Petrie's excavations at Wadi Maghara revealed numerous artefacts, including evidence of copper-smelting *in situ*. The three components of the site – hilltop settlement, wadi-floor settlement, wall/dam – reflect the isolation and vulnerability of the miners, housed in a tightly clustered, defensive main settlement combined with unprotected accommodation in reasonable proximity to the mines themselves.

In the Old Kingdom and early Middle Kingdom, the region to the south of the first Nile cataract at Aswan represented the hostile southern frontier of Egypt proper. Exploitation of the amethyst mines at Wadi el-Hudi, about 35 km southeast of Aswan, appears to have peaked in the Middle Kingdom, a period of many inscriptions and graffiti at the site (Fakhry 1952; Sadek 1980; Shaw and Jameson 1993; Klemm *et al.* 2002). Three distinct areas of Wadi el-Hudi were in use during the Middle Kingdom: a low hill adjoining an amethyst quarry and surmounted by the remains of a rough stone fortified enclosure, containing about forty dry-stone workmen's shelters; another hill, about 200 m southeast of the first, with a large number of Middle Kingdom texts and drawings carved into the rocks at its summit; a rectangular dry-stone fortified settlement (70 × 50 m), a further 400 m to the south and associated with two amethyst quarries (see figs 8.2 and 8.3).

Texts and ceramics at Wadi el-Hudi suggest two successive major phases of amethyst exploitation, dating to the 11th and to the 12th–13th Dynasties. The 11th Dynasty hilltop settlement at

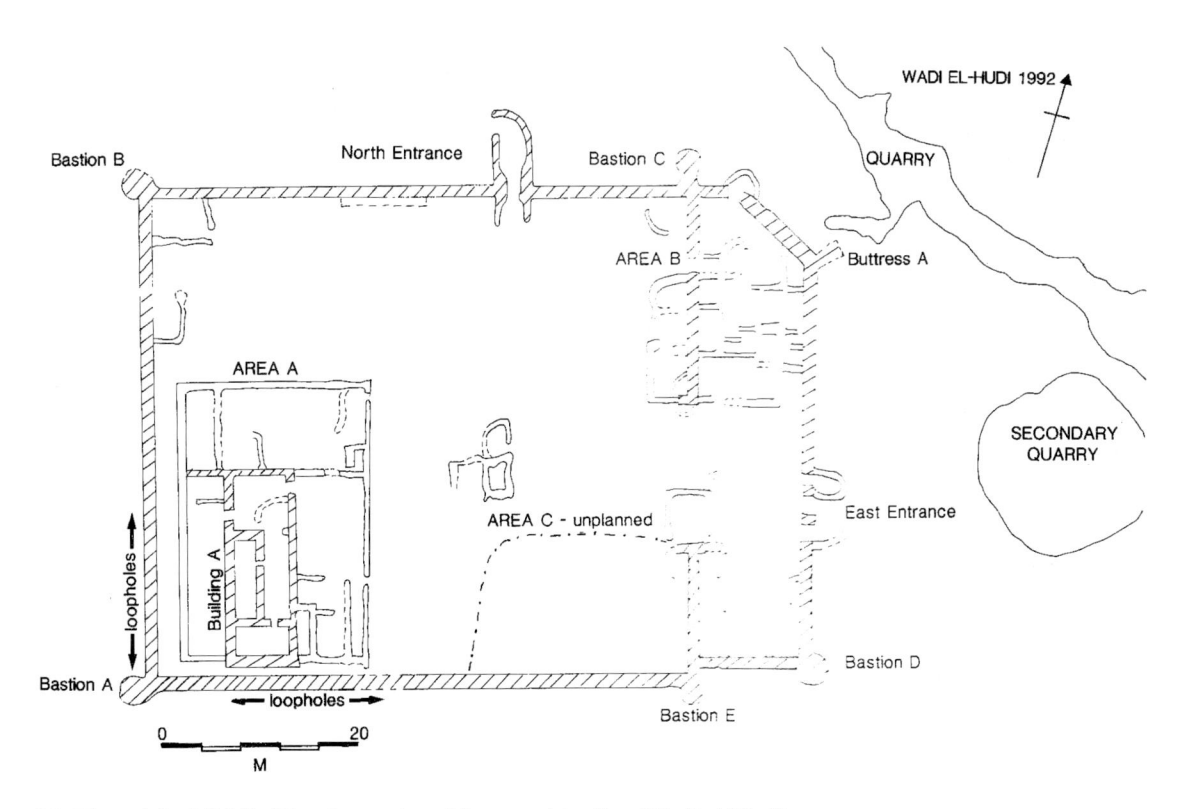

Figure 8.2. Plan of the Middle Kingdom miners' fortress (site 9) at Wadi el-Hudi.

Figure 8.3. Part of the dry-stone wall surrounding the fortress (site 9) at Wadi el-Hudi.

Wadi el-Hudi (site 5) is clearly comparable with the Old Kingdom settlement at Wadi Maghara: both are densely concentrated and crudely fortified versions of the more dispersed dry-stone encampments at Hatnub and Umm el-Sawwan, adaptations of the conventional quarrying or mining settlement to more dangerous circumstances. The 12th Dynasty fortified settlement at Wadi el-Hudi (site 9) – a small dry-stone version of the archetypal Nubian fortress – is more than a local adaptation: it is an expression of new Egyptian attitudes both to quarrying expeditions and to Nubia.

Lower Nubia had effectively become a colonized province of Egypt after the reign of Senusret I (*c*.1971–1926 BC). The area between the first and fourth cataracts was controlled by 12th Dynasty fortresses and watchtowers, some as much depots as garrisons, concerned with military control over the Nubians and with trading and mining expeditions into the Middle Nile and surrounding deserts. The 12th Dynasty amethyst mining settlement appears to have been affected by this new military style of organization and bureaucracy that characterises most Egyptian activities during the period. Quarry-workers were housed like colonists in a quasi-permanent settlement and amethysts were procured in a more military context.

This distinctive 12th Dynasty approach to mineral exploitation was not restricted to Nubia: there is another rectangular, planned quarrying settlement (measuring about 115 × 80 m) at Qasr el-Sagha, 75 km southwest of Cairo at the northern end of the Faiyum basin. This village and its adjacent cemetery were linked by an ancient paved road with the basalt (dolerite) quarries of Widan el-Faras quarries, about 10 km to the north (Arnold and Arnold 1979; Sliwa 1992). There are two other zones of pharaonic remains at Qasr el-Sagha: to the north, a small stone temple (10 × 5 m), assigned to the Middle Kingdom on the basis of its architectural style, and to the northeast a second, more amorphous area of mud-brick settlement (about 140 × 100 m). Both of the settlements are dated to the 12th Dynasty by their ceramics. Like the roughly contemporary pyramid-town of Kahun, the rectangular village clearly housed a specialised community under direct state control. However, it is by no means clear whether the Qasr el-Sagha settlement was directly associated with the basalt quarrying operations.

Although Qasr el-Sagha is only 25 km from the Umm el-Sawwan gypsum quarries, the differences between the two sets of settlement remains are striking. Umm el-Sawwan dates mostly to the Old Kingdom and Qasr el-Sagha to the Middle Kingdom, but there is also a significant difference in terms of the two materials and the needs they served. Good quality basalt – heavy, bulky and used for building and sculptural projects – was held in such high esteem by the Egyptian elite that a paved road and planned village appear to have been constructed to facilitate its procurement on a fairly ambitious scale. Gypsum, on the other hand, could be exploited in smaller quantities by individuals and without the full backing of the state. Neither Qasr el-Sagha/Widan el-Faras nor Umm el-Sawwan are marked by the stelae and graffiti that characterize Hatnub or Wadi Hammamat, but then the two former are in less isolated areas.

The quarrying and mining sites described above, less elaborate than longer-lived pharaonic sites in the Nile valley, such as Abydos or Thebes, nevertheless constitute valuable information on the fundamentals influencing Egyptian settlements. Their archaeological remains also incorporate such features as wells and dams (Dreyer and Jaritz 1983), evidence for religious activity, and the use of a variety of tools (reflecting the level of technology, the nature of the material extracted and the availability of local materials from which different tools could be made). The settlement patterns demonstrate that the essential characteristics of each site result from the interaction of technology, economics, environment and topography. Prominent aspects of these factors are:

1) the nature (and necessary quantities) of the material procured

2) the degree to which the material was processed *in situ*

3) the distance from sources of food and water

4) the perceived need for a relatively constant supply of the material being mined/quarried

5) the risk of attack

6) the stability and character of the Egyptian socio-economic system at different periods and in different areas

7) the composition of the workforce, i.e. the proportions of skilled and unskilled, local and professional workers

8) the primary destination of the material and its range of intended uses

The permanent settlement sites so far identified in the Nile valley comprise such specialised and elaborate types as temple-towns, provincial capitals, workmen's villages and agricultural communities. Survey and excavation at these major sites (e.g. von Pilgrim 1996; Ziermann 2003; Kemp 1989: 137–80; Lehner and Wetterstrom 2006) indicate the rich variations not only between different settlement types but also between different sections and suburbs of individual towns and cities. In the same way, the subtle differences between the comparatively rudimentary and ephemeral accommodation associated with quarrying and mining sites express the Egyptians' ability to adapt their settlement strategies to changing contexts and circumstances. Like the string of functionally and topographically variable Middle Kingdom fortresses and garrisons in Nubia, they suggest a high degree of flexibility and spontaneity in Egyptian civilization.

8.4 Hatnub in the context of other quarrying and mining settlements

The Hatnub Old and Middle Kingdom settlement is much more comparable with the Umm el-Sawwan alabaster-gypsum quarries in the northern Faiyum and the Gebel el-Asr gneiss quarries in the Western Desert, 80 km from Tushka. It also resembles the dispersed encampment surrounding the travertine quarries at Wadi Gerrawi, near Cairo, estimated to have accommodated about 200 workers (see section 2.4 above, and see also Petrie and Mackay 1915: 38–40). Mining and quarrying sites in Egypt proper may not generally have been considered to be under threat, whereas expeditions to locations such as Wadi Maghara and Wadi el-Hudi, at the northern and southern frontiers of Egypt, were regarded – in the Old and Middle Kingdoms at least – as forays into relatively hostile territory.

The New Kingdom encampment at Hatnub is a set of temporary, mainly one-room shelters hastily and loosely assembled from large limestone slabs and boulders. The difference between the earlier and later settlements echoes the evidence of the inscriptions; the state-sponsored Old and Middle Kingdom expeditions were housed in dispersed communal structures, whereas the New Kingdom settlement bears the hallmarks of a small group of individuals without much bureaucratic or organizational backing from the local or national government. It is therefore not surprising that the quarry walls bear almost no written commemoration of the New Kingdom phase of exploitation (Shaw 1986: 201–3).

Appendix 1

Chronology of the Site

The combination of textual and archaeological evidence (particularly the pottery) from Hatnub allows a rough chronology of the various parts of the site to be compiled. The earliest surviving texts anywhere at Hatnub are Inscriptions I and II, the former consisting of the Horus and *nsw-bỉt* (throne) names of the 4th Dynasty ruler, Khufu (*c*.2589–2566 BC), and the latter comprising a damaged version of Khufu's Horus name and a fuller writing of his throne name (*ḫnmw-ḫw.f*). There also appears to be no pottery from the site significantly earlier than the 4th Dynasty, judging from the results given in Chapter 5 above. The texts alone suggest that Quarry P was exploited in the 4th and 6th Dynasties, with no less than three inscriptions from the time of Teti (*c*.2345–2323 BC), and one inscription and perhaps as many as six graffiti from the reign of Pepi II (*c*.2278–2184 BC). However, it should be borne in mind that travertine was already being used for funerary vessels in the Predynastic period (Lucas 1962: 421, 427), and by the 1st Dynasty (*c*.3000–2890 BC) had begun to be used for architectural elements in royal tombs. It is not yet clear which travertine quarries were exploited in the late 4th and early 3rd millennia BC, but the possibility at least exists that Hatnub was already being exploited in the late Predynastic (although if this were the case some pottery might be expected to have survived from this phase of use). It may be noted, however, that the anorthosite gneiss quarries at Gebel el-Asr were undoubtedly exploited from the Neolithic period onwards, yet the recent work at the site has not yet revealed any pottery earlier than the Early Dynastic period (see Shaw *et al.* in press). This is particularly revealing in the case of Gebel el-Asr since this is the only known Egyptian source of anorthosite gneiss

One of the principal factors that emerges from the archaeological study of the Quarry P region is the new evidence for a reasonably substantial New Kingdom phase of quarrying activity. There was previously only a tenuous textual indication of New Kingdom travertine quarrying at Hatnub, in the form of Inscription XIV at Quarry P (Anthes 1928: 17, tf. 8), comprising the name and title: 'Ani, chief of the sculptors of the two lands', which can be dated palaeographically and prosopographically to the New Kingdom. However, the discovery of an encampment of 18th Dynasty quarry-workers suggests that the textual record at the quarry has led to an under-estimation of the New Kingdom phase of work.

Given the archaeological record, it is possible to revisit the textual evidence for New Kingdom links with the Hatnub quarries, which in fact turn out to be somewhat richer than usually assumed. A further piece of textual evidence for New Kingdom activity at Hatnub is a stone heart-scarab (Museo Egizio, Turin: 5993) of apparently unknown provenance but clearly dating to the Amarna period (see Wiedemann 1895: 155–6). Its inscription incorporates an Amarna-style *ḥtp dỉ nsw p3 ỉtn ʿnḫ* formula, as well as the name and titles of its owner: 'Apy, chief of works (*ḥry* k3wty) at Hatnub'. Apy is a fairly common name during the Amarna period, accounting for six of the entries in the *Répertoire onomastique amarnien* (Hari 1976), and it is faintly possible that the Apy mentioned on the Turin scarab might be the same as the Apy who is owner of rock-tomb 10 at Amarna (Davies 1903–8, IV: 19–20, pl. 30), although there is no mention of Hatnub in the latter's titles. Urbain Bouriant, who copied the scenes and texts in tomb 10 in 1893–4, comments:

> La reste du tombeau n'est pas terminée, ce qui laisse à croire qu'Apii [sic] ne fut pas entrer en cet endroit. D'autre part, le nom d'Apii n'était point rare à cette époque. C'est pourquoi j'hésite à identifier le propriétaire du tombeau avec l'Apii, chef des ouvriers des carriers d'albâtre de Hatnub...dont le scarabée existe à Turin
> (Bouriant et al. 1903: 92).

A third, and somewhat more tenuous, piece of textual evidence concerning New Kingdom exploitation of Hatnub can be found in line 28 of the great Speos Artemidos inscription of Hatshepsut, in which the queen claims 'I have built his great temple in white stone of Ain, its gates in travertine of Hatnub (*šs n ḥwt-nbw*)' (Gardiner 1946: 47). With reference to the Speos Artemidos text, Harris (1961: 77) argues that 'the phrase *n ḥwt-nbw* must at this period (i.e. the New Kingdom) be a designation of quality rather than provenance', but the combined archaeological and textual evidence now suggest that this phrase may indeed be a reference to the specific geographical source of the stone, especially given the fact that Speos Artemidos is located near Beni Hasan, only about 55 km to the northwest of Hatnub.

There are a few pieces of archaeological and epigraphic evidence to suggest that a small amount of travertine quarrying may have taken place at Hatnub after the New Kingdom. Archaeologically, Late Period sherds have been found immediately to the north of Quarry Ra (see section 4.1 above), one Roman amphora was found in the vicinity of Quarry P (in hut A35), and a single Coptic sherd was found in structure NN38. Epigraphically, Quarry T contained rock-cut images that may date to the Roman period. The paucity of post-New Kingdom evidence suggests that the Amarna period or early Ramesside period may represent the point at which Hatnub ceased to be exploited as a significant source of travertine.

Appendix 2

The Inscriptions

The translations of texts from Hatnub in appendices 2–6 are only intended to serve as a context for the archaeological information in this monograph. I have made no attempt here to provide any genuinely new edition or commentary on the inscriptions and graffiti from the Hatnub quarries (although such a project is long overdue), and I am therefore almost entirely indebted to the facsimiles, transliterations and translations of Blackden, Fraser, Griffith, Möller, Anthes and Eichler. These translations, will at least provide anglophones with a full rendition of the Hatnub texts for the first time, including not only the 15 inscriptions and 56 graffiti recorded in situ at the site itself, but also 3 unprovenanced graffiti in private collections and 3 fragments of graffiti in the Berlin Museum.

I. *Khufu: Horus name and throne name* (Anthes 1928: 13, tf. 4).

From right to left, this inscription consists of the abbreviated throne (*nsw-bit*) name of Khufu (i.e. only *ḫwfw*), followed by his Horus name (*mḏdw*). Beyond this is a raised relief of a seated, right-facing figure of the king wearing the red crown, holding a long staff in his left hand and a mace in his right (the rest of the inscription is carved in sunk relief). The king is seated on a simple stool with no backrest, and a hawk (presumably Horus) hovers above his head holding an ankh-sign, with the word *bḥdt* carved in front of it. The inscription to the left of the king's figure, comprising two vertical columns, reads *sꜣ ḥꜣ ꜥnḫ ḏd wꜣs ꜣwt-ib ḏt*…. To the right of the inscription is an offering table. Some traces of paint have survived on the hieroglyphs.

I

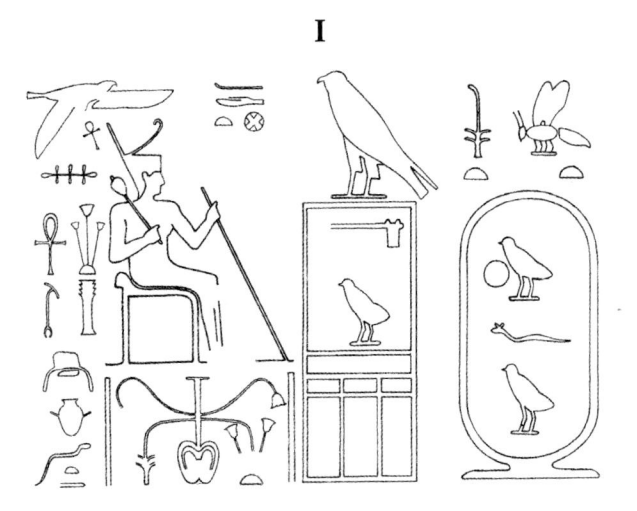

II.   Khufu: Horus name and throne name (Anthes 1928: 13, tf. 4).

This inscription, from right to left, simply consists of the Horus name of Khufu in a serekh (presumably *mḏdw*, but it has been entirely erased) and the full throne (*nsw-bit*) name of Khufu (i.e. ḫnmw ḫw.f).

III.   Pepi I: Horus name and throne name, and several lines of text (Anthes 1928: 13, tf. 4; Sethe 1933a: 95, 14–15; Hornung 1991: 169).

The inscription has now been almost entirely destroyed, although fortunately either Anthes or Blackden and Fraser made a cast of the upper edge. This fragment is supplemented by Blackden and Fraser's copy (numbered XV.1 in their sequence). Sethe 1933a (Urkunden I) supplements and improves the reading of the text in the last line.

> *(1) Horus mry-t3wy, (2) he of the sedge and the bee mry-rc. (3) given life forever… (4) Year 25, 1st month of the season of akhet, day… first occurrence of the heb-sed festival. [Royal commission that] (5) the sole companion, chief [of the six courts of justice], …, (6) first under the king, master of se[cret things] …, controller of the two thrones, governor of the palace, real governor of the south, great lord of the Hare nome, Khuu's son, Khnumenankhses.*

IV.   Pepi I: Horus name and earlier throne name (Anthes 1928: 13, tf. 4).

Sturdy but damaged inscription. Apart from the king's name (*nfr-s3-ḥr*) and the text beneath (*ḫnty-?*), the cast shows traces of characters 7 cm left of the name and further out. They seem to be ordered in horizontal lines, thus almost forming the heading of a long text.

V.   Pepi I: Horus name and later throne name (Anthes 1928: 14, tf. 5).

Inscription comprising the Horus name (*mry-t3wy*) and later throne (*nsw-bit*) name of Pepi I (*mry-rc*). Below the Horus name is the phrase ꜥnḫ ḏt and below the throne name is di ꜥnḫ nb ḏt.

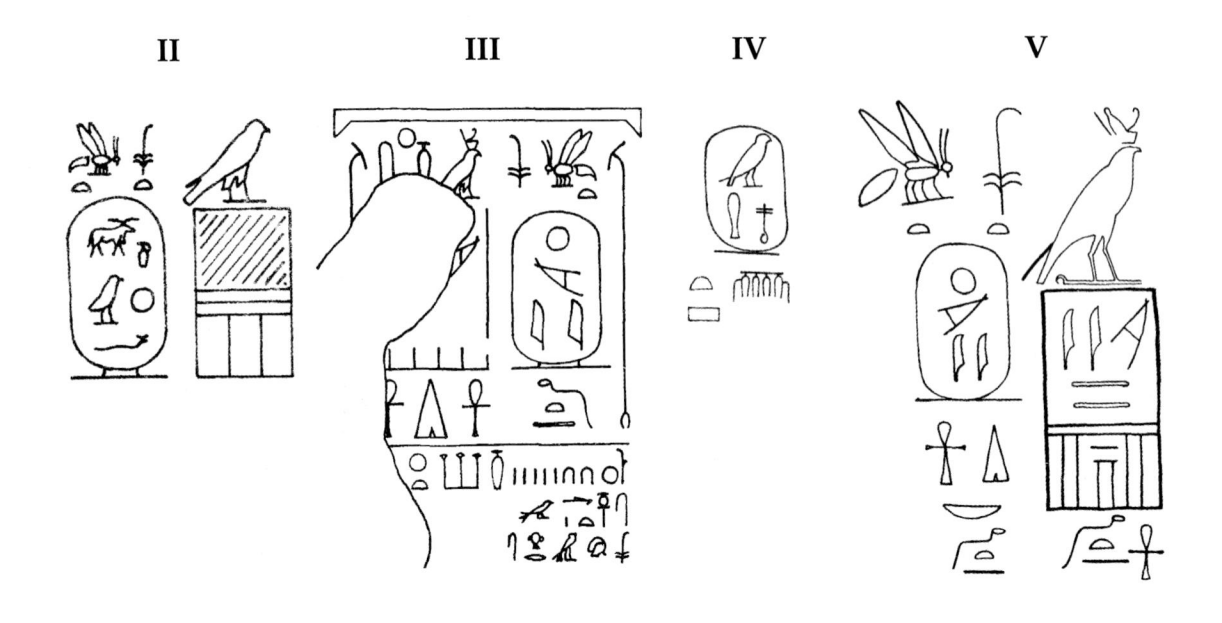

VI. *Merenra: Horus name and throne name* (Anthes 1928: 14, tf. 5; Sethe 1933a: 256, 14–17; Simpson 1977: 1043).

This is a more complete version of Inscription I, but this time for Merenra rather than Khufu. From right to left, this inscription consists of the throne (*nsw-bit*) name of Merenra (*mr-n-rꜥ*), followed by his Horus name (*ꜥnḫ-ḫꜥw*). Beyond this is a raised-relief, seated, right-facing figure of the king wearing the red crown, holding a long staff in his left hand and a mace in his right (the rest of the inscription is carved in sunk relief). He is seated on a simple stool with no backrest and a hawk (presumably Horus) hovers above his head holding an ankh-sign, with the text *bḥdt nṯr nfr nb tꜣwy* carved in front of it. To the left of the king's figure the inscription, in two vertical columns, reads *sꜣ ꜥnḫ hꜣ nb.f mi rꜥ ḏt*. The text below reads *'year after the 5…'*

Anthes' drawing was produced after a sketch made by Möller, who was unable to make a cast. It is this inscription that may perhaps refer to the expedition led by Weni, described in his Abydos funerary inscription (see section 7.2 above).

VII. *Pepi II: Horus name and throne name twice (Anthes 1928: 14, tf. 5).*

This inscription simply consists of the Horus name of Pepi II in a serekh in the centre (*nṯr-ḫꜥw*) and the throne (*nsw-bit*) name of the same king (*nfr-kꜣ-rꜥ*) written twice, facing inwards towards the Horus name on either side. On the right-hand side the *kꜣ* sign is illegible, and on the left-hand side *nfr-kꜣ* is illegible. The copy was made after Möller's sketch; Blackden and Fraser suggest that the Horus name includes the *nṯr*-sign in mirror-writing.

VIII. *Horus name and probable throne name of an unidentified Old Kingdom ruler* (Anthes 1928: 14, tf. 5).

The only legible signs in the serekh are two *i* signs and the only legible sign in the cartouche to its right is a *mr* sign. The only portion of text visible in a horizontal line below the two king's name consists of *ꜥnḫ di ꜥnḫ*. Möller rejected a reading of Pepi I for the Horus name and cartouche, but Anthes points out that no other Old Kingdom ruler's name seems to fit here either.

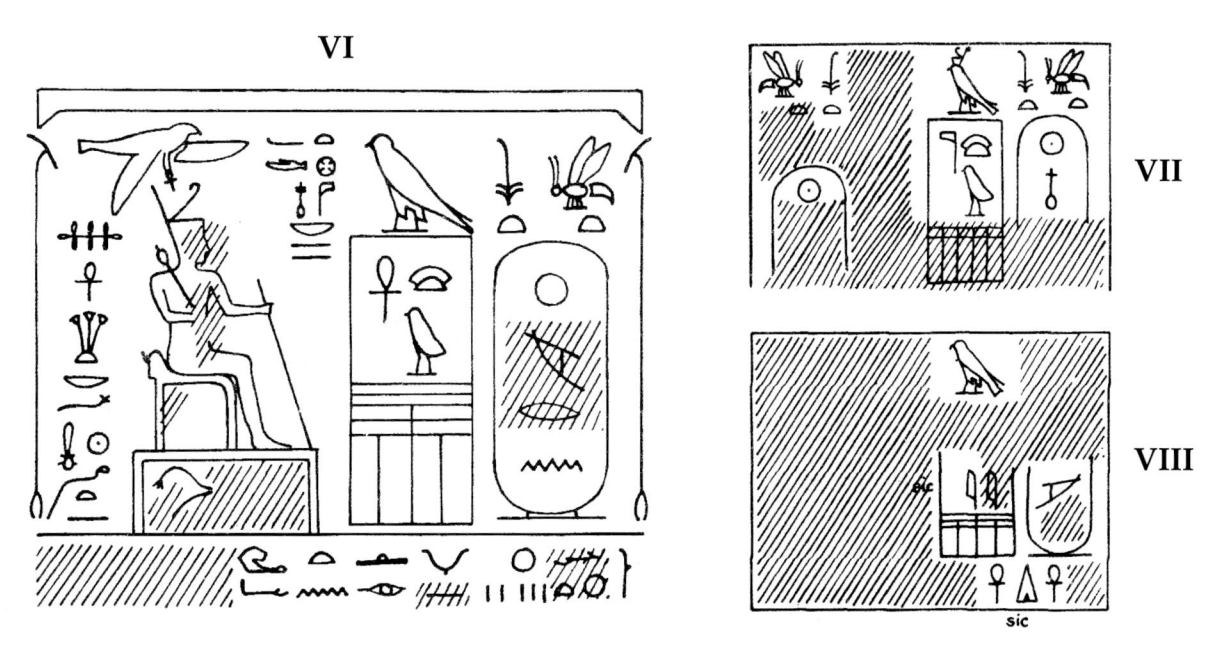

IX. *Seated figure of the nomarch Thutnakht II, son of Thutnakht I, his name and titles, and throne name of an unidentified ruler* (Anthes 1928: 14, tf. 7).

Part of a ruler's name (*mrỉ…*). The head of the ideogram representing a deity in the king's name is not clear enough to help in fully identifying the royal name. The rest of the text refers to the nomarch Thutnakht II, son of Thutnakht I.

(1) He of the sedge and bee, Mery… (2) prince, controller of the two thrones, overseer of priests, royal overseer of…. (3) great overlord of the Hare nome (4) Thutnakht, son of Thutnakht.

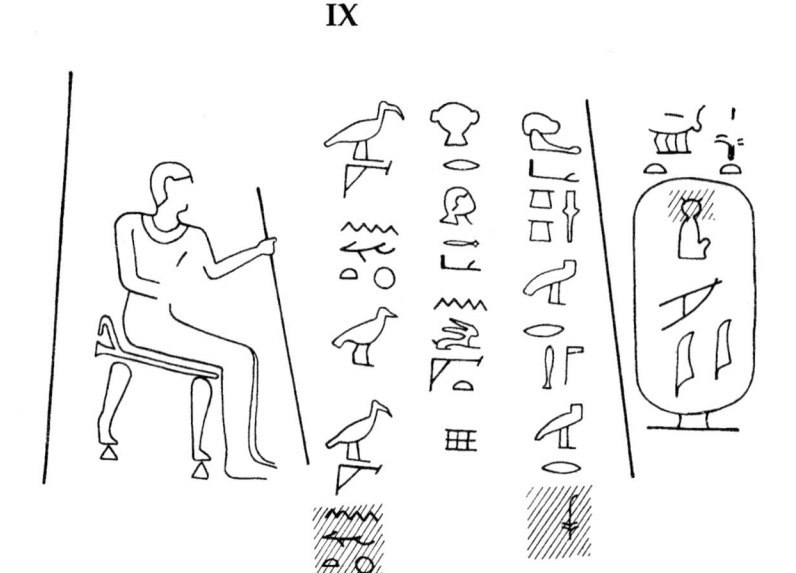

IX

Xa. *Inscription of the nomarch Thutnakht III, son of Khuu* (Anthes 1928: 14–16, tf. 6).

Möller argued that inscriptions Xa and Xb should be taken together, thus allowing Xa to be dated with reference to the 10th Dynasty ruler Khety mentioned in Xb. The writing styles of Xa and Xb are so similar that they appear to have both been written by the same scribe. It is difficult to deduce the original physical locations of Möller's casts of the two inscriptions, although Blackden and Fraser (1892: XV.1) place Xa to the right of Xb, as shown below.

The provincial governor, controller of the two thrones, overseer of the god's servants, chief of Upper Egypt, great overlord of the Hare nome, son of Khuu, Thutnakht (life, health, prosperity) says…

Xb. *Khety, 10th Dynasty: throne name* (Anthes 1928: 14–16, tf. 6).

(1) He of the sedge and the bee, Khety… (2) Meketdjehuty (3) who lives in all eternity, (4) the overseer of the estate of Wepwti (?). (5) I was beloved of my lord, one who was praised in his whole city. (6) I was one who … leads a mḫw, who stretches out his hand to his troops. I have (7) led everyone back to his place, free (8) of mishandling of the townsmen. I have … (9) in every command, and I encountered no difficulties (10) thereby. I was a man of good character, free (11) of …, beloved of all people, (12) with a happy heart, free of sadness (?), (13) one who had no bad characteristics.

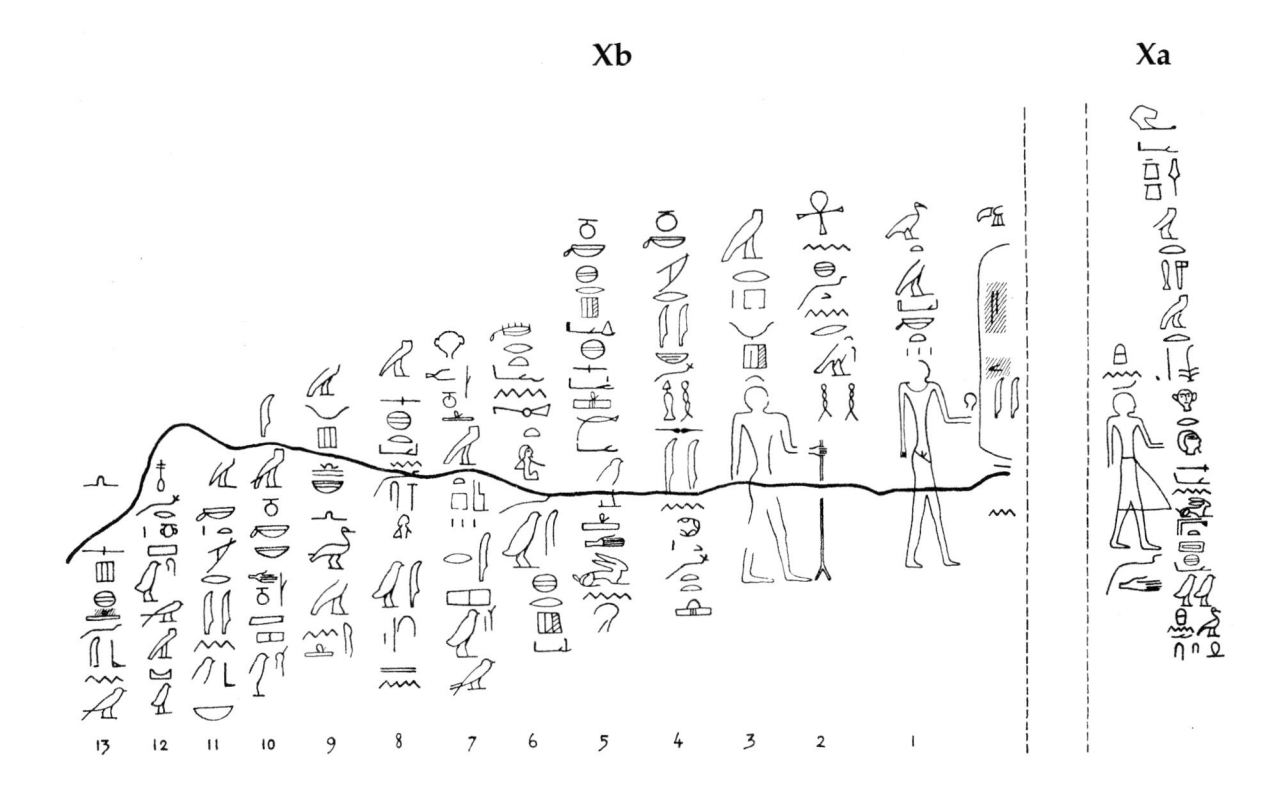

XI. Six casts of engraved hieratic texts, as well as human figures without any identifying text: *α* annotated seated figure of a man, in which two names are legible: Thuthotep and Sobekhotep, son of Khnemui; *β* annotated figure similar to that in *α*. but only the phrase 'son of Khnemui' is legible; *γ–ε* are not separately distinguished (Anthes 1928: 16–17, tf. 7).

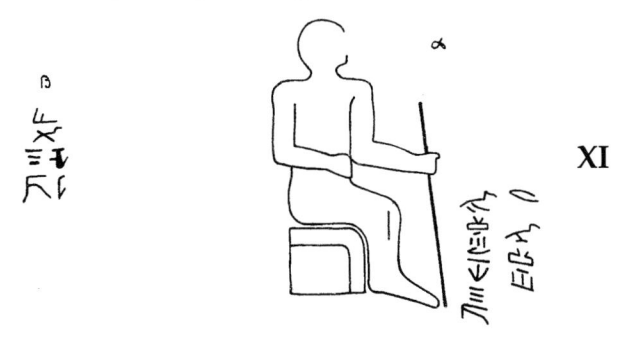

XII Eight small inscriptions and pictures over the entrance to Quarry R. These are, from left to right: *α* dog; *β* falcon; *γ* the name Teti; *δ* destroyed; *ε* the name Teti; *ζ* king's head with cap; *η* Upper Egyptian crown; *θ* the name Teti, with a figure of a standing man in front of it, with bow and very damaged signs over him and in front of him, of which Blackden and Fraser (1892) write 'a very weathered inscription from which I made out that it was cut by a superintendent of the transport'. Möller had not been able to read either the title or anything else (Anthes 1928: 17, tf. 8).

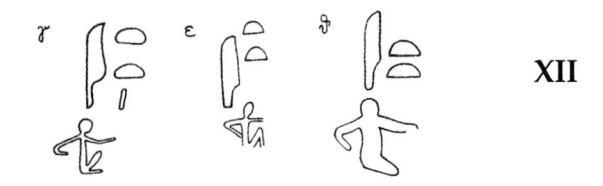

XIII   **Senusret III ($ḫʿ-k3w-rʿ$). Stele of a chief of workmen called Saimeni (Anthes 1928: 17, tf. 8).**

Chief of the workmen of the desert Saimeni.

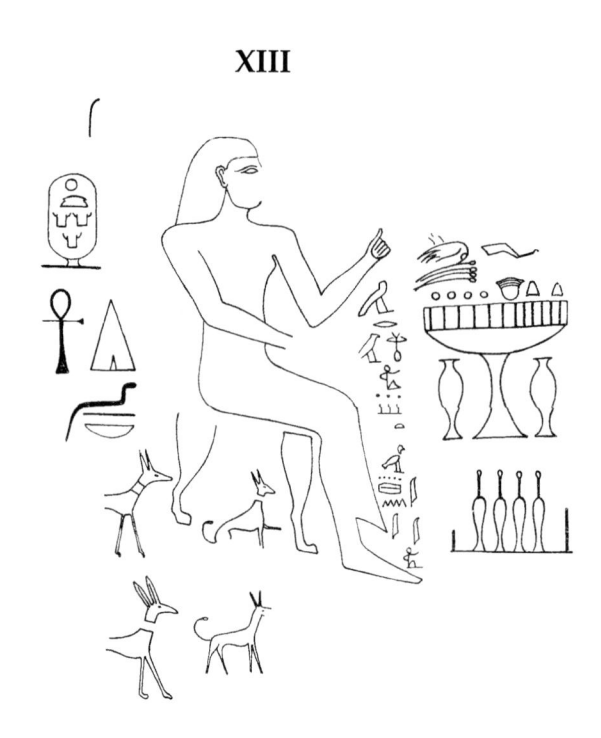

XIII

XIV   **New Kingdom inscription?** Anthes (1928: 17, tf. 8) considers this to be of New Kingdom date on palaeographic grounds (i.e. the use of an unusual sign in place of the $m3ʿ$ $ḫrw$, 'true of voice', phrase), as well as on the basis of the use of the title $ḥry-sʿnḫw$.

Chief of the sculptors ($ḥry-sʿnḫw$) of the lord of the two lands, Ani.

XIV

XV   **Neferefra ($nfr-ḫʿw$)** (Anthes 1928: 18, tf. 2). Only the sequence of titles is discernible in this inscription. It was found not at Hatnub itself but in tomb Dc on the northwestern side of Wadi Nakhla at the Deir el-Bersha necropolis (Griffith and Newberry 1894: 57).

Command of the king to the provincial governor, controller of the two thrones, Iaib.

Appendix 3

The Graffiti

1. Graffito comprising twelve columns and one horizontal line of text, with no accompanying painted images, dating to the reign of Teti (Anthes 1928: 18–19, tf. 9–9a). Anthes suggests that the apparent speed of this expedition (suggested by the use of the phrase 'at once') might have been because of the transportation of the stone along the main quarry road. He also suggests that the reference to 'living domesticated animals' might indicate that fattened animals were taken with the expedition to be slaughtered and consumed at the quarries. The text reads:

> *(1) Year 6 of* sḥtp-t3wy, *3rd month of the shemu season, day…; (2) the overseer of the [army?]* 3ḫt… n *and the … of the ship of* mrw. *(3) We have accomplished this work for he of the sedge and the bee Teti, given life forever, (4) with 300 men … who are in the Residence, (5) while 60 men thereof produced the* smỉ-*boats (6) in* wnw… *(7) enclosed … in the … houses … (8) living domestic animals, which were … (9) so that they might eat them [i.e. eat the animals] … (10) all at once (?) … (11) since the power of Teti is so magnificent.*

1a. Small hieroglyphic graffito situated between two others dated to the reign of Teti, therefore probably itself to be assigned to the same reign (Anthes 1928: 19, tf. 9–9a). The text consists only of a pair of names and titles: 'Temple scribe Isesi' and 'Scribe Ser'.

2. Graffito comprising, on the right hand side, the Horus name (sḥtp-t3wy) and throne name (s3 rʿ ttỉ) of Teti, and, to the left, (from top to bottom) 10 vertical columns of hieratic, one horizontal line of text, 14 vertical columns, and three horizontal lines of hieratic (Anthes 1928: 19, tf. 9). There are no accompanying painted images. The text reads:

> *(1) Horus,* sḥtp-t3wy, *may he live for ever, he of the sedge and the bee, son of Ra, Teti, given life.'*
> *(2–26) [List of 25 personal names, presumably members of the expedition]. (27) We have done this work for he of the sedge and the bee, Teti, given life.*

3. Graffito comprising the Horus name of Pepi II and a date, on the right-hand side, and two horizontal lines and nine columns of hieratic on the left, with no accompanying painted images (Anthes 1928: 20, tf. 10-10a). The text reads:

> *(1) Year 14 of* nṯr-ḫw *(Horus name of Pepi II), 1st month of the season of akhet, day 23; (2) the god's seal-bearer/treasurer … (3)* ỉw, *he says: 'I have come to Hatnub to quarry four offering tables of travertine (*bỉt*) and afterwards I built (4) two* wsḫt-*boats in the Ra-kheny (unknown place name) and together with the troop of boat's deputy commanders who were (5) with me: (6) Der-khesef, (7) Sri, (8) Imakhy, (9) the ship man Nehesy, (10) Der-khesef, (11) Wenut, (12) and twenty elders.'*

4. Graffito comprising five columns of hieratic text, with no accompanying painted images (Anthes 1928: 20–1, tf. 10–10a). This graffito, rather than being the usual record of an expedition, has been interpreted as a rock-inscribed draft of a letter sent back to the quarry-workers' headquarters asking for urgent help. Goedicke (1965: 33) suggests that 'apparently the breaking of the stone for whatever project had been commissioned was finished, and the man in charge expected the professionals to come to complete the project'. Two other points of interest in this graffito are firstly that the same official, Der-khesef is also mentioned in Gr.3, dating to the 14th annual census of Pepi II, and secondly that the phrase '80 people' (rmṯ ḫmn) could also be translated as 'stone finishers', according to Goedicke (1965: 32–3). The text reads:

> (1) The inspector of boats Der-khesef son of Neferkha, he says: (2) 'I have travelled down…1000 men behind me… (3) after these 80 people have come downstream [northwards], they shall come (out here) on the way (4) at mrt-snfrw. I have come down after I had commissioned a vessel to be made… (5) I brought back from there by water and I kept the troops alive'.

Note that Goedicke's alternative translation is as follows: *The ship man Nefercha's son Der-khesef, he says 'The servant here sends to you concerning the needs of … people. Afterwards, when those "stone finishers" come downstream, they shall come (out here) on the way at the well of* mrt-snfrw. *May you come down, when the vessel is ready… may you bring therewith a flood of water, may you revive the troop.'* (Goedicke 1965: 32–3).]

5. Hieratic graffito with no accompanying painted images (Anthes 1928: 21, tf. 10–10a):

> *The royal [seal-bearer?] and chief of the …, Sankhy, his son, the ꜣṯw and chief of the army(?) Khui. 'I came to Hatnub with a hundred men, who do more than a full thousand would. The chief … in their …'*

6. Hieratic graffito with no accompanying painted images (Anthes 1928: 21–2, tf. 11):

> *(1–2) He of the sedge and bee, nfr-kꜣ-rꜥ. (3) The … of the temple(?), companion … says: (4) 'I was sent down to Hatnub by the nomarch … (5) and I brought back 300 blocks of travertine (bỉt) in a single day … totally, together with the troop… (6) I came into this desert with 1600 men, together with my brothers, the companion Djehuty(?) … and Impy and the tpy ḥr (?) of the pharaoh and scribe of the temple Mry; and this work was completed, since(?) the power of nfr-kꜣ-rꜥ is so magnificent. (7) Young men (?) [from three different places?] each numbering 500, 600 and 500… (8) there came down 300 stone-blocks all at once, through this work-gang, and… (9) I loaded two boats for the house of the provincial governor, sole king's companion, chief of the tenants of the palace, chief of the two houses of… Idi along with … (?) Khuit'.*

7. Hieratic graffito without any accompanying painted images (Anthes 1928: 22–3, tf. 12–12a). Möller's diary indicates that this graffito had deteriorated, probably due to the effects of a Bedouin fire, since it had been first recorded by Blackden and Fraser. The main text reads:

> *(1–2) Hare nome…year 31 of Horus nṯr-ḫꜥw, he of the sedge and bee nfr-kꜣ-rꜥ, may he live, day 20 of month 1 of the shemu season. (3) The… sole king's companion, chief of the tenants of the palace, (4) lector-priest, chief of the priests of living Khnum, called Ankhy, says: (5) 'I was sent from the*

Residence to undertake (6) work in Hatnub; I have broken off (7) 2000(?) blocks of travertine (bỉt), given life and handed over(?) in ... two boats... (8) in accordance with... which was commanded in the Residence... (9) shipped in the ḥʿw-ships, which were... (10) with me from Hatnub to the Residence... (11) three days [upstream]... (12) from this Hatnub, along with my father, the [royal] sealbearer, sole companion, lector-priest and chief priest Khnumankh'.

8. Hieratic graffito without any accompanying painted images (Anthes 1928: 23, tf. 12-12a):

The captain Ser says: 'I have come to this Hatnub and then I came also to Behekes. I have not found (it) done by another as I have done'.

9. Hieratic graffito without any accompanying painted images (Anthes 1928: 23-4, tf. 13-13a):

(1) The provincial governor, controller of the two thrones, overseer of Upper Egypt, chief priest, great chief of the Hare nome, Iha (life, health, prosperity), (2) 2nd month of the season of akhet, year 31... (3) This work was undertaken for him in Hatnub, by the following:... (4) Khnum (5-6) [list of other illegible names]... they say: (7) 'I was sent to this Hatnub to undertake work for the provincial governor and overseer of Upper Egypt, (8) Iha (life, health, prosperity) along with 1600 men. I have created there a ḫwsw (9) in the... rock-face of this Hatnub, its length measuring 40(?) cubits, and its width... cubits. (10) I ... however travertine (bỉt) on this wḫdw; I shipped from there 700 blocks (ỉnr) and 803 stones (ʿȝt) (11) for the provincial governor, controller of the two thrones, chief priest of Thoth, lord of ḫmnw, Iha (life, health, prosperity), (12) that Iha who is praised and loved each day. The wheat came down (13) with me each day – (12a) it was my lord (life, health, prosperity) who allowed me to come back – the god's treasurer Khnum, the scribe of the... Thuthotep, six ... men ... ḳʿw(?) ..., 44(?) (men of ?)... Iaib. ... (14) ... the power of this Iha, of the lord, living for ever'.

10. Graffito of prince Khnumiker, dating to the 20th year of the provincial governor Ahanakht (Anthes 1928: 25, tf. 13-13a). This comprises a painted image of a standing male figure, holding ḫrp-sceptre and staff, with two horizontal lines of hieratic above him and five columns of text to his left. The uppermost line is the date, reading: 'Year 20 of the provincial governor Ahanakht', and the second line identifies the individual as 'His son, Khnumiker'. The main text reads:

(3) These are the words of the scribe Khnumiker: I was a scribe to everyone's liking, (4) calm of heart, one who suppresses his passion, he who is praised (5) by those whom he meets; [I was one] who is free of blasphemy. (6) I have come here to Hatnub to obtain travertine (šs), and to erect a monument (7) for Wenut, the lady of wnw, for the health of Ahanakht (life, health and prosperity)'.

11. Graffito of the official Thutnakht (Anthes 1928: 25-8, tf. 14), dating to year 30 of the provincial governor Ahanakht (or perhaps his son). See 11a below for the associated painted image. The text comprises one horizontal line at the top (the date), with eleven columns below, reading:

(1) Year 30 of the provincial governor, (2) controller of the two thrones, [chief priest,] great leader of the wnw, ... *(3) at the forefront of this land, sole companion(?) ... serpent-spirit (?), strong... (4) since he was so greatly loved by Thoth lord of* ḫmnw, *Aha[nakht]... (5) The official Thutnakht, son of Tjehef, speaks: 'I was an excellent scribe, a ... (6) if he travelled upstream and downstream to each place, I headed downstream ... (7) I came back from there as one who was prudent, and then I had led back out from the place where I was sent. (8) [I was one who] guards his coming for the one who has sent him on the journey... (9) Moreover I was one who was loved by his lord and praised by his city. (10) Neither have I hated any kind of person, nor have I ... either the wretched or the strong. (11) And nor have I done anything for which I might be reproached... of all men. I have(?) ... (12) along with ...'.*

11a.   Image of a standing male figure holding a ḫrp-sceptre and staff, wearing a collar around his neck and also wearing an apron-style kilt (Anthes 1928: 25–6, tf. 14). Above this is one line of hieratic identifying him as: 'The official Thutnakht, Tjehef's son'.

12.   Graffito of the official Thutnakhtankh, dated to the 13th year of the provincial governor Ahanakht (Anthes 1928: 28–31, tf. 15). There are no painted images directly associated with this graffito, but the adjacent text Gr.12a comprises two standing male figures and three lines of hieratic (see below). The text of Gr.12 consists of two lines and sixteen columns of hieratic:

(1) Year 13 of the provincial governor, controller of the two thrones, chief priest, great ruler of wnw, *Ahanakht, life, health, prosperity. (2) This is what the scribe Thutnakhtankh said: (3) 'I was a scribe of the divine book, the son of an overseer of agricultural land. I was a scribe (4) of the royal consort(?), a* ḏfḏfw, *one who has strong fingers, one who is skilled (5) in his occupation. Moreover I was an excellent lector-priest, skilled in (6) judgment concerning an illness. I acted correctly as a ruler, (7) one who investigated the heart, one who assessed the giver according to his property; I gained praise from (8) all people, both those who know me and those who don't, and I made no distinction [between them]. I was one (9) who was beloved in his district, and I did not neglect the need of an envoy(?). (10) I was one who is a sweet city for his people, a gem of his family, (11) without having a worry. I was a son to the old, a father to the young, (12) a commander of the citizen in all places; my food belongs to the hungry and my ointment to the (13) unannointed. I gave clothes to him who was naked. I have used magic on the sick countenance, (14) and I have exorcised the stench(?). Moreover I was one who buried the blessed dead. I accomplished (15) a task with truth and power, so that two (opponents) came out of the law-court both contented in their hearts. (16) I increase property across my district, and I do that which my lord loves. (17) Moreover every traveller who should raise his hand to this image, (18) he will become healthy in his house, when he has performed that for which he has come...'*

12a.   Graffito consisting of two painted images of standing men, each holding a ḫrp-sceptre and staff (Anthes 1928: 28–9, tf. 14), with three lines of hieratic text:

The overseer of agricultural land, Thuthnakht (Khnumiker's son), and his son Thutnakhtankh.

13.   Graffito comprising a painted image of a standing male figure holding a ḫrp-sceptre and staff (Anthes 1928: 31, tf. 14), and above him three columns of hieratic. Anthes suggests that this is actually simply another fragment of the expedition report in Graffito 12/12a.

(1) ... send(?) 600 men (2) ... in order [to bring?] stone to the temple (3) of Thoth, lord of ḫmnw.

14.   Graffito of the official Netjeruhotep, overseer of boats (Anthes 1928: 32–3, tf. 17). Anthes points out that the crucial information concerning the precise objective of Netjeruhotep's expedition, probably originally described at the end of line 13, has unfortunately been destroyed. Towards the left-hand side of the graffito is a painted, standing male figure wearing a projecting triangular kilt and holding a staff in his left hand; the right hand is clenched but holds nothing. To the right of his kilt, below his left arm, several offerings are depicted, with a bull's forelimb and head at the top. A line of text immediately above the figure identifies him as 'overseer of boats Netjeruhotep', while a short column below the depictions of offerings reads '1000 of bread and beer'. The main hieratic text, mostly to the right of the figure, comprises one large horizontal line, one smaller line, and 14 columns:

(1) Year 4 of the provincial governor, controller of the two thrones, chief priest, great ruler of wnw, Nehery, son of Thutnakht, son of Kay, life, health, prosperity. (2) This is what Netjeruhotep, the overseer of boats, said: (3) 'I was an excellent official, one who was praised by his lord. I have done my duty in (4) my city and there was no clamour over me. I was made the guardian of clothes, (5) the chief of the granary and the overseer of the garden, then I became the herald and also the overseer of boats. (6) I have sailed upstream and reached Elephantine, and I have sailed downstream and reached the Delta, (7) in the service of my lord, undertaking tasks for the royal palace. I came rejoicing back from there, (8) after I had done that thing concerning which I was set the task, while the officialdom of the royal palace rejoiced thereto, because (9) the love of my lord in the centre of the hall(?) was so great. I was an excellent and beloved herald, one who knew the law; (10) one who separated two rivals; one who announced to the governors the widows who no longer had husbands; one who (11) ensured that two (opponents) would come out of the law-court both (equally?) contented; (12) one who knows respect in the inner part of the audience chamber; one who is skilled in... (13) I was sent here to Hatnub as a man aged 73 years; I led(?)... (14) Moreover, in all that I have said there is no falsehood, so truly am I loved by Nehery son of Kemy'.

15.   Graffito of Heryshefnakht, the king's chief physician and Ahanakht, the priest of Sekhmet (Anthes 1928: 33–5, tf. 19). The date of this text is uncertain: Möller suggests, in his diary, that it dates to year 4 of the governor Nehery

(1) Year 4 of the provincial governor, controller of the two thrones, overseer of the priests, great ruler of the Hare nome Nehery(?), son of Thutnakht son of Kay. (2) These are the words of Heryshefnakht the priest of Sekhmet: (3) 'I was overseer of the priests of Sekhmet, overseer of the magicians, chief physician (4) to the king, he who read the book each day, he who ... if he is sick, (5) he who lays his hand on the patient(s) and thus knows him [i.e. his state], who is skilled (6) in examinations with the hand, (7) Heryshefnakht the priest of Sekhmet, son of Satsekhmet'. (8) Ahanakht, the scribe of the gate, says: (9) 'I was a priest of Sekhmet, a strong man, a man skilled in his profession, (10) he who lays his hand on the patient(s) and thus knows him [i.e. his state], who is skilled in (11) examinations with the hand; he who knows the bulls...'

16. Graffito of prince Kay, written by a man called …nakht (Griffith 1894: 50-1, pl.23; Anthes 1928: 35-8, tf. 16; Brovarski 1981: 22; Giuliani 1997). This is evidently written by the same scribe who was responsible for Graffiti 17 and 18 below. The hieratic text reads as follows:

(1) Year 5 [of]… provincial governor, controller of the two thrones, chief priest, great overlord of the Hare nome, chief of the city, courtier, judge and vizier, chief of Upper Egypt, foremost of the provincial governors in the king's house, Kay son of Nehery, may he live for ever. (2) The royal seal-bearer, the sole companion, chief of the city, chief judge and vizier, royal acquaintance, while he still(?) remains in his father's tent. A (3) strong citizen without equal; a master of power, greatly beloved; he who turns the opinion of one who argues with him. While (4) I was still a child, there was no one there to replace me. I prepared my troops of young men. (5) I entered the battle, together with my city. I acted as its rearguard (?) in šdyt-š3,[a] although there was no-one with me (6) except for my followers, Medjay, Wawat, [Nehesyw], Aamu, (7) Upper and Lower Egypt being united against me. I returned after a happy success … (8) the whole of my city being with me, without loss …Moreover, I was one who protected the weak from the strong; (9) I have made my house into a gate for each fearful one who came on the day of the rebellion; I was nurse and carer (10) for every sick one who came, until he was healthy; I have given clothing to each naked one who came; I was(?) bread (11) for the hungry, beer for the thirsty ones who came. Moreover I was wheat(?) … [without making a difference(?)] (12) in it (i.e. the city); their great ones were like their lesser ones; a son of the governor of the Hare nome… (13) Every traveller who will raise his arm to this image will (14) healthily reach home, after he has executed that for which he has come… (15-21) [Whoever should destroy these] (22) images, [he will be punished] by the gods of the Hare nome…

[a] As in Gr.17 below, the term *šdyt-š3* should perhaps be translated as 'marshy meadow-land' or instead may be a toponym.

17. Graffito of the prince Thutnakht (Griffith 1894: 52-3; Anthes 1928: 38-41, tf. 16), created for him by a scribe called '…nakht' (evidently the same scribe as the one who created Graffiti 16 and 18).

(1) The …-bìtì, sole companion, overseer of the priests, high priest of Thoth, who opens [the face], (2) who renews the clay sealing: with firm foot and immaculate arms: who sprinkles water to the one doing justice (Thoth): who is festive (3) in the wsḫt-hall: who offers incense to his lord (Thoth) while his arms carry something beautiful: who offers … (4) who slaughters birds for the ka of Thoth: who fetches ìbr-oil and ḥknw-balm: who makes him (?) up: [to whom?] (5) Thoth [says?] 'come close' because it is beautiful what he does for him: who places cattle dung (?) on the incense burners[a] ….. (6) who turns it into a burnt offering for the ka of Thoth: whom Thoth likes to see daily: with fattened (7) bulls and fat ìw3-cattle, wnḏw-cattle and birds: who lets the house of god prosper (8) with bread for the ka of Thoth: the priests rejoice (?) when they see him in the portico (?) of the ʿḫnwtì; a lord of bread and (9) sweet beer so that he may satisfy the entire temple: a popular strong townsman, a man of character, great in (10) strength; whom his entire town loves, women together with men: who gives no evil word (?): (11) plenty in beer, sweet in myrrh, so that he may satisfy his companions and attendants (?): a son of the ruler of the Hare nome: (12) one who is rich and great altogether; who feeds his town when it has nothing; who sustains its widows: who formed

its rearguard (13) in šdyt-š? when all the people had fled: (son of) Kay (son of) Thutnakht (son of) Nehery, Thutnakht who lives eternally. (14) Every traveller who will raise his arm to this image will healthily (15) reach home, after he has executed that for which he has come.

ᵃ Actually 'placed', in contrast to the following, clearly preterite, *irr* and *mrrw*.

18. Note made by the scribe of Graffiti 16 and 17, with no accompanying painted images (Anthes 1928: 41, tf. 16). One line and nine columns of hieratic text:

(1) The [scribe?] …nakht it was, (2) who had these (3) images made (4) for the (5) children (6) of the ruler of (7) the Hare nome, when he (8) came to bring back stone (9) for the provincial governor Nehery, life, health, prosperity, (10) in the fifth year of his reign.

19. Graffito of the goldsmith Ahanakht, incorporating painted images of himself and both of his sons (Anthes 1928: 41–2, tf. 20). The figure of Ahanakht is the largest, showing him standing, wearing a triangular, projecting kilt and holding a staff in his left hand, while his son Thutnakht, to the left, appears to hold his right arm. Thutnakht's right arm is clenched around a small, unidentified item. The second son, Sobeknakht, is depicted lower down and to the left; like the father he holds a long staff in his left hand. Above each of the two painted figures of the sons are single lines of hieratic comprising the following descriptions: 'His son Thutnakht' and 'His son Sobeknakht'. The main text, consisting of two lines and six columns, reads:

(1) Year 4 of the provincial governor, controller of the two thrones, chief priest, great chief of the Hare nome, Nehery, son of Thutnakht, son of Kay, may he live forever. (2) The overseer of craftsmen, Ahanakht son of Nakht. (3) 'I was one who was a … is skilled in his occupation; a worker of silver and gold, (4) one who sits on the mat near his lord; one who is effective(?) with silver and gold; an 'ox-herder' (5) of all precious stones, Ahanakht the metalworker.' (6) Whoever should destroy this image, (7) he will be punished by the gods of wnw.

20. Graffito of the provincial governor Nehery I, written by the scribe Ahanakht (Griffith 1894: 48–9; Anthes 1928: 42–7, Tf18).

(1) Year 6 of the provincial governor, controller of the two thrones, overseer of priests, great chief of wnw, *one known to the king, forefront of Upper Egypt, Nehery son of Kemi, (2) the only one remaining in this land of his princely line (?), when all men were in confusion, (3) a powerful citizen within the team of the camp(?), one who is careful of his goings in every place, (4) possessor of prowess, great of love, turning the opinion of he who argues with him: one of whom the king says (5) 'Would that he would come on the day of conference, then would this whole land follow every plan (6) that he might advise', a true son of Thoth, born of the two enneads of Ra, begotten (7) by the bull of truth, rescuing the widow, supporting (8) the wretched, burying the aged, nurturing the child, (9) making his city live with allotments of land, feeding it when there was nothing; who gave (to it), not making distinctions in it, its great ones (10) like its lesser ones. His companions came out to say, 'Who came for wheat?', (11) giving them presents to satisfy them with fields and years of allotments (?), opening the house (12) to every visitor on the day of the rebellion, a healing medicine for him who came sick, (13) clothes to him who*

came naked, a [firm] stronghold in the midst of the district, (14) which all held onto; beloved of his whole city, men together with women, (15) without plotting evil; organising its troops of youths to (16) his satisfaction(?) that they might be numerous, devising its plan, provisioning it, (17) restoring a man to the possessions of his father, endowing a women for her children; lord of justice, (18) repressing his(?) evil, causing brothers to go out satisfied with the judgment of the council. Wealthy in oxen, rich (19) in fat oxen, possessing geese, abounding in wild fowl, (20) sweetening the odour of the temple, possessing what is good, loving incense, one who enjoys (21) a festive day, Nehery born of Kemy. (22) Moreover every traveller who should raise his hand to (23) this image he will return in health to his house, when he has performed that (24) for which he has come.

21. Graffito of a scribe (Anthes 1928: 47, tf. 20). Three columns of hieratic with no accompanying painted images. The text reads:

(1) Moreover it is the scribe of the ʿrryt and the priest of Sekhmet, Ahanakht son of Nakht, who has created this memorial (2) for the provincial governor, the controller of the two thrones, the chief priest, Nehery I (life, health, prosperity) in year 6, in the year of...; (3) I came to carry out the instruction of the lord (life, health, prosperity).

22. Graffito of the official Sobekemhat (Griffith 1894: 49-50; Anthes 1928: 48–52, tf. 22). This comprises the painted image of Sobekemhat wearing an elaborate collar and a projecting triangular kilt; he holds a spear(?) in his left hand and a small unidentifiable object in his right. In front of him are two male offering bearers, the smaller one, just below his left hand, holds out a vessel towards him, while the larger one, probably a dwarf, stands at his feet and holds out a duck towards him. Above the lower offering bearer, and roughly in front of Sobekemhat's waist and kilt, is an offering table, with three vessels on it and various food items portrayed above and to the left (including a duck and the foreleg and head of a bull). There was evidently also a third small male figure lower down, below the graffito, which Möller copied separately; this may possibly also be a dwarf, having an unusually large head in proportion to the body, but appears to hold no offerings.

The text takes the form of one horizontal line above Sobekemhat giving the date (line 1 of the text translated below), one column to his left (i.e. behind him) comprising the conventional invocation to respect the monument (*Moreover every traveller who should raise his hand to this image he will become healthy in his house, when he has performed that for which he has come'*), one brief column beside the uppermost offering bearer (*Khuu, son of Neferkhau*), and 19 columns on the right-hand side (lines 2-20 below):

(1) Year 7 of the provincial governor, controller of the two thrones, overseer of priests, the great leader of wnw, *royal acquaintance, foremost of upper Egypt: Nehery, son of Kemy, who lives for ever. (2) The chief of the garden Sobekemhat says: 'When I was a child, I was a (3) courtier and a resident of the palace without equal, like the fragrant* str *-plant (4) filled with* ꜣmt *-blossoms, which is held to the nose on the "Day of Illuminating" in the hands of all the people, (5) [and one says] let me smell him. My favour with (6) my lord was greater than that of a son, as everyone knows. I speak the truth. When I was (7) praised I deserved(?) it. I did not rob another of his inheritance, I did not expel the peasant (8) from his field, and there was no-one (9) among all*

people who complained about me; there is no-one (apart from me?) who experienced his favour, but (10) one robbed. I was overseer of the garden under the governance of provincial governor Nehery (life, health, prosperity); (11) my favour with my lord was greater than that extended to son or brother. He treated me kindly once more (12) as before; I was on duty for him in his house, without allowing me (13) to see the shadow of another place. He sent only(?) (14) me to Hatnub so that I would go for someone of the royal palace; the document was complete (15) for me, as for a son or brother, because I myself (16) came here; moreover I carried out the task in this desert while I was cool and calm, not ... [with] the strong ones? ... (17) Popularity; I opened(?) because of(?) my popularity, which they gave to me; however they were against me in the same way and no-one of them ... that(?) he hates me. I, (18) moreover, did that which no other person who came before me had done; I stretched out the hand to them, the butchers do not spare the cattle, not ... (19) to celebrate on a festive day. I have left here happy, having done that thing for which I came here. I have done more than all people, for I have such love from Nehery, (20) Kemy's son; I speak the truth. (21) Moreover every traveller who should raise his hand to this image he will become healthy in his house, when he has performed that for which he has come.'

23.   Graffito of Thutnakht, written by the scribe Ahanakht (Griffith 1894: 47–8; Anthes 1928: 52–3, tf. 20).

(1) The [treasurer] of he of the sedge and the bee, the king's sole companion, the overseer of priests, great wʿb-priest of Thoth, the one who performs mꜣʿt, (2) firm of foot, clean of hands, he who is festive in the wsḫt-hall, overlord of the entire temple, one whose position Thoth advanced, his own true son born of the two enneads of Ra, (3) (sole) surviving ḳrḥt-snake in this land, when all men were in confusion, when the commoner was powerful, without his equal, a man of character, great of strength, towards whom these two lands showed love, (4) while there is no dissatisfied face to be seen. I saved my city on the day of plunder from the painful terrors of the king's house. Moreover I was its fortress on the day of its struggle, its refuge (5) in its marshy meadow-land. I kept it alive, while it was entirely sustained through means of the ṯsw (6) of the land, when there was nothing, its great ones were treated as its lesser ones, and no (7) unsatisfied face was to be seen in ḥmnw and also in wnw. I opened (8) my storehouse to everyone. Moreover I was a man of friendly appearance, of kind-hearted (9) disposition, one who owns provisions, a lover of myrrh, (10) one who enjoys a festive day, Thutnakht son of Thuthotep, (11) who lives for all eternity.

24.   Graffito of the prince Kay, created by the scribe Ahanakht (Griffith 1894: 51-2, pl. 22; Anthes 1928: 54–6, tf. 24).

(1) The ... -bity, sole companion, overseer of the town, chief judge-vizier Kay says: 'I was the son of a (noble) man, strong and wise, who for his town looked (attentively) at infinity, who drove it forth on the way of prosperity; who knew him (?) who (?) praises ... his coming (?); who (2) looked at eternity; an acquaintance of the king and his officials; unique in his manner, without an equal; to whom Upper Egypt came in prostration. I was the son of a (noble) man, who had no [adversary?]; a lord of fear, great in power; a lord of terror, great in popularity; (3) with friendly face and kind nature; open-hearted, free of darkness; whom this land shows love; (whom) humans and gods exult at the approach of his statues on the day of their procession to the temple; with

fattened bulls and fat iwȝ-cattle, (4) a lord of geese, with many birds, great in incense burners and pure in offering pieces, so that he may make the smell of the temple sweet; son of Thoth in rightness, semen of the bull of truth; who steps in front of him in his house early to praise his ka – daily because [he] loves [(Thoth?) (his town?)] so much [and (?) because] (5) it is good what he does for it. I have done the right things, sharper (?) than a beard of barley(?); I have rescued the wretched from the hand of the mighty; I have let the widow breathe who has no husband; I have raised the orphan who has no father. (6) I have conscripted its (i.e. the town's) crew of youths so that its holdings (sc. of a crew fit for military service) may be numerous – its (old) crew however had entered the townsmen and lived in their houses while they had not undertaken any campaign at the time of the fear of the (7) royal house. I have rescued my town on the day of the raid from the dire terror of the (8) royal house. I however was its stronghold on the day of its battle, its bastion in the marshy meadow-land; a son of the ruler (9) of the Hare nome, a rich and great altogether. I have however kept my entire town alive in the ṯsw (10) of the land, when nothing was there; (its) great were (treated) like its little ones; no dissatisfied face was (seen) in ḫmnw (11) and likewise in wnw; I opened my granaries to all people. I was a lord of beautiful things, a favourite of myrrh, (12) a companion of the festival day: son of Nehery, Kay mȝꜥ-ḫrw, who lives in all eternity.'

25. Graffito of the nomarch Nehery I, written by the scribe Ahanakht (Griffith 1894: 51-2, pl. 22; Anthes 1928: 56-9, tf. 26). The date is written horizontally, while the rest of the main text comprises 19 columns of unequal length. There are also two horizontal captions and one vertical caption accompanying three small-scale figures to the right of the main image of the standing figure of Nehery I himself, who is shown in a triangular kilt and holding a pear-shaped mace in his left hand and a ḫrp-sceptre in his right. Below Nehery's left arm are several offerings, including the foreleg and head of an ox. The uppermost of the small figures is seated facing away from Nehery with arms stretched out in front of him, the middle one is also facing away, in a standing posture with both arms upraised, while the lowest of the three figures is facing towards Nehery (i.e. to the left) and bowing down in the presence of the nomarch. To the left of the middle figure is an offering table bearing three vessels. The main text reads:

(1) Year 7 of the provincial governor, controller of the two thrones, overseer of the priests, great chief of wnw, king's acquaintance, head of Upper Egypt whom all its^a gods love: son of Kay, son of Thutnakht, Nehery who lives ... (2) year 7 of the nomarch, controller of the two thrones, overseer of the priests, great chief of wnw, king's acquaintance, head of Upper Egypt, intimate of the king without an equal; (3) a man to whom the heart has to open itself; he was (?) brought to the council together with the officials without being recognized (?) by the people; the inhabitants of the residence were satisfied with the orders which he issued; one who is reliable (mtỉ) for the king; (4) to whom the rulers of Upper Egypt came, ..., (5) a strong townsmen of the crew's tent; one who guards [his coming] [for (?) every place]. (6) The king spoke: make yourself a body of men (?), look I will be at another troop (?); (7) the heart of the inhabitants of the residence was filled by his strength. – battle stronghold in the marshy meadow-land, (8) to whom all people [clung (?)]; before whom a trembling was in the people, a terror in [the hearts?], as before (9) Sekhmet on the day of battle, ... [at?] every place; whose (10) end (?) Thoth has ordered for the furnishing of all its/ his districts; whose property Thoth has made large (11) for the prosperity of the

temple and its^b (people?); someone rich (in?) all things; a lord of bulls and Asiatic cattle (?); (12) a lord (?) of .... wind for all people; who rescued [his town?] (13) from the royal house; ...... of the one travelling downstream and the one travelling upstream; a landing post [for] all people; (14) sweetness and faience/brightness^c of the entire land; [into] md3w people, Asiatics and (15) desert dwellers (ḫ3styw?) the love for him^d has penetrated – Nehery, son of Kemy, m3ʿ-ḫrw, who lives (16) in all eternity. (17) Each traveller however who will raise his arm to this image, he will reach (18) home in health, after he has executed that for which he has come. (19) It was the scribe of the ʿrryt, son of Nakht, Ahanakht, who made these images, when he came to fetch travertine (šs), together with the overseer of the garden Sobekemhat.

^a i.e. Upper Egypt's

^b i.e. the temple's

^c i.e. The word translated here as 'faience/brightness' (and by Anthes as 'Glas') is *tḥnt*, i.e. 'faience', perhaps creating an idiom similar to the English 'sweetness and light', since *tḥnt* derives from root meaning 'to dazzle, shine, gleam'. The feminine nature of the noun here means that it cannot be a simple participle referring to Neheri, but must actually be a metaphorical use of the word 'faience'.

^d actually relative link: *'whose popularity ... has penetrated'*

26. Graffito of the prince Thutnakht (Anthes 1928: 59–62, tf. 28). The first of three, Gr.26–8, which all date to year 8 of Nehery I.

(1) Year 8 of the nomarch Nehery (life, prosperity, health). (2) The ...-bity, sole companion, overseer of the priests, high priest of Thoth who sprinkles water for the one doing justice, who opens the face and renews the clay sealing; with pure arms when he offers to the (?) god; (3) administrator (?) of the secret of the god's treasure; who alone hears that to be heard in the ...; who sees the beauty of his lord; whose place Thoth has put in front because he loves him so much; his own son in rightness; created [by the one?] (4) from whom he came forth; born of the two enneads of Re; (sole) surviving krḥt-snake in this land while all (other) people are dirt (?); an acquaintance of the king and his officials; unique in his kind, without an equal; ... embankment (?) ... (5) ...; a strong townsman of the ... who (?) ... the troops (?) of the (?) king on the day of battle; he was (?) brought to the council together with the officials without him being recognized (?) by the people; who knew (?) ... (6) who suppressed (his) passion; of calm heart; free of brashness when it was hot on the day of battle; fore (?) his name was heard as that of a bull; shadow of the entire land on the day of the 'marshy meadow-lands'; who held together the heart of ..., (7) who steadied the foot of the restless; sweetness and faience/brightness^a of the entire land, and no dissatisfied face is (seen) among them; whose property Thoth made large for the prosperity of the temples; with fattened bulls and fat (8) iw3-cattle, a lord of geese, with numerous birds; pure of offering basins at the sacred place; whom his lord loves when he offers and satisfies these living in ḫmnw; one rich in (?) all things; who kept [his town] alive (9) while it was fed entirely and its great ones were (treated) as its little ones, no dissatisfied face was (seen); a lord of beautiful things, a favourite of myrrh, a companion of the festival day; Thutnakht son of Thuthotep, m3ʿ-ḫrw, who lives in all eternity.

^a See line 14 of Gr.25 above, for discussion of the phrase 'sweetness and faience/brightness'.

27.   Graffito of the *wʿb*-priest Khnumhotep (Anthes 1928: 62–3, tf. 28). Image of right-facing, standing figure of a man holding a staff in his left hand and a *ḫrp*-sceptre in his right. Above him is one line of hieratic text, identifying the figure as: *The priest Khnumhotep, Renu's son*. Below the figure, and to the right (below the larger figure of Thutnakht, which actually belongs with Gr.26) are three columns of hieratic:

(1) The priest Khnumhotep, Renu's son, says: (2) 'I was a priest of Thoth. I was a citizen of the residence, one known (3) to this provincial governor, one with whom the high officials are friendly, if they see him'.

28.   Hieratic graffito of the official Renu (Anthes 1928: 63–4, tf. 30). On the left hand side is a painted standing figure of a man wearing a kilt with lower end extended to form triangular projection. His right arm is only visible from shoulder down to just above the elbow, while his partially outstretched left hand holds a spear (or possibly mace) in front of his face. An offering table, on the ground to his right, has at least four vessels on it, and above the table, at about the level of the figure's upper torso, are depictions of several offerings (including a bull's foreleg and bull's head). Above the figure of Renu his name is written in a single line of hieratic: 'Renu'. Further to the right, beyond the offering table, are 15 columns of hieratic text:

(1) Year 8 of the provincial governor, controller of the two thrones, chief priest, great leader of wnw, [one familiar to the king], foremost of Upper Egypt: Nehery, (2) son of Kemy, mꜣʿ ḫrw, who lives for ever. (3) The official Renu says: 'I was an excellent official, one who was praised, one who was sent out by his lord (4) … bed(?) (5) … his lord. I became a priest; I was promoted in my youth because my lord loved me so greatly. (6) I became a district overseer in the time of Nehery (life, health, prosperity). Moreover I was (his) agent… (7) I was prudent in all my offices, one who undertook duties for his lord ceaselessly(?)… [free?] (8) of lies(?) at the … every office(?). I was sent here to Hatnub to (9) bring back a stone block … for one person of the palace. Moreover I did more than (10) any other (expedition-)leader who came previously to this place; I quarried stone and came back … (11) it; so much does Nehery, Kemy's son, love me, I speak the truth. (12) Moreover each person who has (previously) come to [this] place, - if he has accomplished(?) his expedition, so(?) I have found here [his traces]… (13) Moreover I was… (14) Moreover every traveller who should raise his hand to this image (15) he will return in health to his house, when he has performed that for which he has come'.

29.   Graffito of an official and other individuals, dated to the time of the provincial governor Nehery I (Anthes 1928: 65–6, tf. 21):

(1) I was a commander… (2) … (3) … hostility; I went away… (4) great… (5) I deputised there for the… as his comrade… (6) two … previously in the past… (7) wnw and ḥmnw, as we (they?) ought to have been; [I gave back?] the lies to him who said them, much as he loves Nehery, son of Kemy, I speak the truth.

29a.   Hieratic graffito accompanying the furthest to the right of seven red-painted male figures located below Gr.29 (and in addition to the four figures painted on either side of Gr.29). Of these seven figures, the two furthest to the left had no accompanying names or titles, while the four in the middle had originally been identified by accompanying text but the latter had been rendered unreadable by a crack in the rock face. The name and titles at the far right read as follows: *sealbearer, steward, ...seneb*.

30.   Graffito comprising three painted images: two seated male figures (each holding a staff in the left hand and an unknown object in the right) and, below these, an animal which may perhaps be a gazelle; the right-hand male figure has an offering table in front of him, with three vessels on it, and a number of food offerings portrayed above it, including a bull's head and foreleg (Anthes 1928: 66, tf. 23). The left-hand seated figure is identified by a single line of hieratic written above him :*Sobekhotep [son of] Henu*, while the right-hand figure has the name *Kanakht son of Khnum son of Sabu* written above him.

The main text, consisting of two short columns of hieratic, reads:

(1) I was an artist who was loved, [concerning the] laughing (?) [of the ... one who is praised] ...
(2) by his troop, one who is beloved by the citizens.

31.   Graffito dedicated to the official Kahotep, created by his 'brother' Ip and dated to the 2nd year of the provincial governor Thutnakht V (Anthes 1928: 67, tf. 29). On the left-hand side there is a painted image of a standing, kilted, right-facing man holding a staff in his left hand and a *ḫrp*-sceptre in his right. Above him is a single line of hieratic text giving the date (see line (1) below). To his right are seven columns of hieratic, as well as one short horizontal line of text:

(1) Year 2 of the provincial governor, controller of the thrones, chief priest, Thutnakht, son of Nehery (life, health, prosperity). (2) The official Kahotep, son of Senebi, says: 'I made... (3) wnt[a] *and ḫmnw ... to make/do ... (4) I brought ... (5) provincial governor, controller of the two thrones ...Ahanakht ... (6) in the time of the provincial governor, controller of the two thrones, Nehery(?) ... (7) to [make provisions?] for the royal palace ... (8) in the time of the provincial governor, controller of the two thrones, Ahanakht(?) ...'. (9) This was created for him by his brother Ip.*

[a] Presumably just a variant on the usual writing, *wnw*.

32.   Graffito comprising two painted images of standing, kilted, right-facing men, each holding a staff in his left hand and a *ḫrp*-sceptre in his right, dated to year 20 of the provincial governor Thuthotep I. Above the two figures are three lines of hieratic text, and between them are six columns (Anthes 1928: 67–8, tf. 29). The uppermost horizontal line gives the date, while below it is a line probably originally giving the name of the right hand figure, of which only the determinative remains. The line of text on the left reads: *his son Kanakht...invocation offerings ... all good things...* The date plus the six columns of hieratic comprising the main text read:

(1) Year 20 of the provincial governor Thuthotep I, son of Nehery. (2) I came like [anyone?] who has come [in the past?] to bring travertine (šs) for my lord; (3) I have left here with a happy heart, and after I had done that (4) for which I came; I have descended ... (5) after I had carried out

the orders of my lord Thuthotep I (life, health, prosperity). Moreover anyone who (6) had come similarly but had not brought it, although he was supposed to bring it(?). Moreover anyone (7) who should raise his hand to this image he will reach his house in health.

33.   Graffito incorporating a possible image of a brewing woman (Anthes 1928: 69–70, tf. 25). A red-painted figure seems to show a naked woman with her arms inside a large pottery vessel, with hieratic text both above and to the right:

(1) Whoever should destroy this [stele] (2) will be destroyed by Thoth, (3) but whoever…over(?) this…(4) … (5) 1000 of all that is good…for your ka. (6) Ka, son of Khnum [says:] (7) 'I was a swšw;[a] *I was a … ; I was a … ; … (8) I [came?] to Upper Egypt; [I? caught?] fish; (9) I [caught?] mice; I hunted that which was in the desert. I was a strong man … (10) … (11) …'*

[a] Anthes notes that he is unsure whether the word *swšw* should be connected with *swš* ('twisting thread').

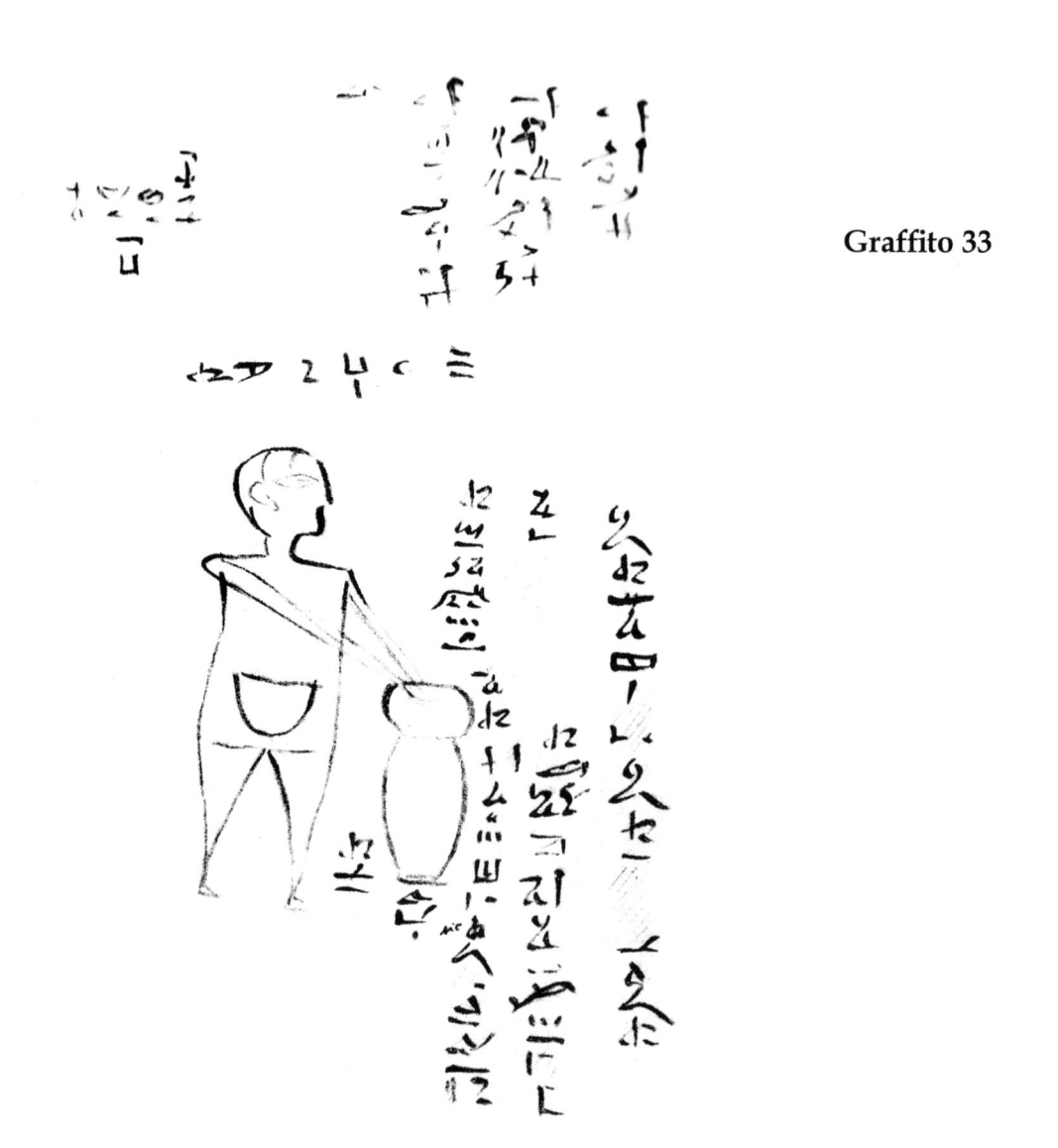

Graffito 33

34.   Graffito commemorating Ikem (Anthes 1928: 70, tf. 21). Image of a seated male figure holding a staff in his left hand. Above him is a single line of hieratic, reading:

Ikem son of Neferu.

35.   Graffito commemorating a father and son (Anthes 1928: 70-1, tf. 23). Image comprising two seated male figures, each holding a staff in their left hands. Above them is one line of hieratic, and immediately below them is another horizontal line, as well as two short columns. The uppermost line identifies one of them as:

Nerekhef(?), son of ..., son of Inerer(?).

The lower line reads:

If anyone should destroy these images, the gods of wnw *will punish him.*

Anthes (1928: 70-1) suggests that the remaining few signs may be the upper part of a destroyed long inscription, or they can perhaps be read together (and in isolation) as:

Moreover this was made for him by Shenut(?).

36.   Graffito of the official Kanakht (Anthes 1928: 71, tf. 21). Image of a standing, kilted, right-facing man holding a staff in his left hand and a *ḫrp*-sceptre in his right. Above him is one line of hieratic text identifying him as:

Sealbearer Kanakht son of Hetepi.

37.   Graffito of Thuthotep (Berlin 18555; Anthes 1928: 71, tf. 28). Image of a standing, kilted, right-facing man holding a staff in his left hand and a *ḫrp*-sceptre in his right. Above him is one horizontal line of hieratic text identifying him as:

Thuthotep son of Nakht.

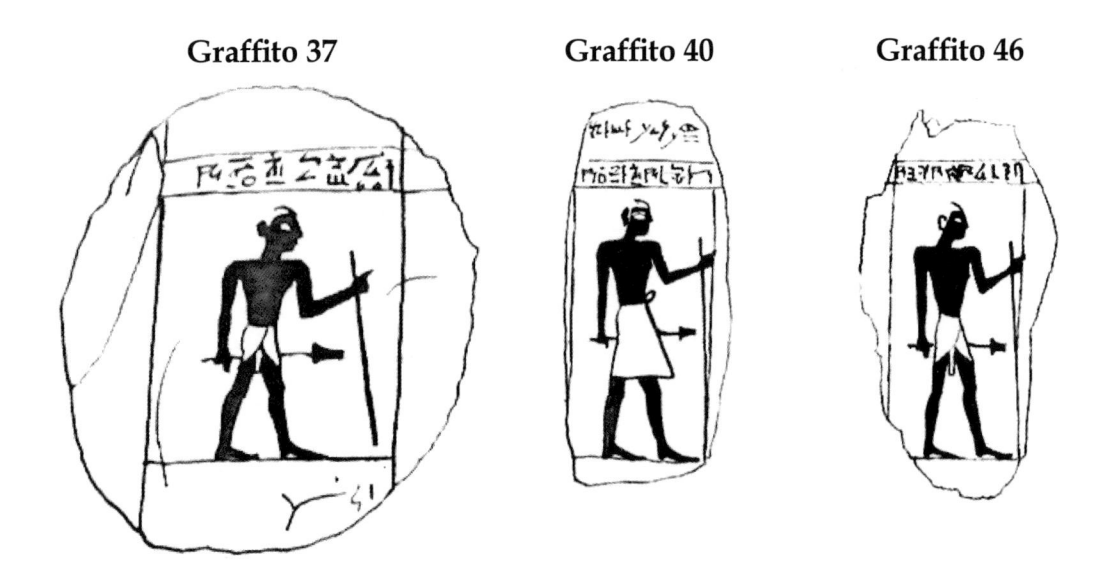

Graffito 37 **Graffito 40** **Graffito 46**

38. Graffito of an unknown official, which Möller dated to the 12th Dynasty on palaeographic grounds, but which Anthes considered to date to the First Intermediate Period (Anthes 1928: 71–2, tf. 25). To the right of the text is the rough outline of a man holding staff and sceptre with an offering table in front of him (both the figure and the table being described but not illustrated in Anthes 1928). Above the figure are two very unclear horizontal lines of hieroglyphs, the first of which ends with the 'placenta' sign (Gardiner Aa1) followed by the seated man determinative (Gardiner A1), and the second begins with *ir.n.i*. The main text comprises three columns of hieroglyphs:

> *(3) [I was a lord?] of beautiful things, a man of ..., one beloved of the good, one praised by all people. The inhabitants of my town... (4) ... when my expedition had arrived to thank me, one year like the other. I am a strong townsman (nḏs) .... (5) I did everything for which I had (?) come as a prudent person for every year. The refugees (?) however...*

39. Graffito of Ahanakht (Berlin 22609; Anthes 1928: 72, tf. 25). Image of a standing right-facing man holding a staff in his left hand and a *ḫrp*-sceptre in his right. Above him is one horizontal line of hieratic text giving his name, and behind him are three columns of text describing his achievements:

> *(1) Ahanakht son of Khnum. (2) I was an entertainer (?); I was a popular dancer; (3) I was one who is a joy for his troops and who is loved by his entire city, (4) and there is no unfriendly face to be seen in it.*

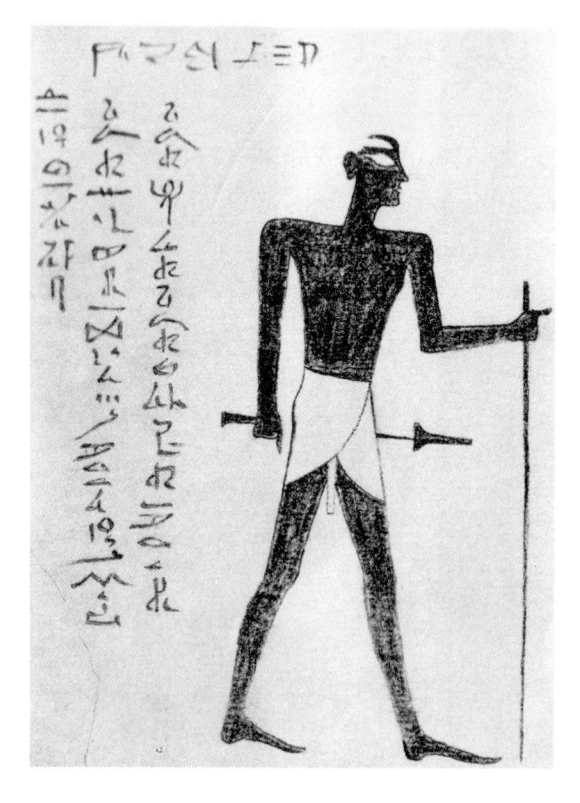

Graffito 39

40. Graffito of Iaib (Berlin 18556; Anthes 1928: 72, tf. 27). Image of a standing right-facing man holding a staff in his left hand and a *ḫrp*-sceptre in his right. Above him are two horizontal lines of hieratic text:

> *(1) Sealbearer Iaib, son of Inta. (2) This was made for him by his brother Ipy.*

41.   Graffito of Ahahotep (Berlin 22610; Anthes 1928: 72, tf. 27). Image of a standing right-facing man holding a staff in his left hand and a *ḫrp*-sceptre in his right. Above him is one line of hieratic text simply naming him and giving two generations of his filiation:

Ahahotep, son of Henu, son of Thuthotep.

42.   Graffito of the provincial governor Thutnakht IV (Anthes 1928: 72-3, tf. 14. Image of a right-facing, standing, kilted man holding a staff in his left hand and a sceptre in his right, with a row of four *ḥs*-jars in front of him, at eye-level. The body of the man is painted dark red, while his headgear and kilt are white. Above him, and to his right, are two horizontal lines of hieratic (lines 1-2 below), while a column of hieratic (line 3) drops downwards from the other side of the row of jars.

(1) *Prince, controller of the two thrones, chief priest, Thutnakht son of Ahanakht, mȝꜥ-ḫrw.* (2) *The official Sobekhotep has made this for him.* (3) *If anyone should destroy this, Thoth will punish him.*

43.   Graffito of an unknown official (Anthes 1928: 73, tf. 14). Image of a standing kilted man facing right, with a staff in his left hand and a *ḫrp*-sceptre in his right. Behind him are four columns of hieratic:

(1) *...I have departed(?) from here as one who is prudent...* (2) *in order to bring back travertine (šs) for the royal jubilee(?) as one(?)* (3) *whom the court loves, if(?) he...; he who comes and looks after his troop since it is so large...* (4) *says, 'I was a..., a strong citizen of the residence, one who is praised and loved...'*

Graffito 43

44. Graffito of Khnumi (Berlin 22611; Anthes 1928: 74, tf. 24). Image of a standing kilted man facing right, with a staff in his left hand and a *ḥrp*-sceptre in his right. There are also offerings depicted above and below his left arm.

There are two brief horizontal lines of hieratic (lines 1-2 below) above his head, and two vertical columns of text to right and left of his staff (lines 3 and 4 respectively). Anthes (1928: 74) suggests that the missing words in lines 1-2 may be Khnumi's filiation.

(1) Gift [given to the king] by Khnumi.... Khnumi. (2) This was made for him by his brother Khnum. 1000 jars of beer are pure for your ka.

45. Stele of two cousins, Nakht and Ankh (Berlin 22612; Anthes 1928: 74, tf. 24). Two vertical lines of hieratic text read: *Nakht son of Ankh son of Khnum* and *Ankh son of Nakht son of Khnum*.

One horizontal line below reads: *This was made by their brother Khnum.*

46. Stele of Khnum (Berlin 18557; Anthes 1928: 74, tf. 27). The hieratic text, written above an image of a standing, kilted man holding *ḥrp*-sceptre and staff, reads: *Khnum [son of] Sabu, [son of] Nakht.*

47. Stele of an unknown man (Berlin 22613; Anthes 1928: 74-5, tf. 21). The main text of this graffito reads: *this was made for the official ...emhat, son of Kefa*. To the right of the hieratic dedication text is a figure of a man holding a staff and sceptre, with an illegible graffito inscribed below him.

48. Stele of Hetepi (Berlin 22614; Anthes 1928: 75, tf. 24). Standing figure of a man wearing a short kilt, holding a long staff in his left hand and a *ḥrp*-sceptre in his right. The horizontal line of hieratic above his head identifies him as: *Hetepi son of Intef*, while a vertical line of hieratic behind him reads: *This was made for him by his brother Menti, son of Keri*. As Anthes points out, this text is confusing in that the two 'brothers' appear to have different fathers.

48a The number Gr.48 is used to refer to several stelae (Anthes 1928: 75-6) that are not mentioned by Möller but are preserved partly through Möller's diary and partly through 14 fragments transferred to the Ägyptisches Museum, Berlin (22615-9), of which only 3 now survive, the rest having been lost or destroyed in World War II.

49. Middle Kingdom graffito dedicated to the provincial governor of the Hare nome, Amenemhat, dating to year 31 of Senusret I (Griffith 1894: 53-4; Anthes 1928: 76-8, tf. 31). The standing, bearded figure of Amenemhat, wearing a blue-painted kilt and necklace, is depicted to the right of the main body of the hieratic text; he is holding a staff in his left hand and a *ḥrp*-sceptre in his right. Möller's notes indicate that there was originally an offering table in front of him, with an offering formula written above it, and also, to the right of the table, originally a figure

of his wife, now totally destroyed. Even further to the right, under the graffito, three men were depicted, each facing to the right and painted a deep reddish brown, one of them holding a throw-stick. To the left of the main text there is a right-facing male figure (a son or servant?) carrying a goose in his left hand and an unknown object in his right. Below the figure of Amenemhat are images of two dogs, while a single line of text above Amenemhat's head reads: *The royal sealbearer Amenemhat, born of ?.* The main hieratic text reads:

(1) Year 31, first celebration of the jubilee of he of the sedge and bee ḫpr-k3-rꜥ, given life for ever. (2) The prince, provincial governor… royal [sealbearer], sole companion, son of Kay, Nehery's son, Amenemhat, (3) says, 'I have come here to Hatnub to obtain mnw-stone for he of the sedge and bee ḫpr-k3-rꜥ, given life for ever. (4) I am one who is praised by his lord and whom he loves every day for as long as (5) Senusret I lives. I speak the truth. I was a watchful one who is free from (6) sleep while engaged on business on behalf of the king's estate. Moreover I was (7) a silent man who bends his back (in respect), as the entire … knows, (8) in truth and not in falsehood; the royal [sealbearer], sole companion, (9) chief priest, son of Kay, Nehery's son, Amenemhat, true of voice before Nemti lord of ṯrtỉ. (10) Every craftsman, every sailor, and all of the people who raise their hands towards this image, (11) will be rewarded. As for those who, however, might seek to destroy my name or image, the gods (12) of wnw will exclude their children from office till their deaths.'

50.   Middle Kingdom stele dating to year 20 of Amenemhat II and bearing two horizontal lines of hieroglyphic inscription incorporating the *ḥtp dỉ nsw* formula (Anthes 1928: 78, tf. 32). The inscription presumably concluded with the name of the man, but this is now missing. Below the inscription there was originally a depiction of a seated man facing to the right towards a table laden with offerings. According to Anthes' footnote, this painted image was badly damaged and therefore not copied by Möller (Anthes 1928: 78, n.1).

(1) Year 20 of he of the sedge and bee, Horus, hmꜥꜥt, nb-k3w-rꜥ, son of Ra, Amenemhat, given life, stability, power, like Ra… gift (2) given to the king for Osiris lord of Djedu and for Anubis on his mountain, he gives offerings every day consisting of all good pure things, the one who is revered with regard to his city god…

51.   Scene dating to the Middle Kingdom on the basis of its palaeography, depicting a man and his servant (Anthes 1928: 78, tf. 33); it is not clear whether the man is sniffing a flower or drinking. According to Anthes, the man is painted red, his wig and chair are pink, and the servant's kilt is white. A vertical line of text behind the man is difficult to read but probably identifies him with the name Sep. Two horizontal lines of text above the servant (lines 1-2 below) list the offerings he brings:

(1) 1000 bread loaves (2) 1000 jars of beer.

52.   No ruler's name is cited in this graffito, but it is tentatively dated by Möller to the Second Intermediate Period, on the basis of the palaeography of some of the ideograms (Anthes 1928: 78–80, tf. 32). This text is accompanied by a painted figure of a standing male statue (not illustrated below), with sceptre and staff (to the right of the columns of hieratic), and the painted images of a hunter, with bow and arrows and two dogs, as well as the front section of a gazelle

(to the left of the text).

(1-2) ... to recognise that I stretch (?) my hand to another (?) (3) For the ka of ... he says (?): (4) 'Everyone however who will destroy this image, his office may be destroyed for him in his hands, ... (5) no servant shall be present in his house. Who however will offer (?) bread and beer to it, he shall be rewarded ... (6) ... Everyone ... who passes this image (7) while he has bread with him and beer with him: if he gives some to it, so he shall ... (8) in ..., the lord of the living (?) ... (9) ... his dogs with (?) him and (10) his gifts (?) with him, in the (?) desert ... [he shall be well?] (11) in eternity, and his children in [his] place .... (12) [N.N.] says: ... (13) ... my lord ..., he will reach ...'

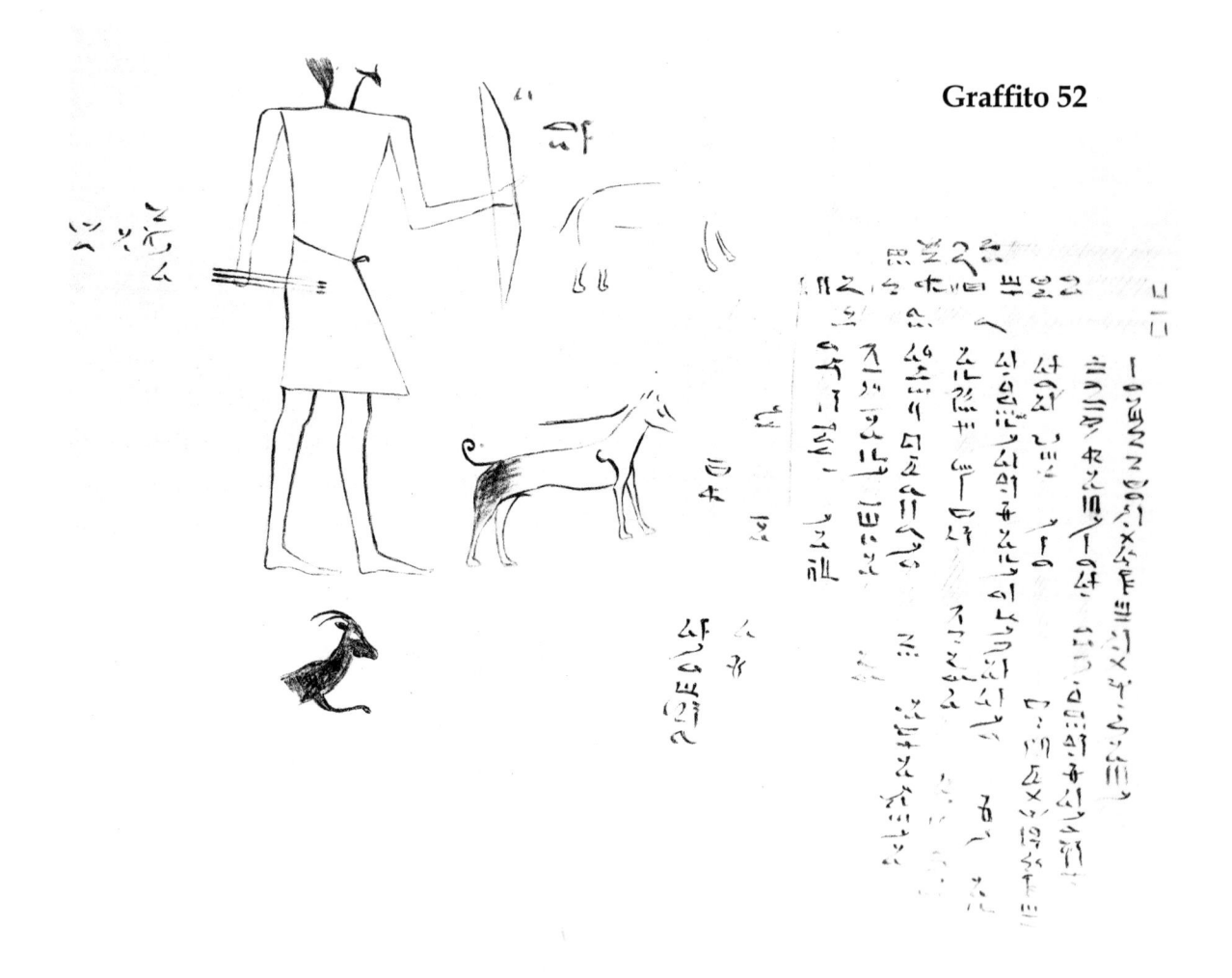

Graffito 52

Appendix 4

Unprovenanced Texts

UT1. Senusret I (throne name and birth name), year 22. Slab of travertine bearing a hieratic inscription (Grdseloff 1951, Posener 1968). This 'stele' appears to have been removed from the wall of one of the Hatnub quarries before the epigraphic work of Blackden, Fraser and Möller, perhaps even in ancient times. The inscription consists of two horizontal lines of text above a standing figure of the writer wearing a kilt and holding a sceptre in his right hand and a long staff in his left (presumably a depiction of the 'assistant' …hotep), with six columns of hieratic text to his right and two columns to his left.

Initially a fragment in the upper right hand corner of this stele was published by Bernard Grdseloff (1951) but later the central fragment was discovered, and the full text was published by Georges Posener (1968). The only other Hatnub text that is definitely dated to the reign of Senusret I is Graffito 49, which mentions the jubilee festival in his 31st regnal year. One of the aspects of quarrying at Hatnub that is reinforced by this text is that the governors of the hare nome seem to have rarely, if ever, visited the quarries themselves, preferring to send trusted

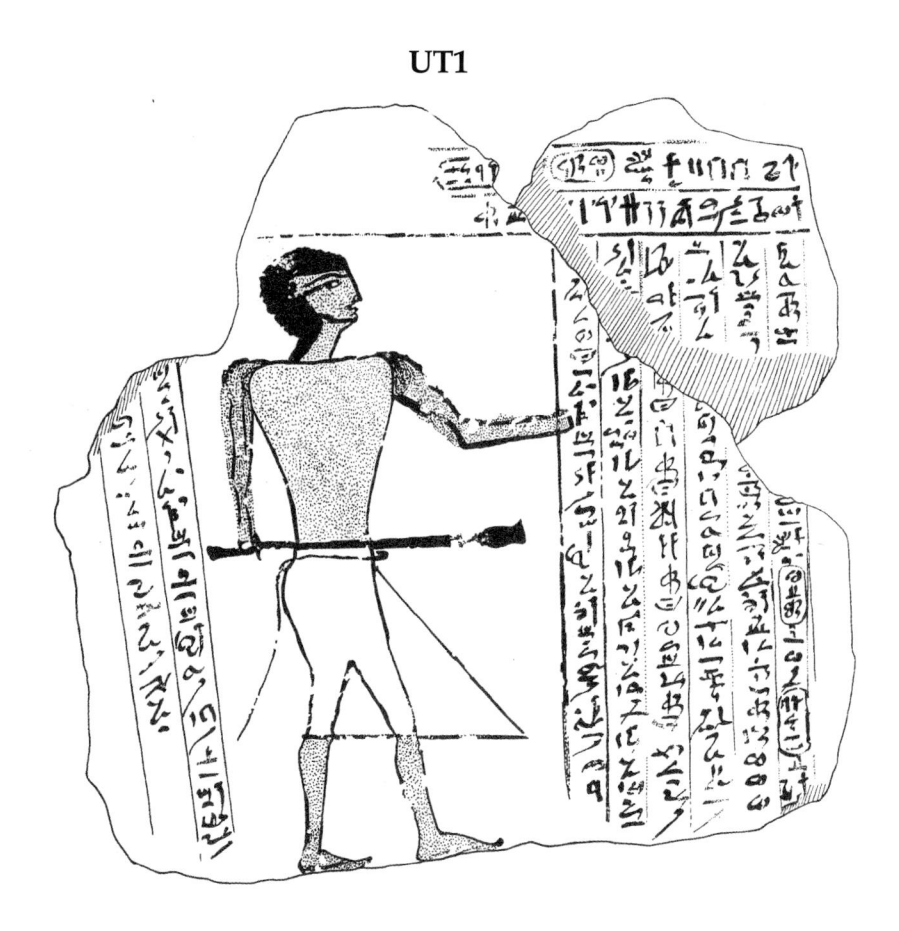

UT1

officials to extract the travertine on their behalf. In the same way, the royal treasurers of the Middle Kingdom often organised quarrying and mining expeditions but do not usually seem to have led them in person, generally delegating the task to their subordinates. Thus the mission in this example is arranged by the 'chief treasurer' Sobekhotep but it is stated in line 2 that the actual expedition was led by an 'assistant' (*imy-sȝ*), which Posener (1968: 70) suggests is probably an abbreviation for *imy-sȝ n imy-r sḏȝw*t (assistant of the chief treasurer).

(1) Year 22 of he of the sedge and the bee ḫpr-kȝ-rʿ, [son of Ra] Senusret, (2) who lives as Ra for ever and always. The assistant ...[ho]tep says: (3) 'I have come here ... for he of the sedge and the bee ḫpr-kȝ-rʿ, [son of Ra] Senusret, who lives as Ra for ever, (4) on a mission from ... the sole [companion], the chief treasurer Sobekhotep, unique without exception, (5) who has no equal, [who enters] first and leaves last, an honourable man to whom one opens one's (6) heart. With regard to every ... every scribe, every quarryman, every leader of a team who shall read (7) [this] stele and who shall [say] "a thousand loaves of bread, a thousand beers, a thousand cattle, a thousand geese, a thousand of (8) [all] good things, each day", for this image, he will return withour hindrance, having accomplished that for which he has come. (9) [As for] anyone who destroys this representation; he will not return to his house, nor embrace (10) (his) children, nor see a happy outcome'.

UT2. Senusret I (Horus name and throne name). This unprovenanced, double-sided, stele inscribed in hieroglyphs and hieratic, the so-called Michaelides Stele (priv. col., Cairo; Simpson 1958; 1961), consists of three fragments. Simpson (1961: 30) points out that, even after the addition of the third fragment of the stele (supplementing the two fragments already published in his 1958 article), 'its possible origin at Hatnub remains a mere conjecture'.

Front: *(1) Life to the Horus ʿnḫ-mswt, (2) he of the sedge and the bee ḫpr-kȝ-rʿ (throne name of Senusret I), living forever. (3) The conscript of the levies of recruits, Khenty ...*

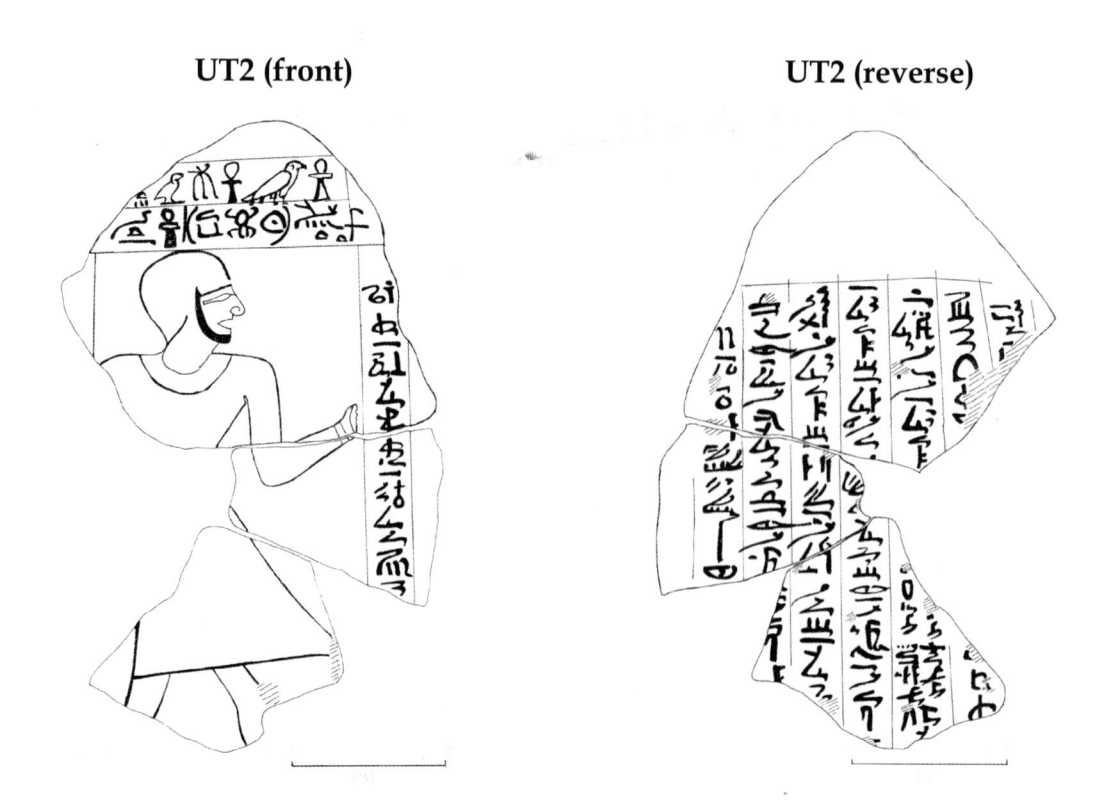

UT2 (front)   **UT2 (reverse)**

Reverse: *(1) with (?) ...[Now as for] (2) every scribe, [every ... (every)] wˁb-priest (?) [who may chance to pass by (?) this...], (3) who will stretch forth his arm to [this] image [and will invoke (?) a thousand ..., a thousand] bread, a thousand* sr *-geese, a thousand pigeons, a thousand ... [...] (4) for this image, he will arrive in peace, (after) he has accomplished that on account of which he has come. [But as for him] (5) who will destroy this image and efface this inscription ... [...], (6) he will not see success, he will not achieve that on account of which he has come. It is [Thoth, lord of] (7)* ḫmnw *and it is Anty, lord of [ṯrtỉ(?), who will punish (?) him].*

UT3. Senusret III (throne name). This fragmentary rock-cut stele, which is in the private collection of George Michaelides (like UT2 above), comprises two fragments, which, although not joining, appear to be part of the same inscription on the basis of both writing style and the similarity of the travertine from which they are carved (Goedicke 1959). Although the section of text referring to the material being quarried is missing, Goedicke is probably correct in his hypothesis that it relates to a 12th Dynasty expedition to quarry travertine at Hatnub. The word translated here by Goedicke (1959) as 'quarry-man' is *ỉḳwy* (see section 8.1, above), which is used with this sense in three of the Wadi Hammamat quarrying inscriptions, all dating to the Middle Kingdom (113, 188 and 123, see also Gardiner 1916: 154)

As Goedicke points out, only one other text at Hatnub refers to quarrying at Hatnub in the reign of Senusret III (Inscription XIII). Unlike Inscription XIII, Goedicke's text includes references to large numbers of workmen, which suggests that activities took place on a fairly major scale. It also seems, judging from the wording of Goedicke's text, that this was probably a one-off mission rather than a more permanent scenario. A crucial question raised by Goedicke is whether this mission could possibly have been linked with the expedition mentioned in the tomb of Thuthotep at Deir el-Bersha, given that this tomb has been dated to Senusret III's reign.

Fragment A: *[Year ... of his majesty, he of the sedge and the bee,]* ḫˁ-k3w-rˁ.

Fragment B: *(1) The chief workman Senusret... (2) says: 'I came here in order to bring [travertine? together with] (3) 1080 quarry-men, 360 artists, ... necropolis workers'.*

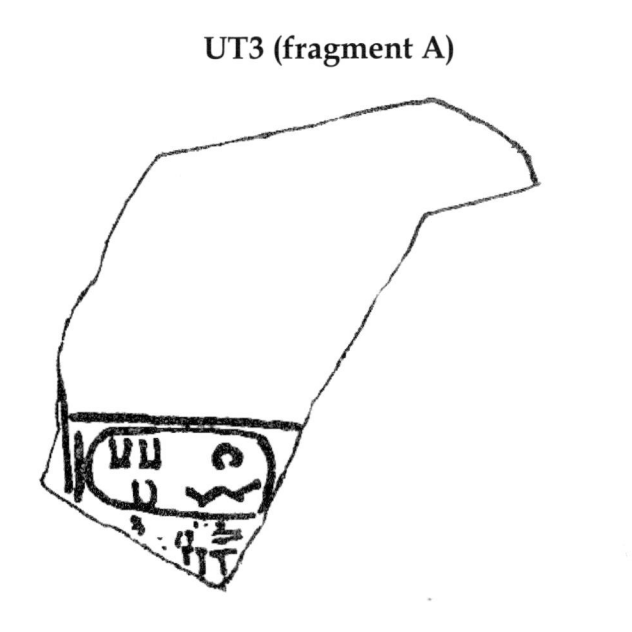

UT3 (fragment A)   **UT3 (fragment B)**

Appendix 5

Chronological List of all Known Texts from Hatnub

[Inscrip=Inscription, Gr.=Graffito, UT=unprovenanced text]

OLD KINGDOM
Inscrip I-II.   Khufu.
Inscrip III-V.   Pepi I
Inscrip VIII.   Pepi I? Merenra?
Inscrip VI.   Merenra
Inscrip VII, Gr.6.   Pepi II

FIRST INTERMEDIATE PERIOD
Inscrip IX-X, Gr.9   Earlier nomarchs
Gr.10-13, 42   Nomarchs Ahanakht and Thutnakht IV
Gr.14-29   Nomarch Nehery I
Gr.31-2   Nomarchs Thutnakht V and Thuthotep I

MIDDLE KINGDOM
Gr.49, UT1-2   Senusret I
Gr.50.   Amenemhat II
Inscrip XIII, UT3.   Senusret III

SECOND INTERMEDIATE PERIOD
Gr.52.   No ruler's name, but dated palaeographically.

NEW KINGDOM
Inscrip XIV.   No ruler's name, but dated prosopographically and palaeographically to the New Kingdom.

ROMAN PERIOD(?)
Quarry T relief and text (Timme 1917: 46, Abb.50)

UNDATED (but all probably First Intermediate Period or Middle Kingdom)
Inscrip XI-XII, Gr.30, 33-41, 43-8, 51.

Appendix 6

Texts formerly and currently in the collection of the Ägyptisches Museum, Berlin

Formerly in the Ägyptisches Museum (lost or destroyed in World War II)

18555   Gr.37: stele of Thuthotep (Anthes 1928: 71, tf. 28)

18557   Gr.46: stele of Khnum (Anthes 1928: 74, tf. 27)

22610   Gr.41: stele of Ahahotep (Anthes 1928: 72, tf. 27)

22611   Gr.44: stele of Khnumi (Anthes 1928: 74, tf. 24)

22612   Gr.45: stele of two cousins, Nakht and Ankh (Anthes 1928: 74, tf. 24)

22613   Gr.47: stele of an unknown man (Anthes 1928: 74-5, tf. 21)

22614   Gr.48: stele of Hetepi (Anthes 1928: 75, tf. 24)

22616   Gr.48a/5: part of a text giving the filiation of an individual (Anthes 1928: 75)

22617   Gr.48a/6: images of two standing men, each with kilt, sceptre and staff (Anthes 1928: 75-6)

22618   Gr.48a/7: images of two standing men, with only the outlines of the bodies surviving (Anthes 1928: 76)

22619   Gr.48a/8: poorly preserved image of a standing man with staff (Anthes 1928: 76)

Currently in the Ägyptisches Museum

18556   Gr.40: stele of Iaib (Anthes 1928: 72, tf. 27)

22609   Gr.39: stele of Ahanakht (Anthes 1928: 72, tf. 25)

22615   Gr.48a/4: standing figure of a man (Anthes 1928: 75)

Bibliography

ABBREVIATIONS

AAR	African Archaeological Review
AJA	American Journal of Anthropology
ASAE	Annales du Service des Antiquités de l'Égypte
BASOR	Bulletin of the American Schools of Oriental Research
BIDE	Bulletin de l'Institut du Desert d'Égypte du Caire
BIFAO	Bulletin de l'Institut Français d'Archéologie Oriental du Caire
BiOr	Bibliotheca Orientalia
BSAE	British School of Archaeology in Egypt
BSEG	Bulletin de la Société d'Égyptologie de Genève
BSFE	Bulletin de la Société Française d'Égyptologie
BSGE	Bulletin de la Société de Géographie d'Égypte du Caire
CdE	Chronique d'Égypte
CRIPEL	Cahiers de Recherches de l'Institut de Papyrologie et Égyptologie de Lille
CSJ	Cairo Scientific Journal
CUP	Cambridge University Press
EEF	Egypt Exploration Fund
EES	Egypt Exploration Society
GM	Göttinger Miszellen
IFAO	L'Institut Français d'Archéologie Orientale du Caire
JAI	Journal of the Anthropological Institute
JARCE	Journal of the American Research Center in Egypt
JAS	Journal of African Studies
JEA	Journal of Egyptian Archaeology
JFA	Journal of Field Archaeology
JNES	Journal of Near Eastern Studies

JRA	Journal of Roman Archaeology
JRS	Journal of Roman Studies
JSSEA	Journal of the Society for the Study of Egyptian Antiquities
JWP	Journal of World Prehistory
LÄ	Lexikon der Ägyptologie, ed. W. Helck *et al.* (Wiesbaden, 1975–86)
MDAIK	Mitteilungen des Deutschen Archäologischen Institut, Abteilung Kairo
MIFAO	Mémoires de l'Institut Français d'Archéologie Oriental
MIO	Mitteilungen des Insituts für Orientforschung (Berlin 1953–71)
MMJ	Metropolitan Museum Journal
OLP	Orientalia Lovaniensa Periodica
OUP	Oxford University Press
PPS	Proceedings of the Prehistoric Society
PSBA	Proceedings of the Society for Biblical Archaeology
RdE	Revue d'Égyptologie
SAK	Studien der altägyptischen Kultur
VA	Varia Aegyptiaca
WA	World Archaeology
Wb	Wörterbuch der Ägyptischen Sprache, eds A Erman and H. Grapow (Leipzig, 1926–31)
ZÄS	Zeitschrift für Ägyptische Sprache und Altertumskunde

Adriani, A. 1940. *Annuaire du Musée Gréco-Romain (1935–1939)*. Alexandria: Société de Publications Egyptiennes.

Akaad, M. K. and M. H. Naggar 1964a. Petrography of the Egyptian alabaster of Wadi al Assyuti. *Bulletin of the Faculty of Science, Alexandria University* 6: 157–73.

Akaad, M. K. and M. H. Naggar 1964b. The deposit of Egyptian alabaster at Wadi el Assyuti. *BSGE* 36: 29–39.

Akaad, M. K. and M. H. Naggar 1965a. Petrography of Wadi Sannur alabaster and its bearing on the mode of formation of Egyptian alabaster. *BSGE* 37: 15–30.

Akaad, M. K. and M. H. Naggar 1965b. Geology of the Wadi Sannur alabaster and the general geological history of the Egyptian alabaster deposits. *BIDE* 13/2: 35–63.

Altenmüller, H. and A. M. Moussa 1981. Die Inschriften der Taharkastele von der Dahschurstrasse. *SAK* 9: 57–84.

Anthes, R. 1928. *Die Felseninschriften von Hatnub*. Leipzig: J.C. Heinrichs.

Arnold, D. 1991. *Building in Egypt: Pharaonic Stone Masonry*. New York and Oxford: OUP.

Arnold, D. and D. Arnold 1979. *Der Tempel Qasr el-Sagha*. Mainz: Philipp von Zabern.

Arnold, D. and E. Pischikova 1999. Stone vessels: luxury items with manifold implications, in Ziegler, C. (ed.), *Egyptian Art in the Age of the Pyramids. Catalogue of an exhibition held at the Metropolitan Museum of Art, Sept.16, 1999 – Jan., 9, 2000*, New York: Metropolitan Museum Press, 121–32.

Aston, B. G. 1994. *Ancient Egyptian Stone Vessels: Materials and Forms*. Heidelberg: Heidelberger Orientverlag.

Aston, B. G., Harrell, J. A. and I. Shaw 2000. Stone, in Nicholson, P. T. and I. Shaw (eds), *Ancient Egyptian Materials and Technology*. Cambridge: CUP, 5–77.

Aufrère, S. H. 2003. L'origine d'albâtre à la 1re dynastie d'après les inscriptions des vases provenant des galleries de la pyramide à degrees. *BIFAO* 103: 1–15.

Badawy, A. 1963. The transport of the colossus of Djehutihetep. MIO 8: 325–32.

Bavay, L., Th. De Putter, B. Adams, J. Navez, L. and André, L. 2000. The origin of obsidian in Predynastic and Early Dynastic Upper Egypt. *MDAIK* 56: 5–20.

Barbieri, M., Lilyquist, C. and G. Testa 2002. Provenancing Egyptian and Minoan calcite-alabaster artifacts through 87SR/86SR isotopic ratios and petrography, in Lazzarini, L. (ed.), *Interdisciplinary Studies on Ancient Stone: Proceedings of the International Conference of the "Association for the Study of Marble and Other Stones in Antiquity" ASMOSIA 6, Venice, June 15–18 2000*, Padua: Bottega d'Erasmo, 403–14.

Barbieri, M., Testa, G., Merola, D., Polychronakis, Y. and V. Simitzis 2002. Comparative strontium-isotope analysis and petrography of Egyptian and Cretan limestone and calcite-alabaster, in Lazzarini, L. (ed.), *Interdisciplinary Studies on Ancient Stone: Proceedings of the International Conference of the "Association for the Study of Marble and Other Stones in Antiquity" ASMOSIA 6, Venice, June 15-18 2000*, Padua: Bottega d'Erasmo, 415–25.

Beadnell, H. J. L. 1927. *Wilderness of Sinai: A Record of Two Years' Recent Exploration*. London: Edward Arnold.

Benham, F. 1985. A consideration of the possible causes and manner of destruction of the Saad el Kafra Dam. *Wepwawet: Papers in Egyptology* (Summer 1985): 1–4.

Bernard, M. 1966–7. *Les vases en pierre de l'ancien empire (Ve et VIe dynasties)*. Unpublished dissertation. Université catholique de Louvain, Faculté de philosophie et lettres, Institut supérieur d'archéologie et d'histoire de l'art.

Birch, S. 1852. Upon a historical tablet of Ramses II, 19th dynasty, relating to the gold mines in Aethiopia. *Archaeologia* 34: 354–91.

Bissing, F. W. von 1907. *Steingefäße. CGC 18065–18793*. Vienna: Adolf Holzhausen.

Blackden M. W. and G. W. Fraser 1892. *Collection of Hieratic Graffiti from the Alabaster Quarry of Hat-nub*. Private circulation.

Bloxam, E. 1998. *The organisation, exploitation and transport of hard rock from 'Chephren's Quarry' during the Old Kingdom*, unpubl. MA diss., Institute of Archaeology, University College London.

Bloxam, E. G., 2003. *The organization, transportation and logistics of hard stone quarrying in the Egyptian Old Kingdom: a comparative study*, unpubl. PhD diss., Institute of Archaeology, University College London.

Bloxam, E. 2006. Miners and mistresses: Middle Kingdom mining on the margins. *Journal of Social Archaeology* 6: 277–303.

Bloxam, E. and T. Heldal 2007. The industrial landscape of the northern Faiyum Desert as a world heritage site: modelling 'outstanding universal value' of 3rd millennium BC stone quarrying in Egypt. *WA* 39/3: 305–23.

Bloxam, E. and P. Storemyr 2002. Old Kingdom basalt quarrying activities at Widan el-Faras, Northern Faiyum Desert. *JEA* 88: 23–36.

Bouriant, U., G. Legrain and G. Jéquier 1903. *Monuments pour servir à l'étude du culte d'Atonou en Egypte VI: Les tombes de Khouitatonou*. Cairo: IFAO.

Bourriau, J. 1988. *Pharaohs and Mortals: Egyptian Art in the Middle Kingdom*. Cambridge: CUP.

Bourriau, J., P. T. Nicholson and P. J. Rose 2000. Pottery, in Nicholson, P. T. and I. Shaw (eds), *Ancient Egyptian Materials and Technology*. Cambridge: CUP, 121–47.

Bowman, H., F. H. Stross, F. Asaro, R. L. Hay, R. F. Heizer and H. V. Michel 1984. The northern colossus of Memnon: new slants. *Archaeometry* 26/2: 218–29.

Bradbury, L. 1988. On travelling to "God's Land" and Punt in the Middle Kingdom. *JARCE* 25: 127–56.

Breasted, J. H. 1906. *Ancient Records of Egypt I: The First through the Seventeenth Dynasties*. Chicago: University of Chicago Press.

Brovarski, E. 1981. Ahanakht of Bersheh and the Hare nome in the First Intermediate Period and Middle Kingdom, in Simpson, W. K. and W. M. Davis (eds), *Studies in Ancient Egypt, the Aegean, and the Sudan: Essays in Honour of Dows Dunham*. Boston: Museum of Fine Arts, 14–30.

Brugsch, H. 1862. *Receuil des monuments égyptiens*. 2 vols. Leipzig.

Brunner-Traut, E. 1970. Gravidenflasche: das Salben des Mutterleibes, in Kuschke, A. and E. Kutsch (eds), *Archäologie und Altes Testament: Festschrift für Kurt Galling zum 8. Januar 1970*. Tübingen: J. C. B. Mohr, 35–48.

de Bruyn, P. 1955. A graffito of the scribe Dhutihotpe, reckoner of gold in the south-eastern desert. *JEA* 41: 121-2.

Bryan, B. 1992. Royal and divine statuary, in Kozloff, A. and B. Bryan (eds), *Egypt's Dazzling Sun: Amenhotep III and his World*. Bloomington IN: Indiana University Press, 125–92.

Budge, E. A. W. 1908. *An Account of the Sarcophagus of Seti I, King of Egypt, B.C. 1370*. London: Sir John Soane's Museum.

Castel, G. and G. Soukiassian 1985. Dépôt de stèles dans le sanctuaire du Nouvel Empire au Gebel Zeit. *BIFAO* 85: 285–93.

Castel, G. and G. Soukiassian 1989. *Gebel el-Zeit I: Les mines de galène (Egypte, IIe millénaire av. J.-C.)*. Cairo: IFAO.

Castiglione, L. 1967. Tables votives à empreintes de pied dans les temples d'Egypte. *Acta Orientalia Academiae Scientiarum Hungaricae* 20: 239–52.

Castiglione, L. 1971. Zur Frage der Sarapis-Füße. *ZÄS* 97: 30–43.

Castiglione, L. 1974. Das wichtigste Denkmal der Sarapis-Füße im British Museum wiedergefunden. *Studia Aegyptiaca* 1: 75–81.

Caton-Thompson, G. and E. W. Gardner 1934. *The Desert Fayum*. 2 vols. London: EES.

Chartier-Raymond, M. 1988. Notes sur Maghara (Sinai). *CRIPEL* 10: 13–22.

Clarke, S. and R. Englebach 1930. *Ancient Egyptian Masonry: The Building Craft*. Oxford: OUP.

Couyat, J. and P. Montet 1912-13. *Les inscriptions hiéroglyphiques et hiératiques du Ouadi Hammamat*. Cairo: IFAO.

Darnell, J. 2002. *Theban Desert Road Survey in the Egyptian Western Desert I*. Chicago: Oriental Institute of the University of Chicago.

Davies, N. de G. 1903-8. *The Rock Tombs of el-Amarna*, 6 vols. London: EES.

Davies, N. de G. and A.H. Gardiner 1915. *The Tomb of Amenemhet*. London: EES.

Debono, F. 1993-4. Un atelier d'artisans au Ramesseum. *Memnonia* IV–V: 37–53.

Deines, H. von 1976. Die Rezepte Eb 808 und 809 im Pap. Ebers, um gs.w bei einer Frau zu behanden. *GM* 19: 17–22.

De Putter, T. and C. Karlshausen 1992. *Les pierres utilisées dans la sculpture et l'architecture de l'Egypte pharaonique: guide pratique illustré*. Brussels: Connaissance de l'Egypte Ancienne.

Description 1809-28. *Description de l'Egypte, ou receuil des observations et des recherches qui ont été faites en Egypte pendant l'expedition de l'Armée française*. Paris: Imprimerie Impériale.

Dorsey, D. 1991. *The Roads and Highways of Ancient Israel*. Baltimore MA: Johns Hopkins University.

Dreyer, G. and H. Jaritz 1983. Die Arbeiterunterkünfte am Sadd-el-Kafara, in Garbrecht, B. (ed.), *Sadd el-Kafara: Die älteste Talsperre der Welt (2600 v.Chr.)*. Braunschweig: Leichtweiss-Institut für Wasserbau der Technischen Universität Braunschweig: Appendix B.

Duell, P. 1938. *The Mastaba of Mereruka*. 2 vols. Chicago: OIP.

Dunham, D. 1947. Four Kushite colossi in the Sudan. *JEA*, 33: 63–5.

Eggebrecht, A. 1966. Zur Bedeutung des Würfelhockers, in *Festgabe für Dr Walter Will*. Cologne, Berlin, Bonn and Munich: Carl Heyman, 143–63.

Eichler, E. 1993. *Untersuchungen zum Expeditionswesen des ägyptischen Alten Reiches*, GOF 26, Wiesbaden.

Engelbach, R. 1938. The quarries of the Western Nubian Desert and the ancient road to Tushka. *ASAE* 38: 369–90.

Ericson, J. E. and B. A. Purdy (eds) 1984. *Prehistoric Quarries and Lithic Production*. Cambridge: CUP.

Erman, A. 1885. *Ägypten und Ägyptisches Leben im Altertum*. Tübingen: H. Laup'schen.

Fahlbusch, H. 1986. *Der Sadd el-Kafara, in Geschichtliche Wasserbauten in Ägypten*. Braunschweig: Leichtweiß-Institut für Wasserbau der Technischen Universität Braunschweig.

Fakhry, A. 1952. *The Inscriptions of the Amethyst Quarries at Wadi el-Hudi*. Cairo: Govt Press.

Firth, C. M. and J. E. Quibell 1935. *The Step Pyramid* I. London.

Fischer, H.G. 1985. More about the *Smntjw*. *GM* 84: 25-32.

Fischer, H. G. 1991. Sur les routes de l'Ancien Empire. *CRIPEL* 13: 59–64.

Forbes, R. J. 1964. *Notes on the History of Ancient Roads and their Construction*. 2nd unrev. ed., Amsterdam: A.M. Hakkert.

Fraser, G. W. 1894. Hat-nub. *PSBA* 16: 73-82.

Garbrecht, G. 1983. *Der Sadd el-Kafara Die älteste Talsperre der Welt (2600 v.Chr.)*. Braunschweig: Leichtweiß-Institut für Wasserbau der Technischen Universität Braunschweig.

Garbrecht, G. 1999. Wadi Garrawi, in K. Bard (ed.), *Encyclopedia of the Archaeology of Ancient Egypt*. London: Routledge, 864-6.

Gardiner, A. H. 1946. Davies's copy of the Speos Artemidos inscription. *JEA* 32: 43–56.

Gardiner, A. H. 1947. *Ancient Egyptian Onomastica*, 2 vols. Oxford: OUP.

Gardiner, A. H., T. E. Peet and J. Cerny 1955. *Inscriptions of Sinai* II. 2nd ed. Oxford: OUP.

Gauthier, H. 1920. Le temple de l'Ouadi Miya (el-Kanais). *BIFAO* 17: 1-38.

Gerisch, R. 2004. *Holzkohleuntersuchungen an pharaonischen und byzantischen Material aus Amarna und Umgebung. Ein Beitrag zur Identifizierung von Hölzern unter Berücksichtigung des Gebrauches von Holz als Brennmaterial und seiner Rolle bei der Rekonstruktion der lokalen Vegetation*, MÄS 53. Mainz: Philipp von Zabern.

Giuliani, S. 1997. A new proposal for the interpretation of Hatnub Graffito No 16. *GM* 159: 53–9.

Goedicke, H. 1959. A new inscription from Hatnub. *ASAE* 56: 55–8.

Goedicke, H. 1962. Psammetik I. und die Libyer. *MDAIK* 18: 26–49.

Goedicke, H. 1965. «80» as a sportive writing. *CdE* 40: 28–33.

Goneim, M. Z. 1956. *The Buried Pyramid*. London: Longmans, Green and Co.

Grdseloff, B. 1951. Un nouveau graffito de Hatnoub. *ASAE* 51: 143–6.

Griffith, F. 1894. Selected inscriptions from the quarry of Het-Nub, in Griffith, F.Ll. and P. Newberry, *El Bersheh* II. London: EEF, 47–54, pls 22–23.

Griffith, F. Ll. and P. Newberry 1894. *El Bersheh* II. London: EEF.

Gunn, B. and A.H. Gardiner 1917. New renderings of Egyptian texts I: the temple of the Wady Abbad. *JEA* 4: 241-51.

Habachi, L. 1960. Notes on the unfinished obelisk of Aswan and another smaller one in Gharb Aswan, in Struve, V.V. (ed.), *Drevni i Egipet*, Moscow: Institut Vostokovedeni i a, Akademi i a Nauk USSR, 216–35.

Halioua, B. and B. Ziskind 2005. *Medicine in the Days of the Pharaohs*, Cambridge MA: Harvard University Press.

Hari, R. 1976. *Répertoire onomastique amarnien*. Geneva: Aegyptiaca Helvetica.

Harrell, J. A. 1989. An inventory of ancient Egyptian quarries. *NARCE* 146: 1–7.

Harrell, J. A. 1990. Misuse of the term "alabaster" in Egyptology. *GM* 119: 37–42.

Harrell, J. A. 2001a. Ancient quarries near Amarna. *Egyptian Archaeology* 19: 36–8.

Harrell, J. A. 2001b. Calcite, in Redford, D.B. (ed.), *The Oxford Encyclopedia of Ancient Egypt*. Oxford: OUP, 223–4.

Harrell, J. A. n. d. Table 2: Ancient Egyptian Softstone Quarries [Online]

Harrell, J. A. and T. M. Bown 1995. An Old Kingdom basalt quarry at Widan el-Faras and the quarry road to Lake Moeris in the Faiyum, Egypt. *JARCE* 32: 71–91.

Harrell, J. A. and V. M. Brown 1992. The oldest surviving topographical map from ancient Egypt: Turin Papyri 1879, 1899 and 1969. *JARCE* 29: 81–105.

Harrell, J. A. and V. M. Brown 1994. Chephren's quarry in the Nubian desert of Egypt. *Nubica* 3/1: 43–57.

Harrell, J. A., M. A. T. M Broekmans and D. I. Godfrey-Smith 2007. The origin, destruction and restoration of colour in Egyptian travertine. *Archaeometry* 49/3: 421–36.

Harris, J. R. 1961. *Lexicographical Studies in Ancient Egyptian Materials* Berlin: Akademie-Verlag.

Heizer, R. F., F. Stross, T. R. Hester, A. Albee, I. Perlman, F. Asaro and H. Bowman 1973. The colossi of Memnon revisited. *Science* 182: 1219–25.

Helck. W. 1987. *Untersuchungen zur Thinitenzeit* Wiesbaden: Harassowitz.

Hellström, B. 1951. The oldest dam in the world. *Bulletin of the Institution of Hydraulics at the Royal Institute of Technology*, Stockholm 28.

Hellström, B. 1970. *The Rock Drawings. The Scandinavian Joint Expedition to Sudanese Nubia, vols 1.1–2*. Odense.

Hester, T. R. and R. F. Heizer 1981. *Making Stone Vases: Ethnoarchaeological Studies at an Alabaster Workshop in Upper Egypt*. Monographic Journals of the Near East. Malibu CA: Undena Publications.

Hikade, T. 2001. *Das Expeditionswesen im ägyptischen Neuen Reich: ein Beitrag zu Rohstoffversorgung und Außenhandel*, SAGA 21. Heidelberg: Heidelberger Orientverlag.

el-Hinnawi, E. E. and S. M. Loukina 1972. A contribution to the geochemistry of "Egyptian alabaster". *Tschermaks Mineralogische und Petrographische Mitteilungen* (Vienna) 17/3: 215–21.

Hoffman, M. A. 1979. *Egypt Before the Pharaohs: The Prehistoric Foundations of Egyptian Civilization*. New York: Alfred A. Knopf.

Hornung, E. 1991. Sedfest und Geschichte. *MDAIK* 47: 169–71.

Hume, W. F. 1912. The alabaster quarries of Wadi Asiut. *CSJ* 6: 72.

Isler, M. 1992. The technique of monolithic carving. *MDAIK* 48: 45–55.

James, T. G. H. 1991. The discovery and identification of the alabaster quarries of Hatnub. *CRIPEL* 13: 79–84.

Jansen-Winkeln, K. 1989. Zu einigen „Trinksprüchen" auf ägyptischen Gefäßen. *ZÄS* 116: 143–53.

Janssen, J. J. 1975. Prolegomena to the study of Egypt's economic development during the New Kingdom. *SAK* 3: 127–86.

Jaritz, J. 1993. The investigation of the ancient wall extending from Aswan to Philae. *MDAIK* 49: 107–32.

Jeffreys, D. J. 1985. *The Survey of Memphis I*. London: EES.

Jones, M. 1990. The temple of Apis in Memphis. *JEA* 76: 141–7.

Jones, M. and A. M. Jones 1982. The Apis House Project at Mit Rahinah, First Season, 1982. *JARCE* 19: 51–8.

Jones, R. forthcoming The inherent pitfalls in using the Djehutihotep transport scene for manpower estimates in the ancient transport of construction material.

Kaiser, W. 1969. Die Tongefässe, in H. Ricke, *Das Sonnenheiligtum des Königs Userkaf,* II. Wiesbaden: Franz Steiner, 49–82.

Kemp, B. J. 1983. Old Kingdom, Middle Kingdom and Second Intermediate Period c.2686–1552 BC, in Trigger, B. G., B. J. Kemp, D. B. O'Connor and A. B. Lloyd, *Ancient Egypt: A Social History*. Cambridge: CUP, 71–182.

Kemp, B. J. 1984. *Amarna Reports* I. London: EES.

Kemp, B. J. 1985. *Amarna Reports* II. London: EES.

Kemp, B. J. 1989. *Ancient Egypt: Anatomy of a Civilization*. 1st ed. London: Routledge.

Kemp, B.J. 1995. *Amarna Reports* VI. London: EES.

Kemp, B. J. 2006. *Ancient Egypt: Anatomy of a Civilization*. 2nd ed. London: Routledge.

Kessler, D. 1981. *Historische Topographie der region zwischen Mallawi und Samalut*. TAVO B30. Wiesbaden: Dr Ludwig Reichert.

el-Khouli, A. 1978. *Egyptian Stone Vessels: Predynastic Period to Dynasty III: Typology and Analysis*, 3 vols. Mainz am Rhein: von Zabern.

el-Khouli, A. A. R., R. Holthoer, C. A. Hope, O. E. and Kaper, O.E. 1994. *Stone Vessels, Pottery and Sealings from the Tomb of Tut'ankhamun*. Oxford: Griffith Institute.

Kitchen, K. A. 1991. Building the Ramesseum. *CRIPEL* 13: 85–93.

Klemm, D. 1984. Steinbruch, in *LÄ* V, 1276–83.

Klemm, R. and D. Klemm 1979. Herkunftbestimmung altägyptischen Steinmaterials: (1) Bericht über die erste Kampagne 1977, (2) Bericht über die zweite Kampagne 1978, *SAK* 7: 103–40.

Klemm, R. and D. Klemm 1981. *Die Steine der Pharaonen*. Munich: Staatliche Sammlung ägyptische Kunst.

Klemm, R., D. Klemm, D. and L. Steclaci 1984. Die pharaonischen Steinbrüche des Silizifierten Sandsteins in Ägypten und die Herkunft der Memnon-Kolosse. *MDAIK* 40: 207–20.

Klemm, R. and D. Klemm 1988. Pharaonischer Goldbergbau im Wadi Sid und der Turiner Minenpapyrus, in S. Schoske (ed.), *Akten München 1985* 2. Hamburg: Helmut Buske Verlag: 73–87.

Klemm, R. and D. Klemm 1991. Calcit-Alabaster oder Travertin? Bemerkungen zu Sinn und Unsinn petrographischen Bezeichnungen in der Ägyptologie. *GM* 122: 57–70.

Klemm, R. and D. Klemm 2008. *Stones and Quarries in Ancient Egypt*. London: BMP.

Klemm, R., Klemm, D. and A. Murr 2002. Geo-archäologischer Survey im Wadi el-Hudi, in B. Schmitz (ed.), *Festschrift Arne Eggebrecht*, Hildesheim: Gerstenberg.

Köhler, K. 1995. The state of research on late Predynastic Egypt: new evidence for the development of the pharaonic state? *GM* 147: 79–92.

Lacau P. and J.-Ph. Lauer 1961. *La pyramide à degrés IV: Inscriptions gravées sur les vases*. Cairo; SAE.

Legrain, G. 1903. Notes d'inspection, no.9: sur une ouabit en albâtre. *ASAE* 4: 225–6.

Lehner, M. 1985. The development of the Giza necropolis: the Khufu project. *MDAIK* 41: 109–44.

Lemaire, A. and P. Vernus 1978. L'origine égyptienne du signe y des poids inscrits de l'époque royale Israélite. *Semitica* 28: 53–8.

Lichtheim, M. 1973. *Ancient Egyptian Literature I: The Old and Middle Kingdoms*. Los Angeles and Berkeley: University of California Press.

Lieblein, J. 1909. Les inscriptions trouvées dans les carrièrres de Hatnub. *Sphinx* 12: 227–30.

Lilyquist, C. 1995. *Egyptian Stone Vessels: Khian through Tuthmosis IV*. New York, MMA.

Lilyquist, C. 1996. Stone vessels at Kamid el-Loz: Egyptian, Egyptianizing, or non-Egyptian? A question at sites from the Sudan to Iraq to the Greek mainland, in Hachmann, R. (ed.), *Kamid el-Loz* 16, Saarbrücker Beiträge zur Altertumskunde. Bonn: Dr Rudolf Habelt GmbH.

Lucas, A. 1962. *Ancient Egyptian Materials and Industries*, rev. J.R. Harris, 4th edition. London: Edward Arnold.

Mackay, E. 1915. Old Kingdom dam in Wadi Gerrawi, in Mackay, E. and W.M.F. Petrie, *Heliopolis, Kafr Ammar and Shurufa*, London: EES, 38–40.

Malek, J. 1986. *In the Shadow of the Pyramids: Egypt in the Old Kingdom*, London: Little Brown and Co.

Meyers, P. and L. van Zelst 1977. Neutron activation analysis of limestone objects in a pilot study. *Radiochimica Acta*, 24: 197–204.

Middleton, A. P. and S. M. Bradley 1989. Provenancing of Egyptian limestone sculpture. *Journal of Archaeological Science* 16: 475–88.

Minault-Gout, A. 1997. Sur les vases jubilaires et leur diffusion, in Berger, C., S. El-Naggar and B. Matthieu (eds), *Études sur l'Ancien Empire et la nécropole de Saqqâra dédiées à Jean-Philippe Lauer*, Montpellier: Univ. Paul Valéry - Montpellier III, 305–14.

Möller, G. 1908. *Bericht über die Aufnahme der hieroglyphischen und hieratischen Felseninschriften im Alabasterbruch von Hatnub in Mittelägypten*. Sitzungsberichte der Königlich Preußischen Akademie der Wissenschaften 32: 679–90.

Moores Jr., R. G. 1991. Evidence for use of a stone-cutting drag saw by the Fourth Dynasty Egyptians. *JARCE* 28: 139–48.

Moorey, P. R. S. 1994. *Ancient Mesopotamian Materials and Industries: The Archaeological Evidence*, Oxford: OUP.

Moussa, A. M. 1981. A stela of Taharqa from the desert road at Dahshur. *MDAIK* 37: 331–7.

Murnane, W.J. 1975. A note on the personnel of the Sinai expeditions under Ammenemes III. *GM* 15: 27–33.

Murray, G. W. 1925. The Roman roads and stations in the eastern desert of Egypt. *JEA* 11: 138–50.

Murray, G. W. 1939. The road to Chephren's quarries. *The Geographical Journal* 94/2: 97–114.

Murray, G. W. 1945–6 A note on the Sadd el-Kafara: the ancient dam in the Wadi Gerrawi. *BdE* 28: 33–4.

Nagel, G. 1938. *La céramique du Nouvel Empire à Deir el-Médineh* I. Documents de fouilles publiés par les members de l'Institut Français d'Archéologie Orientale du Caire X. Cairo: IFAO.

Newberry, P. E. 1893. *El Bersheh* I. ASE 3. London: EEF.

Nordström, H-A. and J. Bourriau 1993. Ceramic technology: clays and fabrics, in Arnold, D. and J. Bourriau (eds), *An Introduction to Ancient Egyptian Pottery*, Mainz: von Zabern, 147–90.

O'Connor, D. 1983. New Kingdom and Third Intermediate Period, 1552–664 BC, in Trigger, B. G., Kemp, B. J., O'Connor, D. B. and A. B. Lloyd (eds), *Ancient Egypt: A Social History*, Cambridge: CUP, 183–278.

Partridge, R. 1996. *Transport in Ancient Egypt*, London: Rubicon Press.

Peet, T. E. and C. L. Woolley 1923. *City of Akhenaten I*, London: EEF.

Petrie, W. M. F. 1888. *A Season in Egypt*, London: EEF.

Petrie, W. M. F. 1892. *Medum*, London: EEF.

Petrie, W. M. F. 1894. *Tell el-Amarna*, London: EEF.

Petrie, W. M. F. 1907. *Gizeh and Rifeh*, London: BSAE/Bernard Quaritch.

Petrie, W. M. F. 1940. *The Wisdom of the Egyptians*, London: BSAE/Bernard Quaritch.

Petrie, W. M. F. and C. T. Currelly 1906. *Researches in Sinai*, London: John Murray.

Petrie, W. M. F. and E. Mackay 1915. *Heliopolis, Kafr Ammar and Shurafa*, London: BSAE/Quaritch.

Petrie, W. M. F. 1937. *The Funeral Furniture of Egypt/Stone and Metal Vases*, London: BSAE/Quaritch.

Phillips, J. 2001. Stone vessel production: new beginnings and new visions in New Palace Crete, in Shortland, A. J. (ed.), *The Social Context of Technological Change: Egypt and the Near East, 1650–1550 BC*. Oxford: Oxbow Books, 73–91.

Pillet, M. 1923. Rapport sur les travaux de Karnak (1922–1923), no. 6: un sanctuaire-reposoir de barque sacrée d'Amenhotep 1er. *ASAE* 23: 113–17.

Pliny. *Natural History*, trans. D. E. Eichholz. Vol. 10 of the Loeb Classical Library. London: William Heinemann, 1962.

Posener, G. 1936. *La première domination perse en égypte*. BdE XI. Cairo: IFAO.

Posener, G. 1968. Une stèle de Hatnoub. *JEA* 54: 67–71.

Postgate, N. 1997. Mesopotamian petrology: stages in the classification of the material world. *CAJ* 7/2: 205–24.

Quirke, S. 1990. *The Administration of Egypt in the Late Middle Kingdom: The Hieratic Documents*, New Malden: SIA Publishing.

Reade, J. 1983. *Assyrian Sculpture*, British Museum Publications, London.

Reisner, G. A. 1931. *Mycerinus: The Temples of the Third pyramid at Giza*, Cambridge MA: Harvard University Press.

Reisner, G. A. 1932. *A Provincial Cemetery of the Pyramid Age: Naga-ed-Dêr*, III, Oxford: OUP.

Reisner, G. A. and W. S. Smith 1955. *A History of the Giza Necropolis, II: The Tomb of Hetepheres, the Mother of Cheops*. Cambridge MA: Harvard University Press.

Rice, M. 1990. *Egypt's Making: The Origins of Ancient Egypt 5000–2000 BC*, London: Routledge.

Ricci, S. de 1932. An album of drawings by Sir J.G. Wilkinson, in S. R. K. Glanville (ed.), *Studies Presented to F.Ll. Griffith*. London: EES, 474–6.

Richards, J. 2000. Weni the Elder and his mortuary neighbourhood at Abydos, Egypt. *Kelsey Museum Newsletter* Spring 2000.

Richards, J. 2001. The archaeology of individuals at Abydos, Egypt. *Kelsey Museum Newsletter* Fall 2001.

Riemer, H. and F. Förster forthcoming. *Desert Road Archaeology in the Eastern Sahara*. Cologne: ACACIA.

Roeder, G. 1959. *Hermopolis 1929–39*. Hildesheim: Hildesheimer Ägyptologische Beiträge.

Rose, P. J. 1987. The pottery survey, in B. J. Kemp (ed.), *Amarna Reports* IV. London: EES, 115–31.

Rose, P. J. 2007. *The Eighteenth Dynasty Pottery Corpus from Amarna*. London: EES.

Rothenberg, B. 1988. *The Egyptian Mining Temple at Timna*. London: Institute for Archaeometallurgical Studies.

Ruffle, J. 1977. *The Egyptians*. New York: Cornell University Press.

Sadek, A. I. 1980–5. *The Amethyst Mining Inscriptions of Wadi el-Hudi*. 2 vols. Warminster: Aris and Phillips.

Saleh, A. A. 1974. Excavations around Mycerinus pyramid complex. *MDAIK* 30: 131–54.

Saleh, M. and H. Sourouzian 1987. *Official Catalogue: The Egyptian Museum, Cairo*. Mainz: Philipp von Zabern.

Schott, S. 1961. *Kanais: Der Tempel Sethos I.im Wadi Mia*. Göttingen: Vandenhoeck and Ruprecht.

Schweinfurth, G. A. 1885. *Ein altes Stauwerk aus der Pyramidenzeit*. Hamburg-Berlin: Hoffmann and Campe.

Schweinfurth, G. A. 1922. *Auf unbetreten Wegen in Ägypten*. Hamburg-Berlin: Hoffmann and Campe.

Scoffin, T. P. 1987. *An Introduction to Carbonate Sediments and Rocks*. New York: Blackie.

Sethe, K. 1924. *Ägyptische Lesestücke*, Leipzig: J. C. Hinrichs.

Sethe, K. 1933a. *Urkunden des Alten Reichs* I Leipzig: J. C. Hinrichs.

Sethe, K. 1933b. Die Bau- und Denkmalsteine der Alter Ägypter und ihrer Namen. *Sitzungsberichte der Preussischen Akademie der Wissenschaften* 22 (20 July 1933): 864–912.

Seyfried, K.-J. 1981. *Beiträge zu den Expeditionen des Mittleren Reiches in die Ostwüste*, Hildesheim: Hildesheimer Ägyptologische Beiträge.

Shaw, I. 1986. A survey at Hatnub, in Kemp, B. J. (ed.), *Amarna Reports* III, London: EES, 189–212.

Shaw, I. 1987. The 1986 survey of Hatnub, in Kemp, B. J. (ed.), *Amarna Reports IV*, London: EES, 160–67.

Shaw, I. 1990. Hatnub: mapping pharaoh's quarries in the Eastern Desert. *Minerva* I/4: 2–3.

Shaw, I. 1994. Pharaonic quarrying and mining: settlement and procurement in Egypt's marginal areas. *Antiquity* 68/258: 108–19.

Shaw, I. 2002. Life on the edge: gemstones, politics and stress in the deserts of Egypt and Nubia, in Friedman, R. (ed.), *Egypt and Nubia: Gifts of the Desert*, London: British Museum Press, 244–251.

Shaw, I. 2006. "Master of the Roads": quarrying and communications networks in Egypt and Nubia, in Mathieu, B., D. Meeks and M. Wissa (eds), *L'apport de l'Egypte à l'histoire des techniques: méthodes, chronologie et comparaisons*. BdE 142. Cairo: IFAO, 253–66.

Shaw, I. in press. "We went forth to the desert land...": retracing the routes between the Nile valley and the Gebel el-Asr quarries, in Riemer, H. and F. Förster (eds), *Desert road archaeology in the Eastern Sahara*. Cologne: ACACIA.

Shaw, I. and E. Bloxam 1999. Survey and excavation at the ancient pharaonic gneiss quarrying site of Gebel el-Asr, Lower Nubia. *Sudan and Nubia: Sudan Archaeological Research Society Bulletin* 3: 13–20.

Shaw, I., Bloxam, E., Heldal, T. and P. Storemyr in press. Quarrying and landscape at Gebel el-Asr in the Old and Middle Kingdoms, in Raffaele, F., Incordino, I. and M. Nuzzollo (eds), *Proceedings of the First Neapolitan Congress of Egyptology*. Wiesbaden: Otto Harrassowitz.

Shaw, I. and T. Heldal 2003. Rescue work in the Khafra quarries at Gebel el-Asr. *Egyptian Archaeology* 23: 14–16.

Shaw, I. and R. Jameson 1993. Amethyst mining in the Eastern Desert: a preliminary survey at Wadi el-Hudi. *JEA* 79: 81–97.

Sidebotham, S. E. 1996. Newly discovered sites in the Eastern Desert. *JEA* 82: 181–92.

Sidebotham, S. E., Zitterkopf, R. E. and J. A. Riley 1991. Survey of the Abu Sha'ar - Nile road. *AJA* 95: 571–622.

Simpson, W. K. 1958. A Hatnub stela of the early 12th Dynasty. *MDAIK* 16: 298–309.

Simpson, W. K. 1961. An additional fragment of a "Hatnub" stela. *JNES* 20: 25–30.

Simpson, W. K. 1963. *Heka-nefer and the Dynastic Material from Toshka and Arminna*. New Haven and Philadelphia: Peabody Museum of Natural History of Yale University and University Museum of the University of Pennsylvania.

Simpson, W. K. 1977. Hatnub. *LÄ* II: 1043-5.

Sliwa, J. 1992. Die Siedlung des Mittleren Reiches bei Qasr el-Sagha. *MDAIK* 48: 177–91.

Spalinger, A. 2005. *War in Ancient Egypt: The New Kingdom*. Oxford: Blackwell.

Sparks, R. 2001. Stone vessel workshops in the Levant: luxury products of a cosmopolitan age, in Shortland, A. J. (ed.), *The Social Context of Technological Change: Egypt and the Near East, 1650–1550 BC*. Oxford: Oxbow Books, 93–112.

Spence, K. 1999. Red, white and black: colour in building stone in ancient Egypt. *CAJ* 9/1: 114–7.

Stadelmann, R. 1981. La ville de pyramide à l'Ancien Empire. *RdE* 33: 67–77.

Stocks, D. 1986a. Sticks and stones of Egyptian technology. *Popular Archaeology* April 1986: 24–9.

Stocks, D. 1986b. Egyptian technology II: stone vessel manufacture. *Popular Archaeology*, May 1986: 14–18.

Stocks, D. 1989. Ancient factory mass-production techniques: indications of large-scale stone bead manufacture during the Egyptian New Kingdom period. *Antiquity* 63: 526–31.

Stocks, D. 1993. Making stone vessels in ancient Mesopotamia and Egypt. *Antiquity* 67: 596–603.

Stocks, D. 2003a. *Experiments in Egyptian Archaeology: Stoneworking Technology in Ancient Egypt*. London: Routledge.

Stocks, D. 2003b. Immutable laws of friction: preraparing and fitting stone blocks into the Great Pyramid at Giza. *Antiquity* 77: 572–8.

Storemyr, P., Bloxam, E., Heldal, T. and A. Kelany in press. Ancient desert and quarry roads on the west bank of the Nile in the First Cataract region, in Riemer, H. and F. Förster (eds), *Desert Road Archaeology in the Eastern Sahara*. Cologne: ACACIA.

Stross, F. H., R. L. Hay, F. Asaro, H. R. Bowman and H. V. Michel 1988. Sources of quartzite in Egyptian sculpture. *Archaeometry* 30: 109–19.

Thomas, E. S. 1909. The mineral industry of Egypt – copper and tin, iron and lead. *CSJ* 3: 181–5.

Thompson, J. 1992. *Sir Gardner Wilkinson and his Circle*. Austin TX: University of Texas Press.

Timme, P. 1917. *Tell el Amarna vor der deutschen Ausgrabung im Jahre 1911*. Berlin: Wissenschaftliche Veröffentlichungen der Deutschen Orient-Gesellschaft.

Trigger, B. G. 1983. The rise of Egyptian civilization, in Trigger, B. G., Kemp, B. J., O'Connor, D. B. and A. B. Lloyd(eds) *Ancient Egypt: A Social History*, Cambridge: Cambridge University Press: pp.1–70.

Trigger, B. G. 1987. Egypt: a fledgling nation, *JSSEA* 17: 58–66.

Valbelle, D. and C. Bonnet 1996. *Le sanctuaire d'Hathor, maitresse de la turquoise: Sérabit el-Khadim au Moyen Empire*. Paris: Picard.

Vandersleyen, C. 1995. *L'Égypte et la vallée du Nil II: De la fin de l'Ancien Empire à la fin du Nouvel Empire*. Paris: PUF.

Van Siclen III, C. C. 1986. *The Alabaster Shrine of King Amenhotep II*, San Antonio: Van Siclen Books.

Verner, M. 1973. *Some Nubian Petroglyphs on Czechoslovak Concessions: Rock Drawings of (I) Foot and Sandal Prints, (II) Symbols and Signs, and (III) Erotica from the Czechoslovak Concession in Nubia*. Prague: Universita Karlova.

Warren, P. 1967. A stone vase-maker's workshop in the palace at Knossos, *Annual of the British School at Athens* 62: 195–201.

Warren, P. 1969. *Minoan Stone Vases*, Cambridge: CUP.

Warren, P. 1989. Egyptian stone vessels from the city of Knossos: contributions towards Minoan economic and social structure, *Ariadne* 5: 1–9.

Wartke, R.-B. 1977. Zum alabaster-Altar des Königs Sahu-Re. *ZÄS* 104: 145–56.

Weigall, A. E. P. 1911. The alabaster quarries of Wadi Assiout. *ASAE* 11: 176.

Wendorf, F., R. Schild and N. Zedeno 1996. A late Neolithic megalith complex in the Eastern Sahara: a preliminary report, in Krzyzaniak, L. (ed.), *Interregional Contacts in the Later Prehistory of Northeastern Africa*, Poznan: Poznan Archaeological Museum, 125–32.

Wengrow, D. 2006. *The Archaeology of Early Egypt: Social Transformations in North-east Africa, 10,000 to 2650 BC*, Cambridge: CUP, 218–58.

Westenholz, J. G. and M. W. Stolper 2002. A stone jar with inscriptions of Darius I in four languages. Achemenet November 2002: 1–13.

Wiedemann, A. 1895. Inscriptions of the time of Amenophis IV. *PSBA* 17: 152–7.

Wilkinson, J. G. 1843. *Modern Egypt and Thebes*, 2 vols. London: John Murray.

Wilson, P. 1996. Foot outlines and inscriptions, in Rose, P. J. (ed.), *Qasr Ibrim: The Hinterland Survey*. London: EES, 102–17.

Winkler, H. A. 1939. *Rock Drawings from Southern Upper Egypt II*. London: Archaeological Survey of Egypt.

Yoyotte, J. 1975. Les sementiou et l'exploitation des régions minières à l'ancien empire. *BSFE* 73: 44-55

Internet sources:

http://www.eeescience.utoledo.edu/faculty/harrell/egypt/Quarries/Softst_Quar.html (see Harrell n.d. above)

http://www.umich.edu/~kelseydb/Publications/spring2000/abydos.html (see Richards 2000a above)

http://www.umich.edu/ ~kelseydb/Publications/fall2001/abydos.html (see Richards 2000b above) Breasted, J. H. 1906. Ancient Records of Egypt I: The First through the Seventeenth Dynasties. Chicago: University of Chicago Press.

INDEX

Aamu 148

AAS 24

Abdel-Aziz Saleh 29

ablutions 121

Abrak 127

Abu Aziz 22, 27

Abu Ghurob 16

Abydos xvii, 2, 7, 13, 14, 15, 24, 115, 121, 125, 126, 132, 139

acacia 36, 38, 115

Achaemenid 17

administrative centre 35, 67

Adriani 17

agriculture xviii

Ägyptisches Museum, Berlin 1, 160, 169

Aha 15, 146

Aha[nakht] 146

Ahahotep 159, 169

Ahanakht 105, 145, 146, 147, 149, 150, 151, 152, 153, 155, 158, 159, 167, 169

Ahmose 14, 23, 116

Ahmose-Nefertari 23

Ain 136

Ainu 14

Akaad 21, 23

Akaba 27

akhet 138, 143, 145

Akhetaten 23

Akkadian 13, 14

Alabastronpolis 7

Alexander 17

Alexandria 17

alignments viii, xii, 41, 45, 51, 97, 99, 100, 101, 113

allotments 149

altar 16, 79

Amarna x, xii, xiv, 1, 2, 3, 4, 5, 6, 7, 8, 19, 22, 23, 27, 36, 38, 49, 72, 78, 79, 83, 84, 85, 91, 95, 109, 110, 111, 135, 136

Amenemhat 6, 7, 75, 105, 127, 160, 161, 167

Amenemhat II 75, 161, 167

Amenemhat III 127

Amenhotep I 14, 17

Amenhotep III xvii, 16

Amenirdis 17

amethyst 36, 106, 121, 122, 126, 127, 130, 132

amphora xi, 46, 56, 57, 84, 136

Amun of the pure mountain xix

Ani 135, 142

Ankh 160, 169

ankh 137, 139

Ankhy 105, 144

anorthosite gneiss 9, 119, 135

Anthes 1, 3, 4, 7, 8, 13, 34, 75, 76, 77, 116, 135, 137, 138, 139, 140, 141, 142, 143, 144, 145, 146, 147, 148, 149, 150, 151, 152, 154, 155, 156, 157, 158, 159, 160, 161, 169

Anty 105, 165

Anubis 161

Apis bulls 16

Apis House 14

Apy 135, 136

aquifers 121

Arab 23, 36, 112

Arab Hatim 23

aragonite 11, 12

arrows 161

Artaxerxes 17, 18

artists xix, 28, 128, 165

ash 36, 42, 66

Ashmunein 28

Assyrian 13, 116

Aston xv, xviii, 10, 11, 12, 14, 15, 17, 24, 25, 27, 78

Aswan 29, 115, 116, 121, 122, 125, 127, 128, 130

Asyut 4, 19, 23, 25

Ba'alath 106

Badarian 25

Badawy 3, 28

bakery 22

baking 38, 121

Ballas 92

Barbieri 19, 24

basalt xiii, 8, 15, 16, 49, 117, 118, 123, 124, 132

basin xi, 46, 52, 75, 78, 99, 125, 132

Bastet 14

beer xi, xii, 36, 43, 49, 51, 52, 53, 55, 56, 57, 58, 60, 61, 62, 63, 64, 82, 83, 86, 87, 88, 89, 90, 91, 92, 93, 94, 95, 147, 148, 160, 161, 162

beer jar xi, xii, 36, 43, 49, 51, 52, 53, 56, 57, 58, 60, 61, 62, 63, 64, 71, 82, 83, 86, 87, 88, 89, 90, 91, 92, 93, 94, 95

Behekes 145

Beni Hasan 4, 136

Beni Suef 19, 21

Beni Suef alabaster 21

Berlin 1, 137, 157, 158, 159, 160, 169

Bernard 25, 163

biconical 62, 84

Birch xviii

Bir Umm Fawakhir xviii

Blackden 1, 4, 8, 137, 138, 139, 140, 141, 144, 163

block statues 15

Bloxam xvi, 8, 106, 117, 118, 119, 124, 126, 127

Boghazköy 18

bones 57

Borchardt 5

boring tools 25

Boston 16, 17

bottle xii, 56, 90, 92

Bouriant 136

bow 26, 141, 161

Bradbury xviii, 123

Bradley xvi, 24

bread xii, 36, 46, 56, 57, 58, 60, 61, 63, 64, 83, 84, 95, 103, 121, 147, 148, 161, 162, 164, 165

bread-mould xii, 46, 56, 57, 58, 60, 61, 63, 64, 83, 95

Breasted 3, 28

breccia xviii

brewing 156

Brussels 17

Bryan 28, 29

bull 13, 99, 147, 149, 150, 152, 153, 154, 155

bull-sphinxes 13

bureaucracy xviii, 115, 132

Burton 22

Byblos 18

C-group 120

Cairns:

C1 x, 40, 41, 51, 113

C1-3 41, 113

C2 40

C3 x, 40

C4 41

C5 41, 59

C5-6 41, 59

C7 xii, 40, 41, 45, 48, 55, 97, 98

C8 41, 52, 97

C9 41

C10 41

cairns 68, 73, 104, 105, 109, 113, 119, 121

Cairo xiv, 13, 14, 15, 16, 17, 19, 24, 25, 115, 116, 129, 130, 132, 133, 164

calcareous sinter 12

calcareous tufa 12

calcite xv, 11, 12, 18, 24

camel 23, 119

camp 8, 119, 120

caravan 120, 123

carnelian 106, 107

Carter 3, 4

cartouche 8, 79, 139

Castel xvi, 106, 129

Castiglione 97

Cataract

   First 130, 132
   Fourth 132
   Second 130

Caton-Thompson xvi, 11, 26, 117, 118, 129

cattle 99, 148, 151, 152, 153, 164

cattle-herders 99

causeway xii, 3, 8, 63, 109, 110, 111, 112, 113, 114, 115, 118, 119, 122, 123

chaff 36, 61, 63

chair 161

chalk-pit 31

charcoal x, 36, 37, 38, 64, 66, 68, 70, 103

chert 27

chief of the granary 147

chief of the sculptors 142

chief of works 135

chisel 21, 22, 25

cistern xix

Clarke xvi

collar 146, 150

column 29, 147, 150, 159

commander of the expedition 127

controller of the two thrones 138, 140, 142, 145, 146, 147, 148, 149, 150, 152, 154, 155, 159

cooking 20, 38

copper xvii, 27, 57, 97, 106, 127, 130

copper-smelting 130

Coptic 7, 22, 34, 52, 64, 78, 95, 136

corvée 126, 129

craftsmen 18, 19, 25, 149

Crete 18, 24
crossbeams 124
cubits 115, 145
Currelly xvi, 36, 101, 130
Cyprus 19
Dahamsha 16
Dahschurstrasse 118, 119
Dahshur 52, 118, 121
Dairut 7
Dakhla Oasis 97, 99
Darb el-Agl 109
Darb el-Amarani 75
Darb el-Arba'in 120
Darb Isbeida 7
Darius I 17
débitage 42, 62
Debono 26
Deir el-Bahari 16
Deir el-Bersha 3, 4, 8, 15, 22, 24, 27, 28, 105, 109, 113, 116, 142, 165
Deir el-Medina 84, 85
de Morgan 26
demotic 22
Der-khesef 143, 144
diorite 15
disc 16, 60, 63, 66, 79
Djedu 161
Djehuty 144
Djoser 1, 11, 15, 16
doctors 127
dog 141, 161, 162
dolerite 132
dolmen 103
donkey 27, 111, 119, 123, 127
doorways 16
Dreyer 19, 20, 95, 132
drill 25, 26, 27
drill core 26
drinking songs 18
Drovetti xviii
duck 150
Duki Dawur 120
dung 86, 148
Dunqul Oasis 119
dwarf 150
Eastern Desert xvi, xvii, xviii, 1, 3, 8, 21, 22, 38, 101, 115, 123, 126, 127
economy xvi, xvii, xviii
Edfu xvii, 125

Eggebrecht 15
Egypt Exploration Society 5, 109
Egyptian alabaster xv, 11, 12
el-Hinnawi 24
el-Khouli 15, 25
el-Qawatir 19, 22, 25
Elephantine 26, 147
embalming tables 16
embankment 111, 113, 123, 153
emplacement x, 47, 48, 51, 53, 67, 105, 113
Engelbach xvi, 119, 120
enneads 149, 151, 153
Eocene 12, 19, 24
epigraphic vii, 1, 2, 3, 109, 136, 163
Ericson xvi
Erman 19, 123
Esna 19
Ethiopia 24
ethnoarchaeology 26
ewer 18
expeditions viii, xvii, xviii, 2, 3, 6, 36, 38, 48, 73, 101, 106, 107, 111, 113, 115, 123, 125, 126, 127, 128, 129, 131, 132, 133, 164
Fahlbusch 20
Faiyum 8, 11, 26, 117, 118, 119, 129, 132, 133
Fakhry 36, 121, 130
false door 16, 125
feet 3, 5, 31, 97, 150
fields 8, 149
finger marks 87
Fischer 123
flags 120
flagstones 21
flake 49, 63, 66
flash-floods 20, 130
flint 25, 26, 27, 48, 49, 51, 63, 66, 129
flower 161
foreman 42, 127
fortress xiii, 121, 122, 131, 151
fowl 150
Fraser 1, 3, 4, 8, 31, 75, 78, 97, 103, 109, 111, 137, 138, 139, 140, 141, 144, 163
frontier 130
fuel 38
funerary equipment xvi, xviii, 7, 15, 115, 125
galena 97, 106, 126, 129
gaming counter 46, 56, 58, 60, 61, 66, 89
Garbrecht 19, 20
Gardiner xvi, 6, 7, 16, 42, 123, 125, 126, 127, 136, 158, 165

Gardner xvi, 11, 22, 26, 117, 118, 129

garrisons 132

Garstang 26

gazelle 155, 161

Gebel el-Asr xiii, 9, 106, 107, 111, 118, 119, 120, 121, 123, 124, 133, 135

Gebel el-Silsila 106, 128

Gebel el-Zeit 97, 106, 126, 128, 129

Gebel Gulab xiii, 29, 122

Gebel Qatrani xiii, 117

Gebel Rokham 19

Gebel Sheikh Said 19, 22

Gebel Tingar 122

Gebel Zeit 106

geese 150, 152, 153, 164, 165

geochemical analyses 24

Gerisch 36, 38

Gerrawi xii, 19, 20, 22, 23, 25, 95, 123, 129, 133

Giza 14, 15, 17, 29, 52, 121

glass 18, 83

gneiss xiii, 9, 29, 107, 119, 120, 121, 124, 133, 135

god's treasurer 127, 145

God's Wife of Amun 17

Goedicke 2, 8, 116, 118, 119, 128, 144, 165

gold xvii, xviii, xix, 3, 6, 122, 125, 126, 127, 149

gold-washers 125

goldsmith 149

goose 161

governor 3, 17, 105, 107, 129, 138, 140, 142, 144, 145, 146, 147, 148, 149, 150, 151, 154, 155, 159, 160, 161, 163

granite xvii, 16, 17, 26, 29, 30, 121, 122, 128

Gravidenflasche 15

Grdseloff 2, 163

Great Harris Papyrus 6

Great Temple 85

greywacke 126

Griffith 4, 137, 142, 148, 149, 150, 151, 152, 160

guard-posts 73

guardian of clothes 147

Gulf of Suez 129

gypsum xv, 11, 13, 14, 15, 18, 20, 26, 27, 68, 118, 126, 129, 132, 133

'Hare' nome 3, 4, 105, 138, 140, 145, 147, 148, 149, 152, 160, 163

Hagg Qandil 109

Halicarnassus 18

hammer-stones 35

harbour 3, 7, 8, 22, 109, 110, 122

harbour of Sneferu 8

Harkhuf 123

Harrell xv, xvi, xviii, xix, 1, 6, 12, 19, 23, 25, 117, 124

Harris 6, 13, 14, 136

Hathor 6, 106, 107, 129

Hatshepsut 136

Hawata 7, 8, 109

hawk 79, 137, 139

headdress 21

headrests 13

heart-scarab 135

hearth bowl 72

Heizer xix, 24, 25, 26, 27

Helwan 19

Hemaka 15

Hendrickx 99

Henu 155, 159

herald 147

herbivore 57

Hermopolis Magna 28, 105

Hermopolitan 107

Heryshefnakht 105, 147

Hester xix, 25, 26, 27

Hetep 15

Hetepheres 15, 16

Hetepi 157, 160, 169

Hierakonpolis xvii

hieratic xix, 1, 4, 22, 77, 141, 143, 144, 145, 146, 147, 148, 149, 150, 154, 155, 156, 157, 158, 159, 160, 161, 163, 164

hieroglyphic 1, 4, 14, 16, 17, 21, 22, 25, 143, 161

hilltop settlement 36, 128, 130

Hof 19

Horus 4, 5, 79, 106, 129, 135, 137, 138, 139, 143, 144, 161, 164

Hotepu 127

Hume 23

hunter 161

hymn 115

Iaib 142, 145, 158, 169

Ibhat 125

Iby 26

Idi 144

Iha 105, 145

Ihi 15

Ikem 157

Imakhy 143

Impy 144

INAA 24

incense burners 148, 152

inductively coupled plasma mass spectrometry 24

Inerer(?) 157
infrastructure xviii, 117, 118, 119
inspector of boats 144
Inta 158
Intef 127, 160
Ip 155
Ipy 158
Isesi 143
Israel 17, 117
James xv, 1, 4, 22, 23, 25
Janssen xvii
jar-sealing 120
Jaritz 19, 20, 95, 122, 132
jars xi, 15, 26, 46, 48, 49, 52, 55, 56, 58, 60, 61, 62, 78, 82, 84, 85, 87, 88, 90, 91, 93, 94, 95, 159, 160, 161
Jomard 7
judge 148, 151
Ka 156
Kahotep 155
Kahun 132
Kaiser xii, 56, 71, 81, 82, 86, 90, 91, 93
Kanais 125
Kanakht 155, 157
Kaper 97, 99
Karnak 14, 16, 17
Karnak cachette 16
Kay 105, 147, 148, 149, 151, 152, 161
Kefa 160
Kemi 149
Kemp xiv, xvii, 3, 84, 85, 126, 133
Kemy 147, 150, 151, 153, 154
Keri 160
Kessler 7, 8, 110
Khafra 9, 14, 16, 17, 29, 30
Khety 140
Khian 18
Khnemui 141
Khnum 105, 107, 144, 145, 155, 156, 158, 160, 169
Khnumankh 105, 145
Khnumenankhses 138
Khnumhotep 105, 154
Khnumi 160, 169
Khnumiker 145, 146
Khufu x, 1, 4, 5, 22, 135, 137, 138, 139, 167
Khui 144
Khuit 144
Khuu 138, 140, 150
kilt 146, 147, 149, 150, 152, 154, 159, 160, 161, 163, 169
Klemm xv, xvi, xviii, 14, 19, 20, 21, 22, 23, 24, 122, 130

Knossos 18, 19, 27
Kom el-Dara 17
Kom el-Nana 3, 36, 109, 110, 111
Koptos 7
Lahun 121, 123
lamps 22
laser ablation 24
Late Period 11, 21, 78, 79, 119, 136
law-court 146, 147
lector-priest 105, 144, 145, 146
Lemaire 17
lexicographical 11
libation basin 125
libation tables 16
lid 46, 56, 58, 60, 61, 89
Lilyquist xv, 19, 25
limestone x, xii, xvii, xviii, 1, 8, 11, 12, 14, 15, 18, 19, 23, 24, 26, 29, 35, 42, 45, 47, 48, 51, 52, 55, 63, 84, 85, 86, 97, 101, 113, 115, 116, 118, 125, 128, 133
Lisht 121
lithics 35, 51
Loukina 24
Louvre 16, 17
Lucas 12, 14, 15, 19, 21, 27, 135
Luxor 16, 19, 26, 27
Ma'asara xii, 14, 115, 116
mace 15, 137, 139, 152, 154
Mackay 19, 20, 133
Maghara 22, 27
Maghara, Abu Aziz 22
magicians 105, 147
Mallawi xiv, 19
Mariette 115
marl C 61, 62, 87, 89, 90
Mastabat Fara'un 118
master of the roads 123
meat jars 49
medical 15, 105
medicine 149
Medjay 148
Meidum xi, xii, 36, 46, 49, 51, 52, 53, 56, 57, 58, 60, 61, 62, 63, 64, 72, 83, 89, 90, 91, 92, 93, 94, 121
Meidum-type bowl xii, 36, 46, 49, 51, 52, 56, 57, 60, 61, 62, 63, 72, 83, 93
Meir 26
Meketdjehuty 140
Memphis 7, 16, 27, 119
Menkaura 29
Menti 160
Mentuhotep II 16

Merenptah 23
Merenra 2, 115, 116, 139, 167
Mereruka 26
Meyers 24
mica 122
Michaelides 164, 165
midden x, 36, 37, 38, 42
Middleton xvi, 24
military road 119
milk 15
Min 106
mine-shafts 129
Minemhat 129
mineral xvii, xviii, 12, 24, 123, 125, 126, 128, 132
Minoan 18, 19, 24, 27, 117
Minya xiv, 19, 22
Mitrahina 14, 16
Mohammed Ali 21
Möller 1, 4, 8, 75, 77, 137, 139, 140, 141, 144, 147, 150, 158, 160, 161, 163
Montet xvi, 13, 127
Moorey 13
Mount Sinai 101
mud-brick 121, 122, 132
Muhammad Ali 13, 23
Murray 19, 111, 117, 119, 120
Museo Egizio, Turin xviii, 135
Mycenae 18
myrrh 148, 151, 152, 153
Nabta Playa 99, 101
Nag' Hammadi 27
Naggar 12, 21, 23
Nakht 149, 150, 153, 157, 160, 169
naoi 16
Naqada xvii
Naqlai Oasis 119
Nebtawyra Mentuhotep IV xvii
necropolis 26, 123, 128, 142, 165
Neferefra 142
Neferkha 144
Neferkhau 150
Neferu 157
Nehery 105, 147, 148, 149, 150, 151, 152, 153, 154, 155, 161, 167
Nehery I 149, 150, 152, 154, 167
Nehesy 143
Nehesyw 148
Nemti 161
Nerekhef(?) 157

Netjeruhotep 147
Newberry 3, 4, 12, 15, 28, 113, 116, 142
Nicholson iii, vii, viii, xiv, 31, 36, 81
nomarch 105, 140, 144, 152, 153
Nubia xvii, 97, 99, 126, 131, 132, 133
Nubian xvii, 121, 127, 131
Nyuserra 16
O'Connor xvii
Oasis 97, 99, 119
obsidian 24
ochre 21
offering bearers 150
offerings 3, 16, 18, 21, 51, 67, 103, 105, 129, 147, 150, 152, 154, 155, 160, 161
offering tables 2, 15, 143
officials 2, 4, 116, 125, 126, 127, 128, 151, 152, 153, 154, 164
ointment 15, 146
Onomasticon of Amenemope 7
onyx marble 12
opening of the mouth 6
Orsk 18
orthostats viii, 41, 49, 51, 56, 99, 101, 106
Osiris 21, 161
ovens 103
overseer of boats 147
ox 79, 116, 149, 150, 152
ox-herder 149
P. Smith 17
paint 75, 137
palace 13, 115, 128, 138, 144, 147, 150, 151, 154, 155
palaeography 75, 161
Palermo Stone 6
Palestine xvi, 18, 101, 115
pallets 122
Papyrus Ebers 15, 17
paths 3, 20, 51, 103, 121
patrix 84
paving 14, 16, 124
Pepi I x, 5, 8, 18, 138, 139, 167
Pepi II 13, 16, 128, 135, 139, 143, 144, 167
Pepyankh 26
perfumes 18
Petrie xvi, 1, 2, 3, 4, 5, 12, 13, 20, 22, 23, 25, 26, 31, 36, 75, 78, 79, 97, 101, 103, 112, 118, 119, 130, 133
petroglyphs viii, xii, 97, 98, 99, 101, 103, 106
petrography 23, 24
petrology 13
Philae 122

Phillips 18

phyle 105

physician 105, 147

pigeons 165

planks 124

platter 72

Pleistocene 12

Pliny 14, 16, 19

Posener 2, 17, 18, 163, 164

post-holes 68

Postgate 13

pot-mark 52, 56, 61

potter's wheel 60, 82

pounder 89

priest viii, 3, 105, 140, 144, 145, 146, 147, 148, 149, 150, 151, 152, 153, 154, 155, 159, 161, 165

prospectors 127

Ptah 106

Ptolemaic 36, 97, 117

punches 25

Purdy xvi

pyramid-town 132

Pyramid Texts 7

Qadesh 126

Qasr el-Sagha 117, 118, 128, 132

Quarries viii, xi, 1, 3, 4, 23, 75, 76, 78

Quarry G 22

Quarry P vii, x, xi, xii, 1, 3, 4, 5, 6, 8, 16, 27, 28, 31, 32, 33, 34, 35, 36, 38, 39, 40, 41, 42, 43, 48, 51, 34, 35, 39, 55, 63, 42, 68, 44, 73, 40, 42, 44, 40, 43, 73, 48, 67, 55, 44, 46, 47, 50, 54, 75, 78, 75, 78, 83, 84, 83, 92, 85, 87, 91, 93, 92, 83, 84, 83, 92, 85, 73, 87, 91, 93, 92, 97, 99, 101, 102, 103, 104, 105, 97, 99, 101, 102, 103, 104, 105, 111, 113, 123, 115, 112, 87, 114, 111, 113, 123, 115, 112, 114, 128, 135, 136, 52, 55, 68, 67, 73, 55, 63, 112, 52

Quarry R 1, 75, 77, 78, 79, 113, 141

Quarry Ra xi, 75, 76, 77, 78, 136

Quarry T viii, xi, 79, 112, 136, 167

quartzite xiii, 24, 29, 122

quayside 118

'rilling' lines 84

Ra 75, 76, 77, 78, 113, 136, 143, 149, 151, 161, 164

Ra-kheny 143

radioactivity 12

Ramesses II 13, 14, 16, 23, 26, 126

Ramesses IV xix

Ramesseum 26, 29

ramps xiii, 119, 120, 121, 123

Ras Gharib 129

Rateb 21

reckoner of gold 127

refuse 41

Reisner 15, 16, 25, 30

Rekhmira 26

Renu 154

Residence 143, 145

resin 56

Richards 115

Rifeh 103

Rift Valley 24

rings 22

ritualistic xviii, 3, 97, 106

River Temple 8

road viii, xii, xiii, 3, 5, 6, 8, 19, 22, 23, 38, 40, 41, 45, 51, 55, 59, 63, 109, 110, 111, 112, 113, 117, 118, 119, 120, 121, 122, 123, 124, 132, 143

Road of the Camp 119

rock drawing xii

Roeder 8

rollers 121, 123, 124

Roman xi, 1, 3, 5, 11, 14, 16, 19, 20, 21, 34, 56, 57, 64, 78, 79, 95, 97, 117, 136

ropes 3, 28

Rose iii, viii, xiv, 36, 45, 81, 85, 95

royal jubilee 18, 159

Sabni 116

Sadd el-Kafara 19, 20

Saimeni 142

sakkia 64

Sankhy 144

Saqqara 1, 11, 14, 15, 16, 26, 116, 121

sarcophagus xviii, 6, 16, 125

satrapy 17

Satsekhmet 147

Schweinfurth 19

sculptor 6, 7

sealing 120, 148, 153

Sekhemkhet 16

Sekhmet 105, 147, 150, 152

SEM-EDS 24

semen 152

Senebi 155

Senusret I 7, 16, 17, 105, 126, 132, 160, 161, 163, 164, 167

Senusret III 75, 105, 128, 142, 165, 167

Sep 161

Ser 143, 145

Serabit el-Khadim 97, 101, 106, 111, 127, 128

Serapis 97

serekh 138, 139

Sethe xviii, 2, 7, 14, 21, 38, 116, 125, 138, 139

Seti I xvii, xix, 16, 29, 125

shabtis 15, 113

shaft grave 18

Sheikh Abd el-Gurna 27

Sheikh Said xiv, 19, 22, 27

shemu 143, 144

Shenut 157

ships 28, 38, 145

Shrine N3 xii, 102

Shrine N7 xii, 103

Shrine S11a xii, 104

Shrine S2 xii, 101, 102

silicified sandstone 16, 122

siltstone xviii, 126

silver 149

Simpson 2, 6, 7, 107, 120, 123, 139, 164

Sinai xvi, 2, 19, 42, 101, 106, 123, 126, 127, 129, 130

Sinki 121

slave 36

sledge 3, 116, 119, 121, 122, 123, 124

slip 36, 49, 56, 61, 62, 63, 86, 88, 89, 91, 92, 94

slow-wheel 84

Sneferu 8, 106

Sobek 16

Sobekemhat 150, 153

Sobekhotep 5, 141, 155, 159, 164

Sobeknakht 149

sole companion 138, 145, 146, 148, 151, 153, 161

Soped 106

Soukiassian xvi, 106, 129

Sparks 18

spear 150, 154

speleothems 12

Speos Artemidos 136

sphinx 16

spoil heaps 31, 35, 41, 80

spout 61

spouted vessel xi, 62

Stadelmann 29

staff xiv, 125, 137, 139, 145, 146, 147, 149, 154, 155, 157, 158, 159, 160, 161, 163, 169

stake hole 70

stalactites 12

stalagmites 12

standing stone xii, 100

statuary xvi

statues/statuettes xix, 6, 13, 14, 15, 16, 17, 21, 27, 28, 29, 113, 116, 121, 126, 151

stele ix, xix, 2, 5, 7, 13, 21, 22, 42, 77, 107, 115, 116, 118, 119, 120, 127, 128, 129, 132, 156, 160, 161, 163, 164, 165, 169

steps x, xix, 3, 22, 31, 33, 97, 124, 152

steward 155

Stocks xvi, 25, 26, 27, 113

stone-cutters 42, 127

straw 86

strontium isotope analysis 24

symbolism vii, 11, 14, 15, 17

Syria-Palestine 18, 101

tamarisk 36

temple xvii, xviii, 6, 7, 13, 14, 16, 17, 26, 27, 28, 38, 97, 106, 109, 117, 121, 125, 126, 128, 132, 133, 136, 144, 147, 148, 150, 151, 152, 153

Terra Santa 17

Teti 15, 16, 128, 135, 141, 143

Thebes 6, 23, 24, 26, 27, 129, 132

thin-section 24

Thomas 27, 36

Thoth 105, 107, 145, 146, 147, 148, 149, 151, 152, 153, 154, 156, 159, 165

throw-stick 161

Thuthnakht 146

Thuthotep 3, 8, 15, 27, 28, 29, 105, 113, 115, 116, 127, 141, 145, 151, 153, 155, 156, 157, 159, 165, 167, 169

Thuthotep I 155, 156, 167

Thutmose I 17

Thutmose III xvii, 14, 17

Thutnakht 105, 140, 145, 146, 147, 148, 149, 151, 152, 153, 154, 155, 159, 167

Thutnakhtankh 146

Thutnakht I 140

Thutnakht II 140

Thutnakht III 140

Thutnakht IV 105, 159, 167

Thutnakht V 155, 167

Ti 116

tiles 8, 21

timber 38, 121

Timme 5, 75, 76, 79, 103, 109, 112, 113, 167

Timna 97, 106

Tivoli xv, 12

Tjehef 146

tombs viii, xvii, 2, 3, 15, 18, 22, 26, 115, 121, 129, 135

tournette 84

townsman 148, 153, 158

trace element 24

track ways 113, 123

transportation viii, xix, 3, 13, 27, 28, 109, 115, 116, 119, 121, 122, 127, 143

treasurer 127, 143, 145, 151, 164

treasurers 164

treasury 128

tribute 18

Tumbos 29

tumuli 99

Tura xviii, 14, 125, 128

Turin Mining Papyrus xviii, xix

turntable 60, 82, 84, 90, 91

turquoise 2, 9, 36, 97, 101, 106, 118, 126, 127, 128, 129, 130

Tushka xiii, 111, 119, 120, 121, 124, 133

Tutankhamun 15, 25

twist-reverse-twist drill 25

Umm el-Sawwan 11, 26, 118, 126, 128, 129, 131, 132, 133

Unas 14

underworld 16

unguents 18

Userkaf xii, 71, 81, 82, 86, 87, 90, 91, 92, 93, 94

Valley of the Kings 26, 27

Valley Temple 17, 29, 30

vandalism 9, 21

van Zelst 24

Vermeersch 99

Vernus 17

vertebra 55

Vienna System 87

vizier 148, 151

von Bissing 25

Wadi Abbad xvii, xviii, xix, 123, 125

Wadi Araba 19, 21

Wadi Arabah 97, 106

Wadi Askhar el-Qibli 21

Wadi Asyut 19, 23

Wadi Bershawi xiv, 19, 22, 23

Wadi el-Hol 97

Wadi el-Hudi xiii, 36, 106, 111, 121, 122, 123, 126, 127, 128, 129, 130, 131, 133

Wadi el-Zebeida 22

Wadi Gasus 123

Wadi Gerrawi xii, 19, 20, 22, 23, 25, 95, 123, 129, 133

Wadi Hammamat xvii, xviii, 123, 126, 127, 129, 132, 165

Wadi Hof 19

Wadi Isbeida 7

Wadi Kabrit 129

Wadi Maghara xiii, 9, 36, 106, 118, 128, 129, 130, 131, 133

Wadi Miya 125

Wadi Moathil 19, 21

Wadi Nakhla 142

Wadi Sannur 19, 21

Wadi Umm Argub 19, 21

Wadiyein 23, 27

Wahibra 21

watch towers 36

water xviii, xix, 18, 20, 28, 38, 48, 85, 111, 116, 120, 132, 144, 148, 153

Wawat 148

way marks 118

Weigall 23

weights 17, 124

well xiv, xvi, xviii, 1, 5, 6, 8, 16, 17, 19, 20, 21, 24, 25, 35, 43, 45, 46, 48, 49, 51, 53, 55, 56, 58, 61, 63, 64, 66, 79, 82, 83, 85, 88, 90, 94, 106, 109, 110, 111, 113, 119, 120, 121, 125, 127, 128, 129, 135, 141, 142, 144, 155, 157, 161

Weni viii, xviii, 2, 3, 38, 115, 116, 125, 139

Wenut 143, 145

Westcar 77

Western Desert xvi, 38, 99, 119, 133

wheat 145, 148, 149

Widan el-Faras xiii, 8, 117, 118, 119, 122, 123, 124, 132

Wilkinson 22

Willems xiv, 22, 23, 27

willow 7

Winkler 97

Wissa 16

work-gangs 113

Workmen's Village 84, 85

workshops vii, xvi, xix, 6, 7, 18, 25, 26, 27, 28, 29

Xerxes 17, 18

XRD 24

XRF 24

Zawiyat el-Amwat 7

zir x, 36, 47, 48, 63, 113

Selective Index of Egyptian, Coptic, Akkadian, and Greek Words

ȝmt-blossoms 150
ȝtw 144
iwȝ-cattle 148, 152, 153
ibr-oil 148
imy-r mšʿ 127
imy-r sȝ 42
imy-sȝ 164
imy-sȝ n imy-r sdȝwt 164
inr 14, 145
iḳwy 165
iḳwyw 127, 128 ʿȝt 116, 145
ʿnḫ-mswt 164
ʿnḫ-ḫʿw 139
ʿrryt 150, 153
ʿḥnwti 148
wʿb 14, 105, 151, 154, 165
wpwti 140
wnw 4, 143, 145, 146, 147, 149, 150, 151, 152, 154, 157, 161
wnš 122
wndw-cattle 148
wḫdw 145
wsr-sceptre 79
wsḫt-hall 148, 151
wsḫt-boat 115, 116, 143
biȝ 119
bit 3, 13, 14, 107, 135, 143, 144, 145
bḫn xvii, xviii, xix, 126, 127
bḥdt 137, 139
bk 14
pr-šs 6, 7, 14
mȝʿt 151
mnw-stone 161
mrt-snfrw 6, 8, 144
mrw 143
mry-rʿ 138
mry-tȝwy 138
mḫw 140
mdȝw 153
mddw 137, 138
nw-vessels 21
nbt mfkȝt 106
nbt mntt 107
nbt msdmt 106
nb ḫȝswt 106
nbt ḥnmt 106

nfr-sȝ-ḫr 138
nfr-ḫʿw 142
nsw-bit 135, 137, 138, 139
nfr-kȝ-rʿ 139, 144
nb-kȝw-rʿ 161
ntr-ḫʿw 139, 144
ntr-ḥw 143
nds 158
rwdt stone 13
rmt 128, 144
ḥʿw-ships 145
ḥwt-nbw 3, 6, 14, 107, 136
ḥmʿʿt 161
ḥmwt-smit 30
ḥmwty 25
ḥry-sʿnḫw 142
ḥry kȝwty 135
ḥknw-balm 148
ḥtp di nsw 13, 135, 161
ḫȝstyw 153
ḫʿ-kȝw-rʿ 142
ḫwsw 145
ḫpr-kȝ-rʿ 161, 164
ḫmnw 105, 145, 146, 147, 151, 152, 153, 154, 155, 165
ḫrp-sceptre 145, 146, 147, 152, 154, 155, 157, 158, 159, 160
ḫnmw ḫw.f 138
ḫrtyw-ntr 42, 127
sȝ rʿ tti 143
sȝw n wʿbw 105
swšw 156
smi-boats 143
smntyw 127
smḥ-ship 128
sr-geese 165
sḥtp-tȝwy 143
sšri 143
str-plant 150
sdȝwty ntr 127
šs 3, 6, 7, 13, 14, 16, 17, 107, 136, 145, 153, 155, 159
šst 13
šdyt-šȝ 148, 149
kȝdȝdȝ 14
krḥt-snake 151, 153
kd 14
tpy ḥr 144

ṯrti 6, 7, 8, 105, 110, 161, 165
ṯḥnt 153
ṯsw 151, 152
ḏfḏfw 146

ⲧⲉⲣⲱⲧ 9

gassu 14
gišnugallu 13
parūtu 13

γυψος 14